Konstantinos Arampapaslis
Magic in the Literature of the Neronian Period

Trends in Classics – Supplementary Volumes

Edited by
Franco Montanari and Antonios Rengakos

Associate Editors
Stavros Frangoulidis · Fausto Montana · Lara Pagani
Serena Perrone · Evina Sistakou · Christos Tsagalis

Scientific Committee
Alberto Bernabé · Margarethe Billerbeck
Claude Calame · Jonas Grethlein · Philip R. Hardie
Stephen J. Harrison · Stephen Hinds · Richard Hunter
Christina Kraus · Giuseppe Mastromarco
Gregory Nagy · Theodore D. Papanghelis
Giusto Picone · Alessandro Schiesaro
Tim Whitmarsh · Bernhard Zimmermann

Volume 162

Konstantinos Arampapaslis

Magic in the Literature of the Neronian Period

Realism and Criticism

DE GRUYTER

ISBN 978-3-11-142940-3
e-ISBN (PDF) 978-3-11-142944-1
e-ISBN (EPUB) 978-3-11-143054-6
ISSN 1868-4785

Library of Congress Control Number: 2024934000

Bibliographic information published by the Deutsche Nationalbibliothek
The Deutsche Nationalbibliothek lists this publication in the Deutsche Nationalbibliografie; detailed bibliographic data are available on the Internet at http://dnb.dnb.de.

© 2024 Walter de Gruyter GmbH, Berlin/Boston
Editorial Office: Alessia Ferreccio and Katerina Zianna
Logo: Christopher Schneider, Laufen
Printing and binding: CPI books GmbH, Leck

www.degruyter.com

Preface

This book is the fruit of research carried out during my studies at the University of Illinois at Urbana-Champaign, and essentially a revised version of my thesis. Words are never enough to express my gratitude, first and foremost, to Antony Augoustakis, who offered his advice, help, and support throughout the project. I owe special thanks to Stavros Frangoulidis and Orestis Karatzoglou for devoting their time to discussing problems that came up during the revision process. I would also like to thank Theocritus Kouremenos, Poulheria Kyriakou, Thomas Tsartsidis, and Angeliki Tzanetou for reading various parts of the manuscript, and for providing valuable feedback. Finally, I am most grateful to Antonios Rengakos and the editorial team at De Gruyter for their help and guidance throughout the publication process.

Thessaloniki 2023

Contents

Preface —— V
Abbreviations —— IX
Introduction —— XI

1	**Seneca the Moralist** —— 1
1.1	Medea's imprecation and its magical setting —— 4
1.2	Magic as reversal —— 12
1.3	Magic and anti-Stoicism —— 14
1.4	The chorus' prayer: a folly without precedent —— 15
1.5	Transforming the model: From Ovid's *monstrum* to Seneca's *monstrum* —— 18
1.5.1	Magic behind the scenes: the nurse's speech as preparatory ritual —— 21
1.6	Magic on stage: the main ritual —— 29
1.6.1	Magic on stage: Medea's mumbo-jumbo! —— 30
1.7	Destruction on stage —— 41
1.8	Conclusions —— 42

2	**Lucan, the Didactic Poet** —— 44
2.1	Sextus Pompey: an anti-Stoic and anti-Roman anti-hero —— 46
2.2	Magic as anti-Stoic practice —— 50
2.3	Magic as charlatanry —— 56
2.4	Erichtho, the all-powerful superwitch —— 58
2.5	Erichtho's necromancy —— 61
2.5.1	The preparatory ritual —— 62
2.5.2	The spell proper —— 66
2.5.3	The second spell —— 71
2.5.4	The instructions —— 74
2.6	Is it even possible? The failure of Erichtho —— 75
2.7	Conclusions —— 76

3	**Petronius: Parody of Literature, Mockery of Magic** —— 78
3.1	Popular horror stories: the werewolf in Petronius —— 81
3.1.1	Adding more magic to the legend —— 84
3.1.2	A story only for credulous lads? —— 86
3.2	Popular horror stories: the witches of Trimalchio —— 90
3.2.1	Another story for the credulous? —— 93
3.3	The rituals of Proselenos and Oenothea: priestesses or witches? —— 95

3.3.1	Priapic rituals and magic: Proselenos —— **98**
3.3.2	Priapic rituals and magic: Oenothea —— **103**
3.3.3	Magic: Another failure —— **104**
3.3.4	Magic as charlatanry —— **105**
3.4	Conclusions —— **107**

4 Epilogue —— 109

Bibliography —— 111
Index of Passages —— 121
General Index —— 129

Abbreviations

All journal abbreviations follow the system of *L'Année Philologique*. Ancient authors, their works, and special collections are abbreviated according to *OCD* 4th edition, with only minor changes for clarification. Here are any other abbreviations used:

DT	A. Audollent (1904), *Defixionum tabellae*, Paris.
DTM	J. Blänsdorf (2012), *Die defixionum tabellae des Mainzer Isis- und Mater Magna-Heiligtums, Defixionum tabellae Mogontiacenses*, Mainz.
OCD	S. Hornblower, A. Spawforth, and E. Eidinow (eds.) (2012), *The Oxford Classical Dictionary*, Oxford.
OLD	P.G.W. Glare (ed.) (2012), *Oxford Latin Dictionary*, 2nd ed., Oxford.
PDM (and PGM not included in Preisendanz)	H.D. Betz (1986), *The Greek Magical Papyri in Translation: Including the Demotic Spells*, Chicago.
PGM	K. Preisendanz and A. Henrichs (eds.) (1974), *Papyri Graecae Magicae*, 2nd ed., 2 vols., Stuttgart.
SGD	Jordan, D.R. (1985), "A Survey of Greek Defixiones not included in the Special Corpora", In: *GRBS* 26, 151–197.

The critical and bilingual editions of several authors which are consistently and extensively used in the book are included in the bibliography. In producing my translations, I have consulted the following works:

(For the *Medea*)
Boyle, A.J. (2014), *Seneca: Medea*, Oxford.
Wilson, E.R. (2010), *Seneca. Six Tragedies*, Oxford.

(For Lucan)
Braund, S.H. (2008), *Lucan, Civil War*, Oxford.

(For Petronius)
Sullivan, J.P. (2011), *Petronius: The Satyricon*, London.

Introduction

For years, Neronian authors remained in the shadow of Augustan literature, with the works of Seneca, Petronius, Lucan, and Persius constantly being compared to those of Vergil, Ovid, and Horace. The outcome was almost always unfavorable, downplaying their artistic and literary value, until scholarship began to examine these works not only in comparison with the Augustan models, but also in their own right.[1] This renewed interest eventually led to the reappraisal of Neronian literature as the product of a period of different cultural, social, and political realities.[2] Topics and themes which the Augustan authors rejected as unsuitable for literary treatment, such as low-class life and religion, popular superstitions, witchcraft, crude sexual encounters, gruesome deaths, and torture, became central features in the literature of the post-Augustan era.

The Neronian authors' preoccupation with *superstitio*[3] and its most extreme form, magic,[4] exemplifies the pursuit of novel literary themes and a turn towards

---

[1] The view of post-Augustan literature as the low-value product of a decadent period was put forward in Nisard 1834, and strongly persisted till the last decades of the twentieth century (see, for example, the assessments of Rose 1936, 348 and MacL. Currie 1985, vii). Even the term 'Silver', which characterizes collectively the era of the first century CE, implies a downgrade from the previous 'Golden' Age of Augustus (Dudley 1972, ix).
[2] Cizek 1972, 289–290 notes that Neronian authors may have not used Vergil as a model, but they adopted certain stylistic features and the moralizing tendency underlying his works; in 291–292 he recognizes the novelty in the literature of the period. Morford 1973, and Dominik 1993 also argue for a shift rather than decline in the literary aesthetics. For a more recent discussion on the reassessment of Lucan, Seneca, and Petronius see Littlewood 2017, 79–92 and Dinter 2013, 6–12.
[3] The Latin term '*superstitio*' has been notoriously difficult to define (see Martin 2004, 10–20; Gordon 2008, 72–73). Although customarily translated as "superstition", initially it bore no negative connotations (Martin 2004, 126; Gordon 2008, 77), but subsequently obtained a derogatory meaning (Martin 2004, 127), and began to be viewed as an opposite concept to *religio* (Scheid 2003, 22–23; Šterbenc Erker 2013, 126). The evolvement of its meaning in Latin is discussed in detail in Martin 2004, 125–139, and Gordon 2008, 78–94. Special care should be applied when considering *superstitio* in philosophical discourse and, with regards to its meaning, scholars usually draw a neat distinction between its vernacular and philosophical use. Throughout the book *superstitio* and superstition are used interchangeably, and only with their pejorative meaning.
[4] Some type of conceptual connection between magic and superstition was conceived at least since the time of Pliny (*HN* 30.6–7), who mentions that, according to legend, magic partially sprang from the *superstitio* of Orpheus. My own view is that superstition denotes one's beliefs in strange supernatural powers, which are different from a given epoch and culture's normative religion or from what an ancient author considers acceptable religious practice, while magic is the active expression of these beliefs by means of spells, incantations, and rituals. See also the discussion and the notes on pages 14–16, and 20.

https://doi.org/10.1515/9783111429441-205

the representation of everyday life. Magic had gained such popularity that it came to be regarded as one of the all-important cultural features of the period.[5] The works of the authors of the Flavian and Trajanic/Hadrianic periods also reflect its prominence in their portrayals of Nero. These depictions may have been part of an effort to discredit the last Julio-Claudian emperor and, by extension, the whole dynasty in favor of the new ones.[6]

Nero, the superstitious emperor: the face of a whole period

Textual passages dealing with Nero's attitude toward superstition and magic are part of larger works, hostile to him, and marked by a distinctively negative tone. The observation that there is little substance to Pliny's as well as Suetonius' depiction of the emperor as an irreligious and tyrannical ruler is probably accurate since the evidence from official sources contradicts these authors' descriptions of Nero.[7] Such negative portrayals appeared soon after his demise as, for example, in the anonymous play *Octavia*, where he is characterized as a *hostis deum* (240) and as someone who scorns the gods (89: *spernit superos*).[8] In the general context of tragedy, such characterizations are expected, and serve to enhance the feelings of sympathy toward the protagonist — in this case Octavia, who suffers at the hands of a most cruel enemy.

Negative portrayals of Nero are also found in encyclopedic works and biographies. In his discussion concerning the history of magic, Pliny narrates an anecdotal story about Nero with the aim of illustrating the vanity of the *ars magica*. He

---

[5] Castagna 2002, xv: "Il periodo neroniano è il tempo dell'innaturale e del sovrannaturale: è il tempo della magia e del vaticinio mostruoso". A common assumption supported by material evidence, most notably the increasing number of *defixiones* (see the chronological index in Audollent 1904, 556) as well as "The very great number of magical gemstones ... from the first few centuries of the Christian era suggests that in some way magic had got a stronger hold upon people of those times than ever before" (Bonner 1950, 22). Literary sources also point to this direction with Pliny claiming that, during his own time, men began to wear rings engraved with the figure of Harpocrates and other Egyptian deities (*HN* 33.41), and that there is not even a single individual who is not afraid of being bound by a *defixio* (*HN* 28.19). For the opposite view, downplaying the prominence of magic in the early Imperial period see Meggitt 2013.
[6] Edwards 2000, xx. On passages dealing with Nero's obsession with magic see Andrikopoulos 2009, 55–64.
[7] Šterbenc Erker 2013, 118–126, providing evidence which aptly illustrates that traditional festivals and state rituals were held as usual under Nero. Champlin 2003, 132 also notes that Nero attended to his official religious duties, but Suetonius' description of the emperor as an individual with a tendency to superstition and one who scorned all *religiones* is probably accurate.
[8] For the dating issue of the *Octavia*, see the discussion in Ferri 2003, 5–30, and Boyle 2008, xiii–xvi.

claims that even the emperor, who initially was a fervent supporter and a great enthusiast of the occult (his passion for magic matched his notorious obsession with the performing arts), eventually lost interest after he realized the falsity of such practices, even though the *magus* Tiridates had initiated Nero in the mysteries of the Persian *magoi* (*HN* 30.14–17). This passage represents Pliny's views as a member of the senatorial elite on the value and potency of magic as well as its alleged connection with the practices of the Persian priesthood.[9]

Suetonius' portrayal of Nero as an emperor indifferent to religious observances, sacrilegious as well as extremely superstitious, further serves as a discourse on magic in the Neronian period (*Ner.* 56):

> Religionum usque quaque contemptor, praeter unius Deae Syriae, hanc mox ita sprevit ut urina contaminaret, alia superstitione captus, in qua sola pertinacissime haesit, siquidem imagunculam puellarem, cum quasi remedium insidiarum a plebeio quodam et ignoto muneri accepisset, detecta confestim coniuratione pro summo numine trinisque in die sacrificiis colere perseveravit volebatque credi monitione eius futura praenoscere.[10]

> An incessant despiser of every cult, except only for that of the Syrian goddess; he soon scorned her so much to the point that he polluted her with his urine, having been captivated by another superstition to which he solely and constantly remained attached. Since indeed, after he had accepted a small effigy of a girl from an unknown plebeian as a protection against conspiracies, a plot was immediately uncovered, he kept venerating it as the supreme deity and thrice sacrificing to it each day, and wanted to impose the belief that he could foreknow the future through its admonitions.

Nero showed his contempt for any type of *religio* except for the cult of the *Dea Syria*, which Suetonius indirectly characterizes as superstition by referring to the emperor's subsequent interest as *alia superstitio*. Through the reference to the *Dea Syria*, Suetonius alludes to the un-Roman and exotic rituals of her worship, thus underlining another aspect of superstition and, by extension, magic: its foreign and exotic character.

Nonetheless, Nero's attitude changed as soon as he became acquainted with another form of *superstitio*, that is, the use of magical objects. According to the passage, an unknown plebeian offered him a miniature figure or image of a girl (*imagunculam puellarem*) as a protective talisman against assassination plots.[11] Nero

---

9 Andrikopoulos 2009, 55–56.
10 The text of Suetonius is from Rolfe's 1950 Loeb edition. All translations are my own.
11 Although the origin of such figurines for the purposes of bewitchment and protection can be traced back to native religious ideas of Egypt and the Near East (Wilburn 2012, 132–133, with relevant bibliography in the notes), private manufacture and use of protective talismans spread throughout the Mediterranean in the Imperial period as we infer from the existence of magical

became obsessed with the figurine, after a conspiracy was revealed, and began venerating the statuette as the supreme deity, offering daily prayers and sacrifices. His belief in the magical powers of amulets is the subject of another excerpt from his biography (*Ner.* 6):

> quas tamen aureae armillae ex voluntate matris inclusas dextro brachio gestavit aliquamdiu ac taedio tandem maternae memoriae abiecit rursusque extremis suis rebus frustra requisiit.
>
> However, after he enclosed these (sc. the slough of snakes) in a golden armlet at his mother's will, he wore it for some time on his right forearm and eventually got rid of it as he grew weary of his mother's memory, and sought it again unsuccessfully at his final moments.

When Messalina sent assassins to kill Nero, a snake darted out of his pillow scaring them away and saving his life. Soon it was noticed that the snake was nothing but a serpent's skin, and the emperor, following Agrippina's advice, placed the skin in an armlet, using it as an amulet. After he had his own mother murdered, he disposed of it, but sought it again when he felt that his life was coming to an end. In this excerpt, Suetonius projects upon his portrait of Nero the popular belief that certain artifacts possessed magical powers and afforded their owners control over the future.

The climax of Suetonius' description of Nero as an individual prone to the occult is central in an excerpt detailing his efforts to appease the soul of his murdered mother, Agrippina, through necromantic rituals: *quin et facto per magos sacro evocare manes et exorare temptavit* (Suet. *Ner.* 34.4). Brief, yet most imposing about Nero's sketching as a superstitious person, the story reflects, in a nutshell, the most important aspect of magic, that is, its alleged power to violate the natural order.

Why magic? Social, and cultural developments in the era of imperial globalization

Even though these anecdotal stories contain elements of hyperbole, they tend to exaggerate a personal trait of the last Julio-Claudian emperor, his tendency toward superstition.[12] The passages dealing with Nero's obsession with magic reflect developments in the religious life of the Empire that created the ideal environment for the 'blow-up' of witchcraft. In the first century CE, the Roman world extends to the furthest corners of the world, from the Middle East to Spain, and from Britain to

---

papyri which give instructions on how to produce and use these objects (Wilburn 2012, 134–139; Faraone 2018, 263–287).

12 Champlin 2003, 132.

Egypt, incorporating diverse ethnic groups. People from different cultural backgrounds are now able to travel or immigrate more easily within the boundaries of a large area under the protection of the Roman Empire, facilitating the flow of, and access to, different ideas, customs, and habits.[13] Thus, magic began to fascinate the Roman mind even more either as a mysterious and exotic practice for the curious, or as a means of achieving anything beyond human power for the naïve.[14] At the same time, just like anything different and new, it provoked anxiety to supporters of tradition and the established order. This may also explain why the distinction between *religio* and *superstitio* became a hot topic for debate in the Neronian period, and why certain aspects of it are treated in the works of Seneca, Persius, Lucan, and Petronius.[15]

The centrality of magic in literature was also made possible due to the changes in the institution of patronage which took place in the later Augustan period, when the authors passed under the emperor's control.[16] The existence of multiple literary circles under the patronage of Nero, where leading figures such as Calpurnius Piso, Seneca, and Thrasea Paetus acted only as intermediaries, probably gave authors greater freedom, compared to the scrutiny Augustan patrons had exercised previously.[17] Neronian literature was not completely subordinate to the demands of the imperial propaganda, but also drew inspiration from everyday life.[18] To put it simply, the themes were not imposed from a political and literary elite; instead, they were chosen by the authors, and the patron-emperor gave his approval

---

13 Migration in the Roman world is admittedly a complex issue, touching upon multiple aspects of social, economic, and religious life. See, for instance, the following studies, which deal with several topics: Noy 2000; Tacoma 2016; Lo Cascio and Tacoma 2016.
14 The role of magic in humanity's efforts to sway the events which were out of its control was noted by Tylor 1871, 104, and Frazer 1925, 11. For the different suggestions on the development of the concept of magic in the Roman world see Garosi 1976, 33–74, Graf 1997a, 56–60, and Dickie 2001, 120–136.
15 Šterbenc Erker 2013, 126–131 recognizes this dichotomy in the religious life of the period and its influence on the literary production.
16 Morford 1973, 211; Morford 1985, 2005–2006 notes that this significant change took place under Augustus' reign after the death of Maecenas.
17 Besides, the wealth of Seneca, Lucan, Persius, and (perhaps) Petronius meant that these authors did not depend on the economic support of a patron to keep up with their literary activities (Morford 1985, 2012). For a detailed discussion on the major literary circles of the Neronian period, their members and activities see Cizek 1972, 291–297 (Seneca), 349–358 (Cornutus), 366–369 (Probus), 369–371 (*Calpurnii*), and 381–387 (Thrasea Paetus). Morford 1985, 2011–2012 rejects the schema of literary patronage proposed by Cizek.
18 Griffin 1984, 149: "The flattery of the 'court poets' does not reveal any literary direction from the throne"; referring to the poet Lucilius, Seneca's protégé, on the same page: "His epigrams as a whole reflect the Greek milieu of Rome — its astrologers, doctors, grammarians and athletes".

afterwards.[19] This view is further supported by evidence from Suetonius (*Ner.* 42) and Tacitus (*Ann.* 14.16), whose narratives point to the existence of literary circles where Nero's literary acquaintances would put their compositions up for the emperor to amend or criticize.[20]

These changes provided new opportunities which explain the interest in magic and *superstitio* in Neronian literature. The choice and manner of treatment, however, was a more complex process, informed by the authors' orientation towards the topic: as modes of religious thought and ritual, *superstitio* and magic challenged norms, and transgressed natural, social, and religious boundaries defined by the official state religion.[21] Its atypical characteristics rendered the topic of witchcraft the ideal means for negotiating anew aesthetic norms and earlier literary models. Seneca, Lucan, and Petronius test and expand the traditional aesthetic boundaries delineated in Augustan literature by writing about a topic which was considered, in and of itself, transgressive.

Magic in imperial literature: before and during Nero

Literary descriptions of magic do occur in Augustan literature, but they are generic and do not offer accurate depictions of actual witchcraft rituals. They are typically limited to general observations about the powers and impious activities of witches and sorcerers as well as the effects of magic on nature.[22] For example, in *Aeneid* 7.750–760, Vergil describes the powers of the Marsic priest Umbro, who has the ability to hypnotize snakes with spells (*cantu*) and alleviate the effects of their bite with his skills (*arte*). In *Epode* 5, Horace describes the impious rite of the witches Canidia and Sagana, who have captured a boy and are about to starve him to death in order to use his liver in the concoction of a love potion. These two witches also appear in *Satire* 1.8, where they perform a magic ritual before an effigy of Priapus scares them away with his fart. In *Fasti* 6.141–145, Ovid describes how old women transform into the bird *strix* and attack Proca in his cradle, sucking out his blood. Even Vergil's *Eclogue* 8, which includes the first extant description of sympathetic love magic in Latin literature, and Ovid's extensive narrative of Medea's spell to rejuvenate

---

19 In addition, Persius 1.30–36 shows the poet's disdain toward the practice of offering recitativo performances during banquets, where the participants would give their approval afterwards (*adsensere viri*). See also Castagna 2002, ix.
20 Sullivan 1968b, 454–455.
21 See the observations about magic in Gordon 1987b, 60.
22 However, scholars have also argued for the influence of contemporary reality on the narratives of magic in Augustan authors. See, for example, Eitrem 1941, 63, Tupet 1976, xiii, and Luck 1999, 123.

Aeson (*Met.* 7.179–293), need not be attributed to their respective author's empirical knowledge or hearsay. Although single details that allude to real magic rituals of the *PGM* can be found in both texts, it is generally accepted that these accounts were strongly influenced by earlier literary models.[23] Finally, it is worth noting that descriptions of magic, some of which appear as more realistic, are more prevalent in the works of Ovid than in those of other Augustan authors, thus suggesting a change in literary aesthetics from the late Augustan years onwards.[24] In other words, Ovid can be viewed as the precursor or, rather, a transition point in the process of transformation of the literary aesthetics of Neronian authors.[25]

Neronian representations of witchcraft draw material from earlier accounts, including those of the Augustan authors, but further exhibit a degree of realism which has no precedent in Latin literature. This becomes clear through the comparison of witchcraft scenes with the text of the *PGM* and the *defixiones*, bringing to light verbal similarities as well as structural and conceptual connections, direct or implicit. Of course, contemporary popular views about magic such as those attested in Pliny's *Natural History* were also broadly exploited by Neronian authors with the aim of making the scenes they describe appear more realistic. The change in literary aesthetic, by comparison, reveals a sharper and lively criticism of magic, its practitioners as well as those who believe in its power, and is expressed in diverse forms and through different techniques employed by each author.

Scope of the book

Even though scholars have analyzed the magic rituals in Seneca's *Medea*, Lucan's book six, and Petronius' *Satyrica*, a systematic cross-genre examination of the motif of witchcraft in Neronian literature is lacking.[26] This book aspires to fill this gap and explores the topic of superstition and magic in these three representative works. The study corroborates that realism emerges as the salient trait of Neronian

---

[23] Gordon 2009, 210–211, contra Eitrem 1941, 63 argues that Augustan descriptions of magic do not reflect their respective authors' real-life experiences, but they were shaped under the influence of earlier literary works, such as Varro Atacinus' translation of the *Argonautica*, Catullus' emulation of Theocritus' second *Idyll*, and Ennius' *Medea*, all of which drew upon Classical and Hellenistic sources.
[24] The account of Medea's magic in *Met.* 7.179–293, and his curse poetry *Ibis* are the most conspicuous examples.
[25] Williams 1978, 52; Castagna 2002, xv.
[26] The most detailed treatment of the witchcraft scenes in Lucan and Seneca's *Medea* is Reif 2016; Schmeling and Setaioli 2011 discuss several links between magic and the rituals of Oenothea, Proselenos as well as the tales in *Satyrica* 62 and 63, in the relevant pages of their commentary.

witchcraft scenes on the basis of a thorough comparison with the text of the *PGM* and the *defixiones* as well as the *quasi*-magical recipes found in Pliny the Elder. The imprint of realism in representations of magic rituals, moreover, affords us the opportunity to observe how authors in the Neronian period renegotiated earlier aesthetic boundaries. They did so by deconstructing the 'sterilized' descriptions of the Augustan authors, replacing them with depictions of creative gruesomeness or hilarious sexualization.

The major contribution of the book, however, is to consider realism in the context of each author's purpose. Influenced by Gordon's theory on the different forms of the critique of magic in Graeco-Roman thought and literature,[27] my approach further explains how Neronian authors subordinate such high-degree realism to their own worldview, and foregrounds their intensive engagement with the ills and trickery of magic. More specifically, I show that, on the one hand, the realism of the witchcraft scenes creates an unbreakable bond between reader, real-life, and text that encourages more active participation on the part of the reader. On the other hand, this very realism becomes an indispensable tool which affects the reader's response toward contemporary magic. Realism, in effect, substantiates the criticism of magic. Images of destruction, the horrific, and the ridiculous further serve as the necessary stimuli which facilitate a recognition process on the part of the reader. Casting magic in such a negative light shapes the reader's moral interpretation and, by extension, elicits their critical response to witchcraft.

Chapter I argues that, in the context of Seneca's philosophical drama, his *Medea* can be read as a play illustrating the havoc magic wreaks upon the world with the intent to avert the reader from such practices. My analysis of the heroine's soliloquy in the prologue highlights the passage's affiliation with 'borderline *defixiones*',[28] which betrays the play's preoccupation with the occult, while also illustrating the anti-Stoic and subversive character of magic. The conceptual clash between Medea's utterance and the chorus' subsequent prayer not only underscores the absurdity of magic and its opposition to normative religion, but also foreshadows the eventual dominance of the former over the latter. The feeling of fear and the tension which the prologue arouses in the reader run throughout the play and culminate in the description of Medea's poison concoction. The central scene, with its obsessive focus on the heroine's witchcraft as well as the horror it causes, points up the play's substantive differences from earlier treatments of the myth and further highlights its didactic value. The realistic details in the depiction of Medea's ritual bridge the gap between the mythological witch and reality and accentuate her

---

27 Gordon 1987b.
28 A term coined in Versnel 1991, 63.

negative traits as *pharmakos*. Seneca's emphasis on the horrific aspect of Medea's art further enhances the 'apotropaic' role of the drama that criticizes magic as a force that brings utter destruction to the social, political, and religious order.

Chapter II examines Erichtho's necromancy scene as Lucan's tool of criticism against magic, also turning against its practitioners, and recipients alike. His attacks are first directed toward Sextus, who is sketched as an anti-Stoic and anti-Roman character, and whose passions lead him to resort to magical divination. In the prelude to the witch's appearance, Lucan predisposes the reader about what will follow: his presentation of Thessalian witchcraft invites the reader to view it, at times, as a force that contradicts the tenets of Stoicism and subverts the natural order, and, at other times, as charlatanry. In the central scene, he shows magic to be a malign, yet ineffective force. The sketching of Erichtho as a witch surpassing all her Thessalian sisters, combined with the high-degree realism of her ritual, creates high expectations in the reader. When Sextus, however, does not procure the information he seeks, the reader is stunned at the failure of this iconic witch and begins to question the effectiveness of magic and the power of its practitioners.

Finally, chapter III provides a lucid discussion on superstitious beliefs and magic rituals in the *Satyrica* as a parody of the dominant role of magic not only in the literature of the period, but also in Neronian life. The inset tales of the werewolf and the *strigae*, narrated in the *Cena Trimalchionis*, are examined as Petronius' new creations, a pastiche of earlier traditions of human-wolf transformations and popular beliefs, respectively, which cause the intranarrative audience's chills and fear. These stories, however, have a different impact on Petronius' educated reader, who cannot but mock the credulity and reactions of the intranarrative audience and, by extension, the claims of magic. The tension between the attitude of Petronius' low-life characters and that of the reader persists, albeit in a different form, throughout the Proselenos and the Oenothea episodes. Encolpius' credulity leads him to endure abuse and pain during the priapic rituals in hope of curing his impotence. For the reader, by contrast, the two priapic priestesses are mere caricatures of the witch-figure, with the result that the rites performed, which resemble *quasi*-magical recipes of popular medicine, are nothing more than a pretext for the women to sexually exploit the protagonist. The ridiculous and highly sexualized character of the rites can only cause the reader's laughter, while their eventual failure underscores magic as charlatanry.

1 Seneca the Moralist

The influence of Stoicism on Seneca's tragedies has been asserted early on, provoking a scholarly discussion that is still ongoing. Many of the philosophical interpretations of Senecan drama in general, and the *Medea* in particular, approach the play(s) from the perspective of Stoic psychology and ethics.[1] However, the author's thematic versatility, which is also evident in his prose works, suggests that there are more interpretative paths to take.[2]

Admittedly, Senecan drama articulates a notably anti-Stoic cosmos, in which the negative aspects of reality are stretched to their limits.[3] These exaggerated depictions function in and of themselves as a critique of the conditions upon which they are modelled. As such, they also serve as a springboard for the reader to contemplate on several vexing issues whose possible solutions, for Seneca, are to be sought through Stoic indoctrination.[4] Thus the prose works and the plays form an organic unity, the latter setting forth the problematic aspects of contemporary life, for which the Stoic philosophical teachings offer a cure.[5]

Among the topics Seneca treats *passim* in his philosophical essays and letters are aspects of the divine and traditional religion. His interest on contemporary religious change and practice, which is proved most aptly by the authorship of a now lost treatise entitled *De Superstitione*, can be justified on two grounds: his commitment

---

[1] The *Medea* has been variously viewed as: a mythological *exemplum* illustrating the relation between *adiaphora* and Stoic happiness (Egermann 1940, 41–42); a neo-Stoic lesson on the harmful results of passion on the human soul (Marti 1945b, 229–233); a dramatic exposition of Stoic theories on human psychology (Pratt 1948, 4); a play influenced by Stoic cosmological principles, such as *krasis* and *sympatheia* (Rosenmeyer 1989); a tool for the moral education of the audience through "critical spectatorship" (Nussbaum 1993, 142–148); a probe on issues of identity and self-construction (Fitch and McElduff 2002); an example reproducing the Senecan practice of *meditatio*, illustrating the heroine's introspection of her own struggle, decisions, actions, and subsequent self-recognition to underline the perils of "ethical solipsism" (Bartsch 2006, 231–232); an expansion of the Stoic dogma on consistency and self-restrain, connecting vice and *constantia* in the context of Stoic psychology (Star 2006, 232–241; 2012, 76–83); a dramatization of the Stoic cognitive process (Staley 2010, 81–82 and 94).
[2] Boyle 1997, 33 lists several declamatory topics that run through both the tragedies and the philosophical works of Seneca.
[3] Tarrant 2006, 5–11. Sandbach 1975, 160–161 and Dingel 1974 argued successfully that the tragedies are a 'negation' of Stoicism. See also Lefèvre 2002, 108–110.
[4] Staley 2010, 51: "Seneca's tragedies were probably not tools for teaching philosophy, but they offered an opportunity to think about philosophy and its concerns, both ethical and poetical".
[5] Thematic and stylistic links between the plays and the philosophical works of Seneca are discussed in Tarrant 2006.

to Stoicism as well as his prominent position in Roman public life. For Seneca *superstitio*, an issue very much alive in the first century CE, as we infer from other authors of the period (e.g. Pliny *HN* 8.80, 28.36–39, 29.83; Persius' second satire; Plutarch's Περὶ δεισιδαιμονίας; Quint. *Inst.* 7.3.7, *Decl. min.* 385), touches upon both his philosophical interests but also the practicalities of Roman public life. Though the topic constantly comes up in Senecan drama as several tragedies include depictions of perverted rituals (e.g. *Oedipus'* necromancy, the sacrifice of children and the subsequent *extispicium* in *Thyestes*, Polyxena's death as wedding perversion in *Troades*), it is of paramount significance in the *Medea*, which heavily engages with magic and the occult.[6]

The *Medea* dramatically expounds the issue of superstition through the focus on its most characteristic and excessive form, i.e. magic. The heroine's narrow portrayal as an evil witch, and the presentation of her magic exclusively as a destructive and subversive force, affirms the play's didacticism, no matter how oblique, which aims at the reader's edification. The negative representation of Medea's *ars*, which is in complete accord with Seneca's view of magic as a repugnant practice that contradicts major tenets of Stoic theology, delineates both the protagonist and her actions as a fear-causing *monstrum* — in the words of Strabo φοβερὸν τερατῶδες (Str. 1.2.8). Such horrific impressions have an 'apotropaic' function, averting the reader from superstition and from the tantalizing power of magic.[7]

There is no doubt that the choice of Medea was apt for Seneca as the mythological story of the Colchian witch provided him with all the necessary ingredients to criticize magic and its practitioners: the gender of the protagonist which adheres to contemporary popular views about witches being usually women; her oriental ethnicity, pointing to the birth place of magic and simultaneously separating her from a religiously homogenous community (Corinth); a figure well-known for her supernatural powers, whose myth embodies the antithesis between the civilized Graeco-Roman and the barbaric 'other'; finally, the killings of Creon, Creusa, but especially the murder of her own children exemplify the destruction magic can cause on the natural, social and political order.[8]

---

[6] Dupont 1995, 189–222 discusses ritual perversions in Seneca's plays.
[7] The 'apotropaic' and parenetic function of drama in Stoic thought is discussed in Strabo 1.2. For an overview of the scholarly debate on the educational role of tragedy in Stoicism, with particular emphasis on the views of Seneca, see Staley 2010, 24–31 and Chaumartin 2014, 653–669.
[8] Boyle 2014, lxix–lxxi discusses these as well as other thematics that became central in Roman treatments of Medea's myth. The key features of the myth are also examined and analyzed in Griffiths 2006, 41–50 and 59–63. The political aspects of Seneca's *Medea* are discussed in Lefèvre 2002, 118–119.

However, Medea's wickedness, like that of Oscar Wilde's Dorian Gray, is not reflected in some ugly countenance or appalling form. Her human appearance (compared to that of the witches of Latin elegy, and Erichtho) as well as her divine descent, distance her from contemporary conceptions of the witch.[9] To bring the mythological figure closer to the reader's mental image of an evil sorceress, Seneca subordinates the archetype to contemporary reality by incorporating features that recall the *PGM* and the *defixiones* as well as societal stereotypes in Medea's magic.[10] These elements essentially serve as the anchor between reality and literature, facilitating the process of recognition for the reader, and by extension enhance the 'apotropaic' function of the drama.

At first, Seneca presents the reader with the heroine's soliloquy, to which he gives the form of an imprecation. Such evil utterances epitomize the practice of praying for somebody's harm, which the Romans considered *superstitio* (Cic. *Clu.* 194), and which Seneca criticizes in his philosophical works (Sen. *Ep.* 32.4; *QNat.* 3 pf. 14). Medea's imprecation, the result of the author's interplay between reality and literary precepts, betrays early on the play's preoccupation with magic and the occult. The passage is permeated by sinister and subversive images which impose a gloomy atmosphere that arouses tension and fear in the reader. Intertextual and intratextual ironies further underscore the subversive power of magic and the irrationality of Medea's evil prayer.

A further comparison of the imprecation with the chorus' wedding song, which follows immediately after and serves as a point of reference for the distinction between *religio* and *superstitio* within the play's cosmos, shows in an exemplary way how magic subverts religious norms for illicit purposes. The juxtaposition between these two passages in the readers' mind, who are aware of the play's ending, brings to light several differences that underscore the superiority of magic compared to conventional religion.[11] When death and destruction finally strike Corinth, the reader retrospectively realizes the powerlessness of religion, arousing the feeling of vulnerability which intensifies their horror.

The criticism of magic, however, becomes manifest in the scene of the ritual, in which Seneca transforms Ovid's ambiguous representation of Medea and her practices, with the aim of developing an exclusively evil portrayal of the heroine and

---

9 Gordon 1987b, 73–74 and 83.
10 The most detailed and extensive study tracing features of the *PGM* in the ritual of Medea is Reif 2016, 341–370.
11 Hine 1989 notes the similarities and differences between the two passages and discusses the implications for the reader.

her magic.[12] To this end, he stages a long and accurate witchcraft scene, full of features recalling the spells of the *PGM* that enhance the readers' experience, but most important allow Seneca to surpass its literary antecedent.[13] In other words, Seneca exploits verisimilitude to turn Ovid's *monstrum* (Ov. *Met.* 7.294: the marvelous) into a different type of *monstrum* (Sen. *Med.* 191, and 675: the abominable), simultaneously obliterating the beneficial aspects of Medea's magic as seen, for instance, in Ovid's *Metamorphoses*. The scene in its entirety maximizes the dreadful emotion in the reader's soul just as it does in the intratextual audience, i.e. Medea's nurse.

1.1 Medea's imprecation and its magical setting

The prologue's timeframe, combined with the heroine's isolation, outlines the magical character of her utterance.[14] The scene takes place in the evening, which was an appropriate time for the performance of magic rituals as the instructions in some papyri indicate (e.g. *PGM* I 69: ὀψίας; IV 1853, VII 226: ὀψέ). Since Medea appears alone on stage, when her prayer's malicious content is gradually revealed, the reader infers that the utterance is meant to be inaudible to other characters, and therefore an effort to engage in magic and to hide illegal designs.

Silent prayer was part of Roman religious life (Sen. *Ben.* 6.38.1–5; *Ep.* 10.5), but it is also a *locus communis* of ancient literature, especially for magical and evil prayers.[15] In contemporary reality, evil supplications found their most apt and clear example in the *defixiones*, binding curses inscribed usually on lead tablets.[16] The image of Medea mumbling her magical prayers is already found in Ovid's *Metamorphoses* 7.251 (*precibusque et murmure longo*) in the context of Aeson's rejuvenation, while her use of binding spells is referred to in Ov. *Her.* 6.91 (*devovet absentis simulacraque cerea figit*). In the prologue of the *Medea*, Seneca combines and enlivens these two images, simultaneously expanding them by furnishing the heroine's utterance with features alluding to real curses, to create an unprecedently baleful prayer. The similarities of her imprecation with the text of the *defixiones* and

---

12 Reif 2016, 411. Trinacty 2014, 111–118 on how Seneca reworks and transforms the Ovidian model, with particular focus on her image as a witch.
13 Trinacty 2014, 114.
14 Boyle 2014, 100 sets the time as "late afternoon" and notes that no other character is onstage.
15 van der Horst 1994, 2–12 recognizes several sinister motives for praying silently and supports his argument with specific examples from both Greek and Latin literature.
16 Studies on these binding spells, both Greek and Roman, include Gager 1992; Graf 1997a, 118–174; Urbanová 2018; Ogden 2002a, 210–226; Watson 2019, 57–98; Eidinow 2019, 351–387. McKie 2022 provides a comprehensive study of curses from the western provinces of the Empire.

'prayers for justice' sketch her utterance as a 'borderline *defixio*'.[17] The prologue's structure follows the general pattern of ancient prayer: lines 1–17 list the deities addressed by Medea (*invocatio*), 17–26 detail her requests (*preces*), and 37–55 mention the offerings (*narratio*).[18]

The *invocatio*

> Di coniugales tuque genialis tori,
> Lucina, custos quaeque domituram freta
> Tiphyn novam frenare docuisti ratem,
> et tu, profundi saeve dominator maris,
> clarumque Titan dividens orbi diem,   5
> tacitisque praebens conscium sacris iubar
> Hecate triformis, quosque iuravit mihi
> deos Iason, quosque Medeae magis
> fas est precari: noctis aeternae chaos,
> aversa superis regna manesque impios   10
> dominumque regni tristis et dominam fide
> meliore raptam, voce non fausta precor.
> nunc, nunc adeste sceleris ultrices deae,
> crinem solutis squalidae serpentibus,
> atram cruentis manibus amplexae facem,   15
> adeste, thalamis horridae quondam meis
> quales stetistis:[19]
>
> Conjugal gods, and you, guardian of the bridal bed,
> Lucina, and you who taught Tiphys to govern the new ship
> that would tame the waves,
> and you, stern ruler of the deep sea,
> and Sun, who divides the bright day with your circles,
> and you, who gives your rays, privy to secrets, to silent rites,
> triple-formed Hecate, and gods by whom Jason swore to me,
> and to whom for Medea it is more

---

17 The terms 'prayer for justice' and 'borderline *defixio*' were coined by Versnel 1991, 68 and 63 respectively.
18 Graf 1997a, 192–193 (on Erichtho's magical prayer) and 292 n. 12 for secondary literature; Bremmer 1981, 196 uses the terms 'invocation', 'argument', and 'petition' for the three structural parts of prayers. This is a general structure, though variations such as repetition of the invocation and rearrangement of the sections do exist (Graf 1991, 188–213). Since 'prayers for justice' were essentially petitionary prayers, their structure is similar. Few *defixiones* also exhibit the structure of prayers (see, for instance, *DT* 190).
19 The text is cited from Zwierlein's edition with only minor modifications.

right to pray: chaos of endless night,
the kingdoms hostile to the gods above, and the impious shades,
the ruler of the grim kingdom and his consort,
who was snatched away in better faith, I invoke with an inauspicious voice.
Now, now come goddesses avenging crimes,
squalid with serpents entwined in your hair,
grasping the black torches with your bloody hands,
come, as you once stood terrible
in my wedding chambers.[20]

The invocation opens with an address to celestial gods: the *Di conjugales* (describing collectively Jupiter, Juno, Hymenaeus, and Venus);[21] *Lucina*;[22] *quaeque domituram freta Tiphyn novam frenare docuisti ratem*, (Minerva); *dominator maris* (Neptune); *Titan* (Sun). Following a descending order, Medea then calls upon *Hecate*,[23] whose central position in the play's theology is signaled through the appropriate address: her name, followed by the appellative *triformis*,[24] and a description clarifying that the heroine is invoking her in her capacity as the goddess of witchcraft (*tacitisque praebens conscium sacris iubar*).[25] This section closes with a list of chthonic gods: the deified spirit of Chaos (*noctis aeternae Chaos*),[26] the Underworld (*aversa superis*

---

[20] All translations included in this chapter are my own.
[21] For the identification of the collective *di conjugales* with these deities see Hine 2000, 111 and Boyle 2014, 102.
[22] Green 2007, 136–138 notes that Lucina, more correctly Juno Lucina, was an epithet of Diana in her capacity as patroness of childbirth and women in labor (Varro *Ling*. 5.69).
[23] Hecate's role in binding curses is well attested in the text of the *defixiones* where she is frequently addressed by name or descriptive epithets, such as, for instance, Ἑκάτη χθονία (*DT* 22, 24, 26, 29–33, 35), ῥηξίχθων (*DT* 38), Εἰνοδία (*DT* 41), ἀκρουροβόρη Σελήνη (*DT* 41), and Ἑκάτη τρίμορφος (*DT* 242) — the very last example is the Greek equivalent of the formula Medea uses in line 7 (*Hecate triformis*).
[24] Boyle 2014, 106 observes that the adjective was used to denote Hecate's different faces in the divine realm; in her celestial form she is identified with Luna, in her earthly form she is Diana, and in her chthonic form Hecate.
[25] This line alludes to the association between Medea and Hecate in mythology, which often presents Medea as the goddess' favorite or priestess (Eur. *Med*. 395–397; Ov. *Her*. 12.168, *Met*. 7.74, 194–195; Ap. Rhod. *Argon*. 3.252). Hecate is the deity whose aid Medea will seek insistently when concocting the deadly potion (750–839).
[26] Although *Chaos* occurs only once in the *defixiones*, in a first century CE curse against seven *venatores* (*DT* 251), it is frequently encountered in the magical papyri (*PGM* I 316, IV 443, 1459, 2535, 2849). The pairing of Chaos with the genitive *noctis* might allude to specific formulas such as "Νύξ, Ἔρεβος, Χάος εὐρύ" (*PGM* IV 2857–2858) or "μέλαν Χάος" (*PGM* IV 1247–1248) — in this last case through allusion to the common literary structure "νύξ μέλαινα" (e.g. Eur. *Cyc*. 601; Hom. *Il*. 8.486, 502; Hes. *Theog*. 123; Aesch. *Pers*. 357).

regna)²⁷ and its inhabitants (*manesque impios*),²⁸ its ruling couple (*dominumque regni tristis et dominam*),²⁹ and finally, the Erinyes (*ultrices deae*).³⁰

Extensive lists of chthonic deities feature prominently in the *PGM* and the text of the *defixiones*. However, addresses to celestial gods are a characteristic of 'prayers for justice'. Medea's imprecation also bears further similarities with this category of texts: the periphrastic addresses to Pluto (*dominum regni tristis*) and Persephone (*dominam raptam*), although highly formulaic, recall the use of flattering epithets (*dominus, domina*, δέσποινα, κύριος/κυρία); these adjectives as well as the supplication verbs (*precor, precari*) underscore the submissive tone of the utterance; the stereotypical address *ultrices deae* for the Furies might allude to the conceptual link between *ulciscor* and ἐκδικέω, both denoting some form of retribution for a suffered injustice, which is also confirmed later by the heroine's exclamation (25: *parta ultio est*); Medea's statement that she is invoking the gods to whom Jason had sworn provides an explanation for her appeal to divine justice by implying that he is an oath breaker;³¹ in the middle of her invocation she also reveals her name (*Medeae magis | fas est precari*), thus alluding to the common practice requiring the wronged person to identify themselves.³²

Literary allusions also confirm the affiliation of the utterance with 'prayers for justice' as they point to the injustices Medea has suffered. Juno (implied in the

---

27 The kingdom of the dead is invoked in some spells (*PGM* IV 1460–1461, XXIII 5, LXII 29) because it was considered the abode of demons and evil spirits who could inflict harm on people.
28 An oxymoron according to Hine 2000, 114 as the *manes* were considered *"boni"* (see Maltby 1991, 364). However, as inhabitants of the Underworld, they were also addressed in the *defixiones* as agents of punishment or binding forces for the recipient under various names, such as, for example, *Dii Manes* (*DT* 97, 101, 222), *inferi* (*DT* 96–98, 100), πνεύματα (*DT* 198), *Dii parentes* (*DT* 190), κάτω κείμενοι (*DT* 22, 24, 26, 29–32, 35), and καταχθόνιοι (*DT* 51).
29 Pluto and Persephone are two of the most frequently invoked gods in *defixiones* under various names and descriptive phrases: Πλούτων/*Pluto* (*DT* 1, 22, 24, 26, 29, 38, 111), χθονιθαρχωθ (*DT* 18), φθιμένων βασιλεύς (*DT* 198), Ὅρκος (*DT* 161, 163), *Dis* (*DT* 191, 139), and δόμινους (*DT* 231); Persephone is addressed either as Περσεφόνη (*DT* 74, 75), Φερσεφόνη (*DT* 50, 81), *Persefina* (*DT* 268), or Κόρη (*DT* 3, 9, 10, 13), *regina tenebrarum* (*DT* 288, 289), and δόμινα (*DT* 269).
30 *Furiae* (Erinyes or Eumenides) were the underworld demons whose role was to punish family crimes and transgressions by hunting the perpetrator. Usually three in number (Tisiphone, Allecto, and Megaera), they were considered the personification of curses, thus also identified collectively as *Dirae* or *Arae*. This explains why they feature prominently in *defixiones* (e.g. *DT* 22, 24, 26, 29–31, 33, 35), and why Medea invokes them.
31 Guastella 2001, 214–215 argues that Medea's aim is to exact punishment on Jason also for the benefits he enjoyed as a result of her earlier crimes, most notably the murder of her brother.
32 The distinctive features of the 'prayers for justice' class have been described first in Versnel 1991, 68 and again in Versnel 2010, 280.

collective *di conjugales*),[33] and Titan (assimilated with the Sun),[34] along with the liminal goddess Hecate, were the deities to whom Jason swore to marry Medea and love her forever (Ov. *Met.* 7.93–97 and *Her.* 12). His oath in the *Heroides* ends with a conditional self-imprecation (85–86: *spiritus ante meus tenues vanescet in auras, | quam thalamo, nisi tu, nupta sit ulla meo!*), and since Jason has now abandoned Medea, and plans to marry another wife, these deities serve as witnesses to her husband's misdeeds as well as appropriate agents of punishment for the issue at hand.[35] Medea's petition to Athena and Neptune for retribution might be harder to interpret, but it appears that the heroine considers them somehow responsible for her current sufferings: the former as the goddess who taught Tiphys how to steer the ship, the latter because he allowed Argo to sail safely across his realm. Behind these implications lies Medea's belief that she is entitled to their assistance because, if it was not for their favor, the voyage of the Argo would have never been completed and she would have never met Jason. Therefore, she invokes them to rectify the injustice she has suffered and punish the wrongdoer.

Preces: **Medea's requests and the targets of the curse**

> ... coniugi letum novae
> letumque socero et regiae stirpi date.
> Est peius aliquid? quod precer sponso malum?
> vivat; per urbes erret ignotas egens   20
> exul pavens invisus incerti laris,
> iam notus hospes limen alienum expetat;
> me coniugem optet, quoque non aliud queam
> peius precari, liberos similes patri
> similesque matri – parta iam, parta ultio est: 25
> peperi. ...

Give death to his new wife,
death to his father-in-law, and to the royal bloodline.
Is there anything worse? What torment should I wish for the husband?
Let him live; let him wander through foreign cities as a poor,

---

[33] Hine 2000, 111; Boyle 2014, 102.
[34] Versnel 1991, 70 discusses inscriptional evidence as well as literary prayers, which attest to the central role of Helios/Sol in 'prayers for justice' because of his ability to oversee everything that happens in the world, rendering him the ideal witness to any injustice suffered by an individual. Dido's hostile utterance against Aeneas in *Aeneid* 4.607 refers to this role of the Sun: *Sol, qui terrarum flammis opera omnia lustras*.
[35] Hine 2000, 113 correctly regards this line as 'heralding' Jason's sufferings.

a scared and hated exile, without a home,
an already notorious guest seeking a foreign bed;
let him long for me as his spouse, and –nothing worse I could
pray for– for children like their father
and like their mother –already it is born, my vengeance is born:
I have given birth...

Medea first asks for the deaths of Creusa (*coniugi*) and Creon (*socero*), as well as the destruction of the whole royal bloodline (*regiae stirpi*).[36] These requests recall, respectively, the wish for the death of the target in *defixiones*/'prayers for justice', and several formulas which extended the punishment to the family of the transgressor.[37] The vindictive character of the utterance is further supported by the phrase *dare letum* (17–18), which recalls an ancient legal formula used in funerals (Varro *Ling.* 7.42: *Ollus letum datus est*).[38] She then curses Jason to wander around the world (*per urbes erret ignotas*), poor (*egens*), a scared and hated exile (*exul pavens invisus*), homeless (*incerti laris*), begging for a bed (*limen alienum expetat*). These lines echo the punishment of exile as well as deprivation of sleep, hunger, thirst and beggary, which are encountered in binding spells.[39] Medea also asks that he may long for her as a wife, a curse found in *DT* 227, 230, 270 and 271, where the *defigens* asks that the victim burns with love or lust for them.

The passage also hints at the possible motives that triggered Medea's imprecation. Creusa becomes a target because she is a love rival who removed Jason from her and their children. The inscriptions on lead tablets, amulets, and voodoo dolls suggest that 'love matters' are some of the most common causes for resorting to

---

36 Reif 2016, 278 correctly thinks that the *regia stirps* points to a possible future descendant of Creusa and Jason.

37 Even though the devotee of a *defixio* would petition usually for the binding or the injury of the target, there are cases where the curse intends for the death of the recipient, such as *DT* 187 (ἀποκτείνατε, ὀλέσατε), *DT* 140 (*peroccide*), *DT* 129 (*interemates, interficiates*), *DT* 243 (*occidite*), *DT* 247 (*occidite, exterminate*), and *DT* 250 (*perducas ad domus tartareas*); for a detailed treatment of the threatened punishments in *defixiones* see Urbanová 2018, 77–84. The extension of the punishment to the family of the target is a *locus communis* in both literature (e.g. the curse against the *Pelopidae* or the house of Laius) and real curses: in *DT* 52 the daughters of the recipient also become targets of the curse (καὶ τὰς παιδίσκας αὐτοῦ); *DT* 13 (τοὺς ἐπ' ἐμὲ ἐλθόντας) and *SGD* 104 (εἶεν ἐξόλειαι καὶ αὐτὸν καὶ γενεάς) bind the descendants to the effects of the curse; *DT* 141 is a curse against a husband and wife as well as their children; *DT* 92 wishes for the death of both the recipients and their children (ἀπολλύοιντο καὶ παῖδες αὐτοῖς); for discussion see Kagarow 1929, 57–58 and Watson 1991, 33–35.

38 The use of legal jargon was a feature of 'prayers for justice' as Versnel 1991, 78–79 has shown.

39 E.g. *DT* 266; *PGM* XXXVI 102–133, 134–160 and Watson 2019, 31 with examples on 48 n. 52. For these motifs of punishment in literary curses see Watson 1991, 35–36.

curses.⁴⁰ The cause of her wrath against Creon is less clear, and it might allude to the use of *defixiones* in the context of a legal battle since the dialogue between him and Medea is permeated with legal imagery and vocabulary (179–300), and the heroine's speech in particular (203–251) appears to have been structurally modeled after real court *apologiae*.⁴¹ In the case of Jason, the threatened punishment is a variation of those found also in the conditional self-imprecation for the oath breakers in the vow of allegiance of the people of Aritium to Caligula.⁴² Therefore, we can assume that Medea wishes exile for Jason because he has broken his oath as lines 7–8 imply (*quosque iuravit mihi | deos Iason*). These conceptual links add authenticity to the utterance by bringing to the reader's mind real-life instances, in which binding curses were used.⁴³

The *narratio*: Offerings and past deeds of (im)piety

Immediately after her requests, Medea refers to a sacrifice she must perform (lines 37–39):

> hoc restat unum, pronubam thalamo feram
> ut ipsa pinum postque sacrificas preces
> caedam dicatis victimas altaribus.

---

40 For example, in *DT* 5 and 10 a wife curses the woman who made her husband abandon her and their kids; *DT* 198 curses a woman who deceived her husband. For more *defixiones amatoriae* see the index in Audollent 1904, 472–473. For a study on amatory binding spells see Faraone 1999, 41–95. Unfortunately I could not get my hands on Suárez de la Torre 2021, which focuses on various aspects of amatory spells.

41 Boyle 2014, 184 adopts the following organization: *exordium* (203–206), *narratio* (207–220), *confirmatio* (221–235), *confutatio* (236–243), and *conclusio* (244–251). The prominence of legal terminology and imagery throughout the play is discussed in Boyle 2014, lxxxvii–lxxxviii, and 213. There are several *defixiones*, such as *DT* 60, 93, 96, 101, 217, 221 (against the accusers), and *DT* 87 (against an accuser and his witnesses), which were written before the court day with the intent to cause harm to the opponent as well as their witnesses. For a discussion on the so-called 'judicial curses' see Eidinow 2019, 382.

42 *CIL* II 172: *si sciens fallo fefellerove, tum me | liberosque meos Jupiter Optimus Maximus ac | divus Augustus ceterique omnes di immortales | expertem patria incolumitate fortunisque | omnibus faxint*; "If I swear or will have sworn falsely, then may Jupiter Optimus Maximus, the deified Augustus, and all the other immortal gods deprive me and my offspring of the fatherland, health, and all property". This vow illustrates an important point, i.e. that the punishment described in the self-imprecation was conditional upon the utterer's non-compliance with the terms of the oath (Hickson 1993, 108).

43 For the various reasons leading to the utterance of a curse, see the index in Audollent 1904, 471–473, Urbanová 2018, 20–24 and 163–167, McKie 2022, 60–83.

> This duty only remains, to carry the bridal torch myself to the wedding chamber and,
> after the sacrificial prayers,
> to slay the victims upon the consecrated altars.

The slaughter of the *victima* is primarily related to Jason and Creusa's wedding, for the sake of which the heroine regards herself as a "Fury-like *pronuba*",[44] but it also functions in its traditional way in the context of a 'prayer for justice' — as a δῶρον to convince the invoked gods to respond to the request. In this class of prayers, the word *victima/hostia* often denotes an animal promised to the gods if they punish the culprit, but sometimes it might refer to the targeted individual, whose punishment the utterer consigns to the deity.[45] Accordingly, Medea's use of the word *victima* points to Creon and Creusa, the targets of her imprecation.[46]

In literary prayers the utterer can also recount past deeds of piety to persuade the gods to respond to their current requests.[47] In like manner, Medea refers to her past actions in lines 44–50:

> quodcumque vidit Phasis aut Pontus nefas,
> videbit Isthmos. effera ignota horrida,   45
> tremenda caelo pariter ac terris mala
> mens intus agitat: vulnera et caedem et vagum
> funus per artus – levia memoravi nimis:
> haec virgo feci; gravior exurgat dolor:
> maiora iam me scelera post partus decent.   50

> Whatever impiety Phasis or the Black Sea saw,
> the Isthmos will witness. Savage, unknown, frightful
> evils that cause both the sky and earth to tremble
> my mind revolves: injuries, and slaughter, and death crawling
> through the limbs — I recall crimes too trifling:
> I committed those as a young girl; let my anger accumulate:
> greater crimes are fitting now, after I gave birth.

This excerpt is an example of the *da quia dedi* formula with a significant difference: instead of recalling pious deeds as it is expected, the heroine refers to the crimes she has committed. The word *nefas* is used in Senecan drama to denote a

---

44 Boyle 2014, 122.
45 For the double meaning of *hostia/victima* in the context of 'prayers for justice' see Versnel 2010, 299 with references. Eidinow 2019, 373 n. 113 mentions *SGD* 54 and 109 as instances in which the target of a curse is offered as a gift to the invoked deities.
46 Boyle 2014, 123. Medea refers only to Creon and Creusa, without including her own children as Hine 2000, 118 argued. For other suggestions on the meaning of *victima* see Costa 1973, 67–68.
47 Hickson 1993, 11 and n. 15 on the same page.

transgression of moral or religious norms which is usually the result of heinous crimes (e.g. patricide, fratricide, incest, and filicide).[48] Medea alludes to the murder of her brother Apsyrtus, a crime that evidently upsets the natural order (*tremenda caelo pariter ac terris mala*).[49]

1.2 Magic as reversal

Seneca makes sure to underscore the abnormality of Medea's utterance from the beginning. Her address to infernal spirits is preceded by a powerful remark: *quosque Medeae magis | fas est precari*. The use of the term *fas* would have struck the audience as odd since it was a technical term with considerable religious force denoting, in its strict sense, that which is in accordance with the divine law.[50] Medea's use of the word to describe the invocation of evil spirits and infernal gods is both paradoxical and outrageous, especially since her utterance is partially a curse, and curses were out of the sphere of religious and legal order.[51] Since her prayer is uttered *non fausta voce*, Medea contradicts the precepts of religion, which dictated addressing the gods with auspicious voice.[52] The reversal of religious norms is also apparent in her invocation to the Furies, asking for their presence (*nunc adeste*)[53] in the imminent marriage of Jason and Creusa. According to wedding custom the chorus invoked, among other deities, Hymenaeus, and requested his attendance while praying for the newlyweds' wellbeing. Medea's demand, therefore, appears as an inversion of nuptial prayers as well as an opposite force to the chorus' wedding song, which follows immediately after.[54] From this perspective, Medea's promised offering for the upcoming marriage, which the reader recognizes as the

---

[48] Boyle 2014, 126.
[49] Hine 2000, 119.
[50] *OLD* s.v. *fas*; for a study on the various meanings of *fas* and *nefas*, see Cipriano 1978.
[51] Boyle 2014, 107 claims that the term "is used both appropriately and ironically by Medea". Curses intend to inflict harm on a person, and as such they would have been outlawed under the provisions of the *Twelve Tables*, and later by the *lex Cornelia de sicariis et veneficiis*. For discussions on anti-magic legislation see Pharr 1932, Dickie 2001, 137–147, Collins 2008, 141–150 and Edmonds 2019, 384–390.
[52] Hine 2000, 114; Boyle 2014, 110.
[53] A typical verb of prayers, *adesse* was used to ensure divine presence or assistance (Hickson 1993, 67–69, with notes).
[54] Hine 1989, 415.

murder of Creusa and Creon instead of the expected animal sacrifice, is also a perversion of sacrificial ritual.[55]

Several intratextual and intertextual ironies underscore further Medea's transgressions. Her invocation of Lucina, who was the protectress of childbirth and women in labor, creates an ironic effect because the audience is aware that the heroine will eventually kill her own children. Although she invokes Neptune for help, the heroine threatens to burn Corinth (35–36), the city whose protector deity was Poseidon.[56] The irony in the case of Minerva is more difficult to spot: in some versions of the myth such as those in Callimachus' *Hecale* (Dieg. X 20–21, and fr. 7 Hollis) and Ovid's *Metamorphoses* (7.404–424), after fleeing Corinth, Medea finds shelter in the city of Athens at the invitation of Aegeus. Despite the enjoyed benefits and safety, she attempts unsuccessfully to poison Theseus, the future king of Athens, and child of her savior or, according to the other version of Theseus' paternity, son of Poseidon (Paus. 2.33.1). Finally, Medea's audacity in invoking all these celestial deities becomes even more outrageous in the last scene of the play when she mounts the chariot of the Sun and ascends to the sky (1026–1027), thus overshadowing the gods whose assistance she sought at the beginning.[57]

Medea's invocation of the Furies, whose original role was to punish the shedding of kindred blood, is also paradoxical since the audience knows that she is the one to commit this heinous crime by killing her own children.[58] The irony in this case serves as an indirect criticism against magic, which gives Medea the power to channel the Furies' vengeful force toward her enemies instead of the obvious candidate for their wrath, i.e. herself, as it would have been consistent with their traditional role of punishing kin killers. Her request towards her grandfather, the Sun-god, should be considered in the same light. Asking for his assistance, and more specifically, to borrow his chariot (32: *da, da per auras curribus patriis vehi*) with which she will eventually depart Corinth after she has set the city ablaze, Medea transforms the god into her accomplice.[59] These requests reflect respectively the power of magic to upset religious order and manipulate divine forces into bringing about the witch's illicit aims.[60]

---

[55] Boyle 2014, 123 notes that animal sacrifice was part of the Roman wedding rituals, but here "Medea perverts the wedding sacrifice to one which features other 'beasts/victims', presumably the bride and her father".
[56] Boyle 2014, 104 has already noted the audacity in Medea's invocation of Neptune.
[57] For Medea's ascent to the sky as an allegory of deification, see Hine 2000, 24; Boyle 2014, cxv and 388.
[58] Boyle 2014, 112.
[59] Dingel 1974, 108 claims that this is a motif that runs throughout the *Medea*.
[60] Fischer 2008, 175–176.

The view of magic as an act that goes against the social and divine order becomes most evident in lines 44–50, where Medea recounts her past crimes and actions. Both the use of *nefas* (44) as well as the whole excerpt foreshadow the future murder of her children, but also that of Creon and Creusa by means of magic as the phrase *ignota mala* suggests. The expression can be translated as "unknown evils" in the sense that they are unprecedented crimes (filicide in this case), but it might also be perceived as a reference to magic rites, unknown to the average individual (see, for example, Ov. *Met.* 3.530: *ignota…sacra*). This interpretation is further reinforced through 1. the use of *mala* later in the play to denote the ingredients of the poison (690, 706), 2. Medea's reference to *funus per artus* among these evils, which is an expression alluding to the formulas *membra liquescant/deliquescant* in *defixiones*,[61] and 3. her claims that the current designs can upset nature, a common feature in literary descriptions of magic (Ov. *Met.* 7.199–209, *Am.* 1.8.5–10; Tib. 1.2.41–52; Ap. Rhod. *Argon.* 3.528–533; Luc. 6.461–491).

Throughout the prologue Seneca makes sure to sketch Medea as an imminent danger not only to her enemies, but also to the whole city of Corinth. Tension builds in the reader as they anticipate further negative developments regarding the fate of Jason, Creusa, and Creon. At the same time, the heroine's threat to burn the city using the Sun's chariot (32–36) presents her as a menace for the Corinthians. Recognizing the danger of her magic, the reader is also overcome by fear for the blameless citizens.

1.3 Magic and anti-Stoicism

Several images and statements guide the audience to realize the anti-Stoic mentality of Medea's imprecation that goes against the "purity of mind, good and honest intention" (F88 Vottero) as well as "pious and right disposition" (Sen. *Ep.* 115.5; *Ben.* 1.6.3), which Seneca considered vital in all interactions of humans with the divine, including prayers.[62] Both Medea's general attitude (praying unpropitiously; 12: *voce non fausta precor*) but also her requests asking for the harm of her enemies stand in clear opposition with Seneca's views on the value and role of prayer, which should be characterized by a positive disposition, never seeking to hurt or deprive someone of anything (Sen. *QNat.* 3 pf. 14). Curses, by definition, lack this appropriate sentiment, and they also give rise to passions, specifically fear, if the target becomes aware of their existence (Sen. *Ep.* 94.53: *Nulla ad aures nostras vox inpune*

---

61 The formula is discussed in Franek and Urbanová 2019 with examples from the *defixiones*.
62 For Seneca's view on proper worship see Wildberger 2006, 270–271; Setaioli 2007, 355–360.

perfertur: nocent qui optant, nocent qui execrantur. Nam et horum inprecatio falsos nobis metus inserit). They are thus condemned by the Stoics. Finally, the strong intratextual and intertextual ironies effectively emphasize certain distinctive features of magic as the most representative aspect of *superstitio*, which Seneca chastises in his prose works, that is, the violation of god's benevolent nature, and the reversal of the proper relationship between gods and humans (Sen. *Clem.* 2.5.1: *religio deos colit, superstitio violat*; *Ep.* 123.16: *superstitio error insanus est: amandos timet, quos colit violat*).[63]

Even though the term *magia* does not occur in any of Seneca's prose works, his authorship of the *De superstitione* allows for the assumption that the Stoic would have something to say about witchcraft and its practitioners in its lost parts. Besides, several excerpts from the Senecan corpus which mention the word *veneficus/a*[64] or its derivatives indicate that the philosopher was familiar with the self-proclaimed powers and skills of the magicians: *Ben.* 5.13.4 refers to the *venefici*'s ability to concoct sleep-inducing potions, and *Ep.* 9.16, where he cites a dictum of Hecaton of Rhodes, shows awareness of various methods used in love magic. There is also no doubt about Seneca's negative view of magic. Both *Ben.* 3.6.2 and *De Ira* 1.16.1 indicate that the activities of the *venefici/ae* were considered a crime since in the first passage Seneca explicitly categorizes poisoning as a *maleficium* along with parricide, sacrilege, and homicide, while in the second excerpt he makes a comparison between poisoners and robbers, whom he considers deviant (*errantes*) and pernicious (*sceleratores*). We can assume that these views on poisoners and, by extension, magicians were in agreement with the official views of the state, which long before had outlawed the practice of magic with the intent to cause harm.[65] It thus becomes clear that the characterization of Medea's designs as *nefas* (44), *mala* (46), and *scelera* (50) reflects accurately Seneca's views both as a statesman and a Stoic.

1.4 The chorus' prayer: a folly without precedent

Immediately after Medea's imprecation, Seneca presents us with the chorus' *epithalamium* for the wedding of Jason and Creusa (56–115). As such, it represents a ritual of traditional religion that serves as a point of reference for the reader to

---

63 Setaioli 2014, 393–396 for Seneca's definition and criticism of *superstitio*.
64 Although the word literally translates "poisoner", it was often used in the vernacular to denote the witch/sorcerer. For the various terms employed in Latin for magicians and witches see Burriss 1936, 138–141; Dickie 2001, 12–16.
65 See page 12 n. 51.

distinguish the — often blurry in reality and philosophy — boundaries between religious normality and *superstitio* within the play's anti-Stoic universe.[66] The choral ode's first part (56–74) comprises the prayer for the wellbeing of the newlywed couple, and its position after the prologue creates a stark contrast with the heroine's preceding imprecation, leading to a conceptual comparison between the two passages.

Though the content of the chorus' prayer differs significantly from Medea's imprecation, the structure is similar. It includes invocations to several deities, requests, and offerings:

> Ad regum thalamos numine prospero
> qui caelum superi quique regunt fretum
> adsint cum populis rite faventibus.
> Primum sceptriferis colla Tonantibus
> taurus celsa ferat tergore candido;   60
> Lucinam nivei femina corporis
> intemptata iugo placet, et asperi
> Martis sanguineas quae cohibet manus,
> quae dat belligeris foedera gentibus
> et cornu retinet divite copiam,   65
> donetur tenera mitior hostia.
> Et tu, qui facibus legitimis ades,
> noctem discutiens auspice dextera
> huc incede gradu marcidus ebrio,
> praecingens roseo tempora vinculo.   70
> Et tu, quae, gemini praevia temporis,
> tarde, stella, redis semper amantibus:
> te matres, avide te cupiunt nurus
> quamprimum radios spargere lucidos.

> Let them come to the royal chambers with propitious will,
> the gods governing the sky and those who rule the waves,
> with the people duly silent.
> First, to the scepter-bearing Jupiter, let
> a white-backed bull yield its proud neck;
> let a snowy-white cow, untamed by the yoke,
> appease Lucina, and to the goddess
> who keeps back the bloody hands of violent Mars,
> brings peace treaties to nations at war,
> and keeps wealth in the plentiful horn,
> let a young victim be given so that she becomes gentler.

---

[66] The distinction between superstition/magic and religion has been notoriously difficult to draw. The dictum 'One man's magic is another man's religion', and vice-versa aptly proves the point. From a strictly Stoic perspective, the chorus' *epithalamium* would have been considered superstitious.

And you, who is present with the lawful torches,
and disperses the darkness with an auspicious right hand,
come here, exhausted by your drunken steps,
crowning your temples with a rosy wreath.
And you, star, harbinger of double times,
who always returns slowly for the lovers:
older and younger women impatiently long for you,
to scatter your lucid rays as soon as possible.

The chorus invokes the celestial gods and sea deities (57), Jupiter and Juno (59), Lucina (61), Venus (62–63), Hymenaeus (67), and Vesper (71). Several of these gods were alluded to or directly addressed by Medea: Minerva (representing the gods of the sky, together with the *di conjugales*), Neptune (the ruler of the oceans), the *di conjugales* (Jupiter, Juno, Hymenaeus, Venus), and Lucina.[67] The descriptive address to Hymenaeus (67) also echoes Medea's description of the Furies and their role in her own wedding (15–16: *atram ... facem, adeste*). The Corinthians' request for the presence of all these gods in the upcoming wedding (*adsint, incede, ades*) recalls the heroine's earlier petition toward the Furies as *pronubae* (13 and 16: *adeste*).[68] To make the correspondence between the two prayers even more profound, Seneca includes the promise of the wedding sacrifice in the chorus' *epithalamium*. Just as Medea referred to the sacrifice she will perform after submitting her requests, the chorus mentions the proper victims in the context of the wedding ceremony (60: a bull; 61: a cow; 66: a lamb, presumably).[69]

These mesmerizing similarities serve a twofold purpose. They exemplify in a simple but compelling manner how magic appropriates religious powers, thus highlighting the partially domestic nature of magic which Pliny notes in *HN* 30.1. In the intradramatic level, they emphasize magic's superiority to religion since the reader is aware that eventually Medea will come out victorious from this atypical conflict with the chorus.[70]

There are, however, notable antitheses between Medea's and the chorus' prayer, which reflect contemporary beliefs about magic, illustrating the subversive aspect of the practice. Contrary to the chorus, Medea also asked for the presence of infernal deities, thus conforming to the belief that one can achieve their aims more easily through chthonic powers.[71] While the Corinthians call everyone to attend the

---

67 Hine 1989, 413.
68 Hine 1989, 413; Boyle 2014, 137.
69 Hine 1989, 415–416 correctly views these animals as corresponding to Medea's victims.
70 Hine 1989, 419.
71 Versnel 1991, 64: chthonic gods "carry out tasks not as representatives of right or morality but on the strength of their dark nature".

wedding procession *rite faventibus*, Medea uttered her prayer *non fausta voce*. This feature, though a common motif in literary descriptions of witchcraft that do not attune with the piety demanded also in magic rituals, underscores the reversal of religious conformities.[72] The same can be said about the conceptual comparison between the animal sacrifices and those promised by Medea, the latter alluding to the societal prejudice of human sacrifice in magic.[73] Finally, whereas the chorus is unaware of the heroine's prayer, the latter is able to hear theirs (116: *aures pepulit hymenaeus meas*) because they utter it in public, as required by religious custom. This has certain implications that foreshadow the play's ending, and which are rooted in the popular belief that a prayer could be disrupted by an opposing (usually silent) one.[74] The open, collective prayer of the chorus contrasts with the secret, individual imprecation of Medea, reflecting the common stereotype of the witch's selfish motivation, as well as her ritualistic and social isolation.[75]

1.5 Transforming the model: From Ovid's *monstrum* to Seneca's *monstrum*

The ominous atmosphere of the play set in the prologue, and its preoccupation with magic fully manifests itself in the scene of the incantation, in which Seneca gives a full-scale presentation of Medea's ritual. The centrality of a lengthy and accurate magical rite differentiates his account of the story from earlier surviving treatments of the myth, but most importantly solidifies Medea's image as an evil witch.[76]

With regards to their focus on magic, literary representations of Medea vary:[77] for example, Euripides shows no interest for her spells, while Apollonius provides the reader with a generic description in the Talos episode (Ap. Rhod. *Argon.* 4.1638–1688).[78] The accounts of Ovid, who admittedly exercised the greatest influence on

---

[72] Hine 1989, 415.
[73] Such stereotypes reflect both in literary (Hor. *Epod.* 5; Cic. *Vat.* 14; Sall. *Cat.* 22) as well as archaeological evidence (e.g. *CIL* VI 3, 19747). For a discussion on the connection between magic and human/child sacrifice see Dickie 2001, 133 and 329 n. 62 (citing a list of primary sources); Graf 2007, 140–143 (on inscriptions); Watson 2019, 203–225. For a discussion on instances where human *viscera* were said to have been used in magical rituals see Ogden 2001, 197–201.
[74] See van der Horst 1994, 3 who also provides literary examples.
[75] For the social isolation of Medea throughout the play see Walsh 2012, 74–77 and 91 n. 8.
[76] Reif 2016, 383.
[77] For an overview of the literary treatments of the Medea myth from the archaic to the Roman period see Graf 1997b, 21–43; Griffiths 2006, 14–21; Boyle 2014, lxiii–lxxviii; Reif 2016, 387–396.
[78] Schaaf 2014, 311–329 on the Talos episode. I am a little hesitant to accept the degree of faithfulness Schaaf specifically recognizes in magic rituals found throughout the *Argonautica*.

Seneca, also include descriptions of her magical art:[79] in *Her.* 6.83–94, Hypsipyle briefly refers to the Colchian's charms and herbs (83–84), her power to upset the natural order (85–88), the gathering of materials from tombs (89–90), practicing black magic on 'voodoo dolls' (91–92) as well as her love spells (93–94); in *Metamorphoses* 7, Ovid narrates Aeson's rejuvenation, which includes Medea's preliminary prayer (192–219), a narrative of her gathering of herbs (224–233), magical numbers (234–235), offerings (240–247), the cleansing of Aeson's body (252–261), the preparation of the concoction and its ingredients (262–276), as well as the ritual proper (285–287). The *Metamorphoses* narrative exhibits individual features found in real spells, but as a whole it also appears generic since certain aspects seem incompatible with those of the *PGM*,[80] and the structural unity of the ritual seems somewhat loose.

Surviving sources also present different portrayals of Medea. Before Euripides she appears as a benevolent figure who uses her powers to help people, functioning as the positive polar of her sister/aunt Circe.[81] It is around the first century BCE that Medea is established as an all-powerful sorceress whose skills are used to cause harm and destruction.[82] Ovid, the most notable example, creates an ambivalent portrayal of the heroine: In *Her.* 6.83–94, Hypsipyle sketches her as an evil sorceress by emphasizing the subversive purposes and the negative results of her magic. Medea's description in *Metamorphoses* 7 also refers to the destructive consequences of her art (394–395: *sed postquam Colchis arsit nova nupta venenis | flagrantemque domum regis mare vidit*) but the main episode of the narrative, which is the rejuvenation of Aeson, presents an image of Medea that conforms to the long tradition of her as a beneficent healer/herbalist (*pharmakos/pharmakeutria*).[83] At the end of the ritual, Ovid adds:

---

[79] A common conclusion in scholarship: see Cleasby 1907; Walsh 2012, 71. See also page 4 n. 12. Rosner-Siegel 1982, 235–242 links the increasing use of magic by Medea in *Metamorphoses* 7.1–424 with her progressive transformation from woman into a witch.
[80] Reif 2016, 253.
[81] See also the narrative in Diod. Sic. 4.45–46.
[82] Graf 1997b, 31. The transformation of the character and sketching of Medea in Latin literature is examined in Manuwald 2013.
[83] The image of Medea as a φαρμακεύτρια is found throughout antiquity. For the twofold portrayal of Medea in Ovid's *Metamorphoses* 7 see Segal 2002, 11–19 who shows how the heroine's transition from innocent maiden to murderous witch reflects in her use of magic. Newlands 1997, 186–192 argues for a "fractured" portrayal of Medea which does not explain her shift from vulnerable maiden to a murderess, thus leaving the judgement of her motives up to the reader (207).

Viderat ex alto tanti miracula monstri
Liber et admonitus, iuvenes nutricibus annos   295
posse suis reddi, capit hoc a Colchide munus.[84]

Dionysus had seen from the heavens the wonders of such great marvel,
and realizing that it was possible to give back to his nurses
their youth, he received this gift from the Colchian woman.

This excerpt emphasizes the beneficial effects of magic, which even gods admire. Having seen Aeson's miraculous rejuvenation, Bacchus seeks to rejuvenate his nurses, who grew weary due to their age. Ovid's lines thus oppose a major stereotypical view of magic as a practice hateful to the gods.[85] The ritual of Medea and, by extension, the powers of magic are here described as a gift (*munus*), while herself is seen as a *monstrum* –she is not an abomination, but rather a marvel.

For Seneca, however, there is no beneficial aspect of magic since its essence contradicts the tenets of Stoicism and state religion.[86] To illustrate his condemnation of the magical arts, he restricts his portrayal of Medea to the negative aspect of the Ovidian model, and expands upon it to create a completely awful image of her as a witch.[87] In other words, Seneca embellishes his account of Medea's evil incantation with features which recall real magic rituals to obliterate Ovid's marvelous (*monstrum*) and simultaneously recast it as his own new, and greater *teras* (*maius monstrum*). The scene serves as a catalyst that transforms the heroine into a real abomination, a development already alluded to in 171 (*Medea...fiam*), foreshadowed

---

84 The text is from Miller's edition.
85 Fischer 2008, 176 views these lines as indicative of the magicians' superior position in relation to gods.
86 With regards to both beliefs and practices, it is safe to assume that Seneca's criticism against everyday *superstitio* applies also to magic. In F67 (Vottero) of *De superstitione*, he criticizes the grotesque images of the gods of Roman religion as well as the diversity of divine entities ranging from gods protecting the sewer system (*Cloacina*) to those who presided over human emotions or appearance (*Pavor* and *Pallor*). He also castigates the excessive acts of worship which he witnessed during his lifetime such as the self-castration of Cybele's priests, the Galli (F68), as well as the reenactment of Isis' search for her lost husband, Osiris (F69). Of course, the cults and rituals of Cybele and Isis had become part of the official state religion a long time ago but still, for most Romans, remained exotic because of their origin as well as their strange practices. The connection between foreign religions and *superstitio* is further affirmed by his critique of Jewish religious customs, and especially the Sabbath (F73). See also the points raised on pages 14–16.
87 Walsh 2012, 71 claims that Seneca's account fills the gap left by Ovid in the transformation of his Medea from the *pharmakeutria* that rejuvenates Aeson to the evil witch that kills Creusa and her own children (Ov. *Met.* 7.394–396). She also argues that, by allowing Medea to express her own viewpoint, Seneca reinstates some form of sympathy toward the heroine which was lacking in Ovid.

in Creon's characterization of the heroine as such (191), and affirmed in her own exclamation in 910 (*Medea nunc sum*), which points to the profile of the witch who lays waste on the natural, social, and political order.[88]

The scene opens with the nurse confessing her fear to the readers (670), and her certainty that what they are about to witness is a *maius...monstrum* (674–675) compared to Medea's past deeds — including those of her literary antecedents. These statements function as a guide for the interpretation of the scene: Seneca aims to stir fear in the readers' mind through the ritual of Medea just as the latter does to her nurse (670: *Pavet animus, horret*). And if they already have partial knowledge, like the intratextual audience who has witnessed past events, of Medea's wrath (673: *furentem*), attack on gods (673: *aggressam deos*), and reversal of natural order (674: *caelum trahentem*) from other accounts (see, for instance, Eur. *Med.* 99: κινεῖ δὲ χόλον, 447: τραχεῖαν ὀργὴν ὡς ἀμήχανον κακόν; Ov. *Met.* 7.199–202; *Her.* 6.85–88), Seneca will present them with the heroine's powers in all their grandeur, which will show her for what she truly is.

1.5.1 Magic behind the scenes: the nurse's speech as preparatory ritual

Lines 675–739 describe the events that occur outside the stage. In the style of a messenger's speech, the nurse's monologue, interrupted by a brief direct quotation of Medea's preliminary utterance, details the heroine's gathering of the necessary ingredients for the concoction of the poison.[89] It thus represents, in dramatic context, the preparatory part of the main ritual (674–675: *parat...monstrum*), which conforms to the two-tiered structure of the *PGM* consisting of *logos* and *praxis*.[90]

At the beginning of Act IV, Medea leaves the stage and withdraws to the *penetrale funestum* (676) where she performs the magical rite the audience witnesses in lines 740–848. The word *penetrale* usually denotes an interior or secret location of the house, and metonymically a sanctuary, especially that of the *Penates*.[91] It appears then that Medea is somewhere within the boundaries of the *domus*, where

---

[88] Reif 2016, 411 sees Medea's exclamation as pointing to the rediscovery of her identity as a witch. Guastella 2001, 206 and 209–210 considers Medea's crimes the means to reclaim the identity she lost due to Jason's *repudium*.
[89] Reif 2016, 284 also notes that the nurse's speech is modelled after the standard speech of the messenger in ancient tragedy.
[90] See the table in Reif 2016, 324.
[91] *TLL* 10.1.1061.44–51. *OLD* s.v. *penetrale*.

she builds her altar out of turf (797: *caespite*), far away from indiscreet looks.[92] The particular setting recalls *PGM* XIII 1–343 which instructs the magician to build an earthy altar (βωμὸν γέϊνον) amidst the house. The scene of the incantation just like the utterance of the curse at the beginning takes place in the evening as lines 874–878 suggest.[93] Time and space thus outline the magical environment of the scene.

The preparatory ritual begins with the heroine performing a gesture with her left arm in 680 (*et triste laeva comprecans sacrum manu*)[94] which adheres to the general use of the left hand in magic rituals attested in the *PGM*.[95] But *comprecans* implies that Medea is making the gesture while uttering a prayer, and Donka Markus considers it a reference to a specific worship movement, with the person clenching their left thumb in their fist while raising the right hand. The gesture, which was used predominantly in prayers addressed to underworld spirits, reveals Medea's effort to engage the infernal forces in the ritual, stressing the sinister and coercive power of magic and simultaneously foreshadowing the wickedness of the main rite.[96]

The nurse's narrative then proceeds with the description of Medea's luring of various snakes (681–690) from every corner of the world:

---

[92] This is further supported by the heroine's exclamation in 578 when she announces the building of an altar for the ritual, the flames of which will pour forth from the house (*statuantur arae, flamma iam tectis sonet*). Costa 1973, 129 believes that the altar is located indoors and that *evasit* indicates that Medea left the scene, not the house. Boyle 2014, 299 and Reif 2016, 328 also argue for an interior location for the altar. For instances in which the spell was performed within the boundaries of the house see *PGM* I 56, IV 170, 2468–2469, 2712, LXI 5, LXXII 6 (ἐπὶ δώματος ὑψηλοῦ, *vel sim.*), *PGM* IV 58–59 which instructs the individual to perform the rites at the "eastern section of the town, village, or dwelling" and *PGM* XIII 8 which instructs the person to build an earthy altar (βωμὸν γέϊνον) in the middle of the house.

[93] Boyle 2014, 297.

[94] Costa 1973, 129 and Markus 2000, 149 argue that the meaning of *sacrum* is unclear, and it can refer to 1) the ominous sacrifice and ritual or 2) the shrine of Hecate where Medea performs her rite or 3) the ingredients of the poison that the heroine will concoct. Reif 2016, 297–298 rejects the conjecture *comprecans* in favor of *comparans* and argues that *sacrum* refers to the commonly used ἐπίθυμα.

[95] Markus 2000, 149–150 and Reif 2016, 297. In *PGM* I 279 the person must hold an ebony staff with their left hand while performing the rite; in XXXVI 256–264 the individual is instructed to pick up an *ostrakon* to be used in the ritual with the left hand; in XII 179–181 the devotee must hold in their left hand a piece of linen while uttering a spell to alleviate another person's anger against them; VII 300 includes a spell formula which the individual must write on their left hand.

[96] Markus 2000, 149–150. The gesture to which Seneca seems to allude is that of clenching the thumb while praying, and which is attested in *PGM* IV 2328, XXXVI 162–163, LXIX 3, and LXX 6 (κρατεῖν τὸν ἀντίχειρα). Reif 2016, 298 claims that since magic is a perversion of religious rites, Medea's use of the left hand reflects the reversal of the practice in traditional cults.

> pestes vocat quascumque ferventis creat
> harena Libyae quasque perpetua nive
> Taurus coercet frigore Arctoo rigens,
> et omne monstrum. tracta magicis cantibus
> squamifera latebris turba desertis adest.   685
> hic saeva serpens corpus immensum trahit
> trifidamque linguam exertat et quaerit quibus
> mortifera veniat: carmine audito stupet
> tumidumque nodis corpus aggestis plicat
> cogitque in orbes ...   690

she summons whatever scourge the sand
of hot Libya spawns, and those that mount Taurus
confines under eternal snow while frozen with northern cold,
and every monster. Lured by her magical incantations,
the scaly crowd appears from their abandoned subterfuge.
Here a ferocious snake hauls its immense body,
and reveals its three-forked tongue, seeking whom
it will approach to bring death; when the spell is heard, it is stunned,
it twists its body, swollen by the folded knots,
and rises on its coils.

This excerpt reflects the prominent use of snakes' body parts as ingredients in *quasi*-magical recipes such as those attested in Pliny.[97] However, Seneca conveniently disregards any beneficial use serpents had in traditional medical concoctions by characterizing them as *pestes*, a word denoting anything that brings catastrophe and death.[98] This characterization, combined with the longer description of snakes as ingredients for Medea's deadly poison, compared to the one and a half line for her rejuvenation brew[99] in Ov. *Met.* 7.271–272, allows Seneca to emphasize only the

---

[97] Although such recipes were known to and used by the Romans of the first century, they were still considered part of the art of the Magi. We should note here that Pliny's discussion on natural remedies begins with a general discussion on the beginnings of magic (*HN* 30.2), thus emphasizing the connection. Reif 2016, 298 n. 94 discusses the connections between serpents and witchcraft in the *PGM*. Various parts of serpents were used as ingredients for potions and remedies as Pliny attests (*HN* 29.119–122; 30.22–23), and during the course of magic rituals as we infer from *PGM* III 703, IV 2211–2212, XII 160 (γῆρας ὄφεως), and IV 2003–2004 (αἷμα δρακόντειον). Finally, certain body parts, especially the skin of snakes, could be used as amulets against various medical conditions as well as protective talismans against the evil eye (*HN* 29.67–73). For the popularity of snake-shaped amulets as protection against evil, see Faraone 2018, 50–51 and 313 n. 133 and 134.

[98] Boyle 2014, 300. In *Georgics* 3.418, Vergil describes a snake as *pestis acerba boum*, but the most obvious correlation is with Lucan's book 9 and the Libyan snakes (e.g. 619, 630, 734, 787).

[99] The discrepancy has been noted in Cleasby 1907, 58.

destructive powers of her magic, simultaneously overturning and surpassing the positive image of Medea in Ovid.

The passage also brings the figure of Medea closer to the experiences of the reader with real-life practitioners of magic by sketching her as a snake-handler. The nurse vividly describes how the heroine uses her abilities to lure (*tracta magicis cantibus*) and charm the serpents (*carmine stupet*) with her magical incantations, which would have brought in mind both certain spells (e.g. *PGM* XIII 261–265) and the performances of the *circulatores* (Celsus *Med.* 5.27.3c).[100] However, Medea's powers appear as virtually unlimited since her chants draw near snakes from Libya, but also allow her to lure sluggish serpents in brumation (!) under the snow of Mt. Taurus. To his Medea Seneca unites the powers of all three snake master races of antiquity as her luring of snakes from Libya and Mt. Taurus of Phrygia alludes to the Psylli and the Ophiogeneis, respectively, while herself functions as a representative of the Marsi because of her mythological links with this ethnic minority.[101] The connection of Medea specifically with the Marsi, also underscores her as a foreigner through the allusion to another famous representative of this ethnic group in literature, Umbro. In *Aeneid* 7.752–755, Virgil describes the Marsic priest who joins the alliance against Aeneas as capable of putting poisonous snakes to sleep, minimize their aggressiveness, and alleviating the symptoms of their bite by means of spells and touch.

The narrative breaks at this point, and the nurse recites Medea's own speech in 690–704.[102] The heroine admits that earthy poisons are not sufficient for her

---

[100] The *circulatores* were usually wandering performers, astrologers, and merchants, who were stationed at public spaces and buildings, where they used to sell their merchandise and advertise their skills and abilities for the usual purpose of entertainment. There is no doubt that among them one could find also itinerant magicians as well as individuals adept in charming snakes. For the popularity of the *circulatores* as well as their performances, see Dickie 2001, 216–234 and especially 218–219 for the snake-handlers.

[101] Ogden 2013, 209–214 argues that these peoples were believed to possess special powers of snake-handling, and such reputation can probably be traced back to the activities of real snake-charmers around the ancient world (see also Cels. *Med.* 5.27.3c who explains, among other 'marvels', how the Psylli can put the head of a poisonous snake in their mouths and not get hurt). The tradition presenting the Marsi as snake charmers goes back at least to Lucilius, who mentions that their incantations caused snakes to explode (fr. 575–576 Marx), and it is their magical skills that Gnaeus Gellius attempts to explain by making the son of Medea their ruler (*FrHist* 18; Dickie 2001, 129–130). Their powers were still proverbial in the age of Augustus as we can infer from Ovid's reference to their magical songs (*Ars Am.* 2.102), and Horace's claim that Canidia has afflicted him with headache using a Marsian spell (Hor. *Epod.* 17.29).

[102] Reif 2016, 300 argues that the nurse cites Medea's words because she does not understand the ritual in its entirety, just as the uninitiated have a limited understanding of magic practices.

purpose (690–691), and therefore, she calls upon five mythological serpents to offer theirs (692):

> huc ille vasti more torrentis patens
> descendat anguis, cuius immensos duae,   695
> maior minorque, sentiunt nodos ferae
> (maior Pelasgis apta, Sidoniis minor),
> pressasque tandem solvat Ophiuchus manus
> virusque fundat; adsit ad cantus meos
> lacessere ausus gemina Python numina,   700
> et Hydra et omnis redeat Herculea manu
> succisa serpens caede se reparans sua.
> tu quoque relictis pervigil Colchis ades,
> sopite primum cantibus, serpens, meis.

> Let that serpent which stretches out as a huge torrent
> descend, whose immense knots touch the two
> beasts, the Greater and the Lesser (Bear),
> (the Greater is suitable for the Greeks, the Lesser for the Tyrians),
> and let Ophiuchus at last withdraw his constricting hands,
> and shed venom; let Python be present with my chants,
> who dared challenge the twin deities,
> and let Hydra and every serpent cut down by Hercules'
> hand return, healing its own cuts.
> And you, abandon the Colchians and come, sleepless
> Dragon, the first to be put to sleep by my incantations.

Invocations to supernatural serpents (e.g. Ouroboros, Cnouphi, Apophis), which were considered the primordial manifestation of deities, is a common feature of the *PGM*,[103] while snake figures were inscribed or carved on materials during the course of magic rituals (e.g. Pytho, and more often Ouroboros).[104] Commonly addressed stars in the

---

103 For snakes as the primordial manifestation of gods in spells see, for instance, *PGM* IV 1637–1639, 2613–2614, VIII 11, XII 89 and Betz 1986, 159 n. 53, with bibliography. Most notable cases include: Cnouphi, the lion-headed serpent who is often named in the *voces magicae* and in the Harpon-Cnouphi formula (e.g. *PGM* I 27, II 157, III 435, 561, IV 2433, VII 1023–1024, XXXVI 219); the serpent god Apophis (e.g. *PGM* IV 190–191, VII 558, XIII 262); and finally the Ouroboros, the snake swallowing its own tail (e.g. *PGM* I 145–146, VII 586, XII 203–204, 274–275, XXXVI 184). For general information on these three supernatural serpents see the respective entries in the glossary of Betz 1986, 332–339.
104 See Betz 1986, 337 s.v. *Ouroboros*, with bibliography. For the Pythian serpent see *PGM* XIII 109–110 and 661–667, with Reif 2016, 358.

PGM include the Bear,[105] and Sirius,[106] although Egyptian and Eastern names of zodiacal constellations also occur.[107] The position of Medea's invocations during the preparatory ritual and before the main spell suggests that Seneca imitates the hymnic section of real spells.[108] Such preliminary utterances intended to establish the primary line of communication with the deities invoked in the main spell or ask for the presence of a divine assistant, a πάρεδρος, to help the magician in various stages of the ritual.[109]

In his inclusion of a *paredros* summoning, Seneca might have been influenced by Ovid's *Metamorphoses* 7.192–219. There Medea asks for the presence of several deities, and concludes with a request to her winged serpents (219: *nec frustra volucrum tractus cervice draconum currus adest*) who, functioning as supernatural assistants, will help the witch gather the necessary herbs for her concoction.[110] Similarly, Seneca recreates a spell for obtaining not one, but multiple *paredroi* who will offer their deadly assistance to the witch.

This excerpt, the climax of Medea's preliminaries, underscores the magnitude of her powers: she forces the constellation of Draco (695: *anguis*) to leave its position in the sky and come to her aid; the Ophiuchus cannot resist her commands, releasing the snake he holds despite the constellations' sympathetic relationship.[111] She then asks for the presence of Pytho, Hydra, and the mythological serpent of Colchis. Seneca's Medea surpasses her Ovidian counterpart since she exercises control over several *paredroi*, with each invocation reflecting her uncontested power over the

---

105 E.g. *PGM* IV 1275–1322; IV 1331–1389, with Reif 2016, 357. See also Pachoumi 2017, 38–39.
106 The dog star, often identified with the goddess Isis Sothis (Betz 1986, 131 n. 71); *PGM* XXIII 1–70, *PDM Suppl.* 162–168.
107 This is probably the result of oriental influence. See also the discussion on a Babylonian astral spell which invokes ten constellations, among which one might find Draco and Hydra, in Reiner 1995, 66–68.
108 Hine 2000, 179 notes that the invocation is modeled in the form "of a traditional cletic hymn, with the snakes as the deities".
109 For example, *PGM* IV 3087–3124, which is a spell for revelation, includes a description of the offering to be made to Cronus (3087–3096) while the magician is uttering the formula which summons the god (3097–3110) — usually a single magical line is enough to summon the assistant. A comparison between this spell and the nurse's quote indicates that the latter fits in the whole context of Medea's spell as a formula asking for the presence of the mythological serpents as supernatural assistants. Besides, the heroine herself claims that her utterance is an incantation (*cantus*), and specific verbal elements (*descendat, adsit, ades*) illustrate that its purpose is to summon the serpents and ensure their presence for the spell's completion. For the definition of *paredros* and its various forms in the *PGM*, see Pachoumi 2017, 35–62.
110 Among the powers of the *paredros* listed in *PGM* I 188–191 is the ability to provide the magician with "wild plants".
111 Reif 2016, 300–301.

realms of heaven (Draco, Ophiuchus), earth (Pytho, serpent of Colchis), and the underworld (Hydra).[112]

The passage also hints at the anti-Stoic as well as theomachic character of magic. Medea's ability to manipulate the stars, which in Stoicism function as ministers of the supreme god and possess divine *ratio*,[113] for her malevolent end is at odds with the Stoic idea that God is benevolent (DL 7.147: Θεὸν δ' εἶναι ζῷον... κακοῦ παντὸς ἀνεπίδεκτον; Sen. *Ben*. 4.3.3–4.9.1) and therefore unable to consent to evil or give it aid (Sen. *Ep*. 75.19; 95.49; *De Ira* 2.27).[114] The summoning of Pytho, the serpent that persecuted Leto (Hyg. *Fab*. 140), harassing the unborn Diana and Apollo, is in complete accord with the view of magic as a force threatening the gods. Finally, the pulling down of the constellations that exemplifies Medea's power to upset cosmic laws goes against the rationality of the divine plan, which defines the patterns of movement for each celestial body (Sen. *Prov*. 1.1.2).

The end of the quote marks the return to the nurse's report on Medea's preparations. Lines 707–730 comprise a geographical catalogue, which is commonly found in Senecan drama, functioning as a list of the necessary herbs for the concoction of the poison.[115] Seneca's catalogue contrasts with Ovid's linear, and relatively short narrative of the heroine's gathering of herbs from various places in Greece (*Met*. 7.227–233) as it enumerates several plants from every corner of the world.[116] Whereas Ovid's Medea uses a life-giving herb (233: *vivax gramen*), Seneca's recipe includes only deadly ones (717: *gramen flore mortifero viret*), and their juices (718: *dirusve tortis sucus in radicibus*). These differences amplify the powers of the heroine compared to her literary antecedent, simultaneously stressing only the catastrophic aspect of her magic.

Some of the herbs are collected in the dead of the night (729: *alta nocte*) and others before dawn (728: *dum parat Phoebus diem*).[117] Seneca alludes to the popular belief which considered the effectiveness of plant-based ingredients dependent on specific factors such as, for example, planetary phases or the position of the moon

---

112 Reif 2016, 301.
113 Wildberger 2006, 23 and 500–501 n. 148 for a list of primary sources.
114 Fischer 2008, 177–178 on the issue of theodicy in the *Medea*.
115 Boyle 2014, 305. On this passage and its connection to Medea's magic see Reif 2016, 301–303.
116 Trinacty 2014, 116.
117 Boyle 2014, 310 notes that, in literary representations of witchcraft, the collection of herbs usually occurs under the moonlight in an effort to secure the assistance of Hecate in the course of the ritual (see, for example, Hor. *Sat*. 1.8.20–22; Verg. *Aen*. 4.513; Plin. *HN* 24.12). However, the instructions in the *PGM* show that a time before dawn was also appropriate for plucking herbs to be used in magic (*PGM* IV 286–295). Reif 2016, 349–351 also discusses the importance of time in the context of Medea's spell, and traces parallels with the instructions in the *PGM*.

when collected (Thessalus of Tralles, *De virtutibus herbarum* 27). As in Ovid (*Met.* 7.226–227), the method of collection also corresponds to real life practices: Medea cuts some plants with a knife (728: *ferrum*), ripping off others with her hand while uttering some magical words (730: *ungue…cantato*).[118] This last method of obtaining the herbs recalls *PGM* IV 2967–3006:

> Παρ' Αἰγυπτίοις ἀεὶ βοτάναι λαμβάνονται οὕτως· ὁ ῥιζοτόμος [...] μετ' εὐχῶν ἀνασπᾷ τὸ φυτὸν ἐξ ὀνόματος ἐπικαλούμενος τὸν δαίμονα, ᾧ ἡ βοτάνη ἀνιέρωται, πρὸς ἣν λαμβάνεται χρείαν, παρακαλῶν ἐνεργεστέραν γενέσθαι πρὸς αὐτήν.

> Among the Egyptians, herbs are always collected in this manner; the herbalist [...] tears up the plant while praying, invoking the deity to whom the herb is dedicated, and asking that it becomes more effective toward the use for which it is collected.

The proper manner of collecting herbs was meant to maximize their deadly effects as well as those of the concocted potion. Apart from adding authenticity to Seneca's account, the variations in time and method of obtaining the plant-based ingredients increase the reader's anticipation for a successful result.

Having gathered everything, the scene proceeds with the mixing of the basic ingredients, and the addition of other sinister materials:

> Mortifera carpit gramina ac serpentium
> saniem exprimit miscetque et obscenas aves
> maestique cor bubonis et raucae strigis
> exsecta vivae viscera. haec scelerum artifex
> discreta ponit: his rapax vis ignium,   735
> his gelida pigri frigoris glacies inest.

> She tears off the deadly herbs and squeezes out
> the serpents' poison, and blends both ominous birds
> and the heart of the sorrowful eagle-owl, and the innards
> of the screech-owl, cut while alive. These, the master of crimes
> places separately: some contain the voracious force of fire,
> others the frosty ice of slow-acting cold.

Contrary to Ovid who omits the processing of herbs after they have been collected, and instead describes the ingredients boiling in the cauldron (*Met.* 7.262–274), Seneca presents the reader with a brief procedure during which Medea mixes the basic materials: she tears off pieces of the deadly plants, squeezes the venom out of snakes,

---

[118] Costa 1973, 135 observes that the adjective *cantato* modifies *ungue*, thus "used rather oddly of part of the enchantress's own body", but this does not need to be taken literally. There is no doubt that she uproots plants as she squeezes juice from their roots.

and then blends all these ingredients with bird parts, some of which she had kept separately until now. The process recalls broadly the instructions found in the *PGM*.[119]

Seneca expands Ovid's recipe, which includes a one-line reference to Medea's use of the wings and flesh of a *strix* (Ov. *Met.* 7.269). Both accounts allude to the use of various body parts and fluids of ill-omened birds, especially owls, in magic and medical recipes of *quasi*-magical nature (see, for example, Plin. *HN* 29.81, 113, 117, 127, 143; 30.33).[120] Furthermore, the evisceration of the *strix* while the bird is still alive recalls the instructions of certain spells which require the use of a living animal (e.g. *PGM* IV 2943–2945, XII 30–31, 376, XCV 7–13), thus bringing Seneca's description even closer to real magic rituals. This admittedly gory image increases both the horror as well as the disgust of the reader, and foreshadows the upcoming doom since the *bubo* and the *strix* were linked with death in popular thought.[121] The grim expectations of the reader are enhanced further by the words *mortifera, saniem, obscenas, maesti, raucae*, while the intratextual comment on the opposing elemental nature of the ingredients (fire-ice) anticipates their deadly effect after their mixing.[122]

1.6 Magic on stage: the main ritual

At 737–739 the nurse describes what she hears happening out of her and the reader's sight:

> addit venenis verba non illis minus
> metuenda. – Sonuit ecce vesano gradu
> canitque. mundus vocibus primis tremit.

---

[119] Reif 2016, 347.
[120] In *PGM* I 222–231 the eye of a night-owl is among the ingredients for the crafting of an invisibility anointment; *PGM* IV 26–51 mentions the smearing of the eyes with owl bile as part of a magical ceremony; *PGM* XXXVI 264–274 uses the blood of a night-owl; *PGM* XCVII 7–9 instructs the individual performing the spell to grind the heart of a night-owl, and smear themselves with the product. Reif 2016, 348–349 also discusses the use of animals, including birds, in the spells of the *PGM* and the profound connections with Medea's spell.
[121] More specifically, the eagle owl (*bubo*) was a bird whose mere sighting was considered a bad omen as Pliny attests (*HN* 29.82; 10.34), while the *strix*, on the other hand, was considered accursed (*HN* 11.232), hungry for human flesh (Plaut. *Pseud.* 819–821) and signaling death. For the *strix* in Graeco-Roman literature and folklore see Oliphant 1913.
[122] Reif 2016, 305; and 304 on the analogy between the deaths of Creusa and *bubo*.

> She added to the poisons words, not to be
> feared less — Listen! She makes noise with her wild steps
> and chants. The world trembles at her first sounds.

This excerpt summarizes the main ritual, which consists of *logos* (*verba, canit, vocibus*) and *praxis* (*vesano gradu*), conferring a judgment on the power of magical *verba* which agrees with Seneca's view on the power of words attested in *Ep.* 94.53.[123]

Since the readers are misled to believe that the magical scene is complete, the passage stirs tension in them as they anticipate the final phase of Medea's plan. Thus, when the heroine appears onstage immediately after, they are left totally flabbergasted, and their surprise arouses the emotion of fear.[124] Besides, this is the purpose of the scene in its entirety as the words of the nurse first suggested in 670 and further confirmed through these lines (*verba... metuenda; mundus...tremit*).

1.6.1 Magic on stage: Medea's mumbo-jumbo!

At this point, Seneca provides the reader with the opportunity to witness the main ritual, which is essentially a continuation of the preparatory part. Any similarities between the two aim at emphasizing their unity through partial repetition.[125] The ritual reflects the nurse's description, conforming to the two-tiered structure of the *PGM* (*logos-praxis*), and is modeled after real spells:[126] lines 740–751 constitute the invocation; 752–770 detail Medea's past accomplishments, and 771–784 list the rites and offerings to Hecate (together they comprise the *narratio*); after a brief pause confirming the goddess' assent (785–796), Medea proceeds with the ritualistic moves (797–816); finally, 817–839 include the heroine's requests, followed by the final assent of Hecate (840–842).[127] This combination of speech and action creates a powerful image which is meant to terrify the spectator. The reader, who got a taste of disgust and dread through the nurse's report, will now experience in full the psychological effects.

---

[123] Reif 2016, 305 for these lines as representing *logos* and *praxis*.
[124] Boyle 2014, 312–313. Reif 2016, 328 argues that during both the nurse's monologue and the ritual scene, the two characters are on stage. Hine 2000, 175 also comments on the effect of Medea's appearance onstage.
[125] *Contra* Zanobi 2014, 123–125.
[126] See the table in Reif 2016, 326.
[127] Boyle 2014, 313 adopts a slightly different division based on the meter used in each section. Reif 2016, 332 also applies the traditional structure of prayer in this excerpt.

Invocatio

At the beginning of the incantation scene, Medea stands in front of the turf altar (797) while invoking the gods and spirits of the Underworld. The very first word (*comprecor*) connects the excerpt with the nurse's speech through its allusion to line 680 (*comprecans*):[128]

> Comprecor vulgus silentum vosque ferales deos   740
> et Chaos caecum atque opacam Ditis umbrosi domum,
> Tartari ripis ligatos squalidae Mortis specus.
> supplicis, animae, remissis currite ad thalamos novos:
> rota resistat membra torquens, tangat Ixion humum,
> Tantalus securus undas hauriat Pirenidas,   745
> [gravior uni poena sedeat coniugis socero mei]
> lubricus per saxa retro Sisyphum solvat lapis.
> vos quoque, urnis quas foratis inritus ludit labor,
> Danaides, coite: vestras hic dies quaerit manus.
> nunc meis vocata sacris, noctium sidus, veni   750
> pessimos induta vultus, fronte non una minax.

> I pray to the silent crowd, and you, underworld gods,
> and blind Chaos, and dim house of Hades full of shades,
> and caves of foul Death, surrounded by the banks of Tartarus.
> Souls, with your punishments remitted, run quickly to the new chambers:
> Let the wheel that twists the limbs stop, and Ixion touch the ground,
> let Tantalus, free from troubles, drain the waters of Pirene,
> let a greater penalty be imposed only upon my husband's grandfather-in-law;
> let the slippery boulder roll back upon Sisyphus through the rocks.
> And you, whom the vain toil mocks with perforated urns,
> daughters of Danaus, assemble: this day asks for your help. –
> Now, invoked by my rites, star of the night, come,
> assuming your ill-looking countenance, menacing with all your faces.

Using mostly periphrastic addresses, in imitation of invocations attested in magical texts,[129] Medea asks from several deities, some of whom are the same as those addressed in the prologue, to run to her aid (*currite*).[130] However, she makes an important addition to the list by also invoking the spirits of the deceased (*vulgus*

---

128 Boyle 2014, 315 observes that the use of *comprecor* "picks up the Nurse's *comprecans* ... contributing towards the near seamlessness of this magic act".
129 See pages 6–7, n. 23, 26, 28, and 29, with Reif 2016, 365–366.
130 Boyle 2014, 315 and 318; Hine 2000, 184–186 marks the following parallels: The *ferales deos* (=*manes inpios*), *Chaos* (cf. line 9), the *sidus noctium* (=Luna, a form of *Hecate triformis*), and the *domus Ditis* and *specus Mortis* (=*aversa superis regna*).

silentum; *animae*).[131] The purpose of addressing them is clarified in the immediately following lines (744–749), when Medea requests the presence of the great sinners of Hades, namely Ixion, Tantalus, and the Danaids, in the upcoming wedding of Jason and Creusa. The sole exception is Sisyphus, whose punishment Medea wishes to increase, because he is considered Creon's ancestor, and therefore a probable opponent to her plan.[132]

The crimes of these mythological characters serve as a point of reference for Medea's future crimes. Ixion disrespected the rules of *xenia* by trying to seduce his host's wife, the goddess Hera (Pind. *Pyth* 2.21–48); Tantalus sacrificed his son Pelops and tried to feed him to the gods (Pind. *Ol.* 1.35–55); Sisyphus tricked Death, and avoided the initial punishment imposed on him by Zeus (*Schol. Il.* 6.153); finally, the Danaids killed their husbands (or in some versions of the myth castrated them), thus ending Egyptus' line (Apollod. *Bibl.* 2.1.5). These stories were known to the audience, who, upon reflection, would be able to connect them with Medea's crimes: like Ixion, the heroine violates the rules of *xenia* by murdering her host, king Creon; at the end of the play she kills her children like Tantalus did, thus putting an end to Jason's bloodline just as the Danaids ended that of their husbands; and like Sisyphus, she avoids a possible punishment by fleeing Corinth at the end of the play.[133] Even though Medea invokes the archetypal sinners as divine assistants towards her plan's completion, she will surpass each one of them with her own crimes.[134] And since their transgressions were so abominable to warrant eternal punishment, in the reader's mind the heroine's criminal conduct becomes unprecedented, adding further to her sketching as a monster.

Narratio

In her effort to secure the presence specifically of Hecate (770: *adesse sacris tempus est, Phoebe, tuis*), whom she invokes at the end of her magical prayer, the heroine enumerates her past services to the goddess (*da quia dedi* formula):[135]

---

131 For the role of the dead in curses see Collins 2008, 69–73, and Eidinow 2019, 373–376 with notes.
132 Costa 1973, 138–139; Boyle 2014, 317.
133 Reif 2016, 307 notes that Medea invokes the archetypal sinners because her crime of infanticide will match her with them.
134 Reif 2016, 310 claims that Medea's invocation places the heroine among the sinners, at the same time foreshadowing her crimes against Creon, Creusa, and then her children.
135 Boyle 2014, 320.

Tibi more gentis vinculo solvens comam
secreta nudo nemora lustravi pede
et evocavi nubibus siccis aquas
egique ad imum maria, et Oceanus graves   755
interius undas aestibus victis dedit,
pariterque mundus lege confusa aetheris
et solem et astra vidit et vetitum mare
tetigistis, ursae. temporum flexi vices:
aestiva tellus horruit cantu meo,   760
coacta messem vidit hibernam Ceres;
violenta Phasis vertit in fontem vada
et Hister, in tot ora divisus, truces
compressit undas omnibus ripis piger;
sonuere fluctus, tumuit insanum mare   765
tacente vento; nemoris antiqui domus
amisit umbras vocis imperio meae. –
die relicto Phoebus in medio stetit,
Hyadesque nostris cantibus motae labant:
adesse sacris tempus est, Phoebe, tuis.   770

For you, in my peoples' custom, I have loosened my hair from their band,
and gone around the secret woods with my bare feet,
and produced rain from dry clouds,
and driven the sea to its bottom, and the Ocean has given
great waves, with the tide drawn further from the shores;
the world, with the law of the sky confounded,
has seen simultaneously the sun and the stars, and you, Bears,
have touched the forbidden sea. I have reversed the seasons:
the summer soil has been stunned by my spell
and, forced by it, Ceres has seen winter harvest.
The violent streams of Phasis have turned back to their source,
and reluctant Hister, divided into several mouths,
has confined its wild waters within the river banks;
The waves have resounded, the frenzied sea has swelled
with the wind silent. The home of the ancient forest
has lost its shade by the power of my voice.
As the day is left behind, Phoebus has stopped amidst his course,
and the Hyades, disturbed by my chants, glide.
It is time, Diana, to be present at your own rites.

The excerpt presents Medea's alleged control over nature, a central feature in literary representations of magic (e.g. Ov. *Met.* 7.199–209, *Am.* 1.8.5–10; Tib. 1.2.41–52; Ap. Rhod. *Argon.* 3.528–33), but also a major feat of supernatural entities in the spells of the *PGM* (e.g. I 99, 120–122; IV 191–192, 1354–1355, 1372; XII 241–242, 248–249;

XIII 872–876).[136] These reversals of the natural order are the heroine's tribute to Hecate (*tibi*), which also serve as a means to convince the goddess to respond favorably to her petition.[137] At the same time, these proclamations also enhance Medea's image as an all-powerful witch since the subversion of the natural order, the *par excellence monstrum*, is attributed to supernatural entities in the *PGM*.

Medea's self-description at the beginning of the excerpt points to her foreignness by implying the exotic nature of Colchian rituals (*more gentis*). It also connects her current ritual (738: *vesano gradu*; 804: *passos ... capillos*) with past ones (753: *lustravi pede*; 752: *vinculo solvens comam*), thus foreshadowing the partial reclaim of her old identity, that of the *pharmakos*. From this perspective, the *mos gentis* obtains another meaning as it links the magical ritual with the Colchian element of her identity, and thus sets the foundations for her final transformation into a witch.

At this point, the scene becomes highly dramatic as the heroine first describes her material offerings to Hecate, and then proceeds with the ritual acts, and the casting of the spell.[138] Lines 771–784 are the only instance in Senecan drama where iambic trimeters and dimeters are used alternatingly. As Boyle has observed, this choice is probably based on the meter's association with magic and incantation,[139] thus adding a realistic tone to the utterance:

>   Tibi haec cruenta serta texuntur manu,
>   novena quae serpens ligat,
>   tibi haec Typhoeus membra quae discors tulit,
>   qui regna concussit Iovis.
>   vectoris istic perfidi sanguis inest,   775
>   quem Nessus expirans dedit.
>   Oetaeus isto cinere defecit rogus,
>   qui virus Herculeum bibit.
>   piae sororis, impiae matris, facem
>   ultricis Althaeae vides.   780
>   reliquit istas invio plumas specu
>   Harpyia, dum Zeten fugit.
>   his adice pinnas sauciae Stymphalidos
>   Lernaea passae spicula.

---

136 Reif 2016, 360–364 examines in detail the connections between the commanding of natural phenomena in the *PGM* and Medea's power to upset the natural order.
137 Boyle 2014, 320; Reif 2016, 286 claims that Medea's utterance makes Hecate's intervention indispensable to the heroine's spell. For the analysis of the passage detailing the *adynata*, see Reif 2016, 310–312.
138 For the highly dramatic aspects of the magic ritual see Kohn 2013, 87.
139 Boyle 2014, 323–324, who also includes relevant examples from other texts.

Magic on stage: the main ritual — 35

For you these wreaths are woven with bloody hand,
which bind together nine serpents,
for you these limbs, which belonged to rebellious Typhon,
who shook violently the kingdoms of Jove.
Herein is the blood of the perfidious ferryman,
which Nessus gave while breathing his last.
In this very ash died out Oeta's pyre,
drenched in the poison that killed Hercules.
You see the torch of a pious sister, but impious mother,
the vengeful Althaea.
The Harpy left these very feathers in an inaccessible cave
while fleeing Zetes.
Place upon these the feathers of an injured Stymphalian bird,
which was hit by Lernaean arrows.

Wreaths featured prominently in magic rituals,[140] while the number nine, as a multiple of three, was thought to possess magical powers.[141] The grisly items that Medea names next (773–784), each one accompanied by a ritualistic movement,[142] were probably coined by Seneca in an effort to imitate the codified names given to certain materials used in contemporary magic rituals.[143] All of them point to further developments in the play: as a witch, Medea is a theomach who attacks the gods, like Typhoeus did; she will kill Creusa by tricking her with her wedding gifts, thus recalling the perfidious Nessus, who duped Dianeira into killing Hercules; both the demigod's and Creusa's death come in agony as they are both burnt alive; Medea's filicide assimilates her with Althaea who killed her son, Meleager; like the monstrous Harpy who fled from Zetes and Calais, she will eventually escape any pursuers by flying away on the Sun's chariot;[144] finally, the scourge of the Stymphalian

---

140 See, for example, *PGM* II 27–29, II 70, IV 1058, 1994–1995, VII 874, and CXXIV 1–43 with Reif 2016, 351–352.
141 For the association of number 'three' with magic, see Tavenner 1916.
142 Reif 2016, 314.
143 As we can infer from *PGM* XII 401–444, temple scribes often obscured the names of ingredients used in magic to protect what was considered secret knowledge, and to deter the ignorant masses from engaging in the practice. Betz 1986, 136 n. 114 suggests that the "blood of Typhon" was the codified name for the blood of an ass, and in 150 n. 1 that "Typhon's skull" is the semantic equivalent of an ass' skull. For the association of Althaea's torch, Nessus' blood, and the Harpy's feather with the Argonauts and as foreshadowing Jason's punishment see Boyle 2014, 325–326.
144 These analogies are noted in Reif 2016, 315–316.

birds can be seen as an allegory for herself, who causes destruction and suffering to the community with the burning of the city.[145]

A peculiarly odd element of the ritual is that the heroine performs her offerings without having undergone purification (*cruenta manu*). Since the cleansing of the spell operator appears to have been necessary in magic rituals (e.g. *PGM* I 54–57, III 304–306, IV 26, 1099–1100, VII 981–982, XXIIb 27, XXXVIII 1), Medea clearly violates the rules of ritualistic conduct.[146] And given that purification of the subject was generally considered a major factor in a spell's success (e.g. *PDM* xiv 489–515), the spectators would normally expect that the current ritual will fail solely on religious grounds.[147] Surprisingly though, not only is the ritual completed, but also the plan eventually proves successful. The success, despite the lack of piety, underscores the extreme subversion of even the rules of magic in the play's cosmos, emphasizing the greater *monstrum* Medea produces with her ritual.[148]

After the offerings, Medea recognizes Hecate's assent (786: *favente ... dea*), which manifests itself in the altar's resounding (785: *sonuistis, arae*), the moving of the tripods (785–786: *tripodas ... commotos*), and the moon's descent from the sky (787–796). Identical or similar events which indicate divine favor are attested in the instructions of the *PGM*, thus adding originality to Seneca's composition.[149]

These spectacular images and awe-inspiring sounds horrify the reader (794: *horrore novo terre*), who realizes the irreversibility of the destructive result as the macabre and gloomy appearance of the moon (790: *facie lurida maesta*; 793: *sic face tristem pallida lucem*) indicates.[150] In an unexpected twist, Medea scorns the sound of bronze whose ringing could potentially disrupt the spell, paradoxically claiming that it will instead enhance its effectiveness (795–796). This statement, like Medea's impure conduct in 771–772, also emphasizes the extreme power of her magic, which will succeed even under adversarial circumstances.

---

[145] This interpretation of the reference to the Stymphalian birds (*contra* Reif 2016, 316) is based on the general observation in Ashton 2011, 75 who shows that "it is possible for birds to represent either passive suffering, grief and loss, or active aggression causing suffering to others".
[146] Boyle 2014, 324.
[147] For the importance of purification in religious rituals, and the implications of someone's failure to purify themselves, see Lennon 2014, 29–54. See also n. 118 on page 70.
[148] Reif 2016, 314 views Medea's weaving of the garlands with her impure hands as an inversion of religious precepts but considers it a token of piety to Hecate.
[149] Reif 2016, 355 and n. 297–298 on the same page.
[150] Reif 2016, 318–319.

The spell continues with Medea's movements, the description of the ritual's central *praxis*:[151]

> Tibi sanguineo caespite sacrum
>   sollemne damus,
> tibi de medio rapta sepulcro
> fax nocturnos sustulit ignes,   800
> tibi mota caput flexa voces
>   cervice dedi,
> tibi funereo de more iacens
> passos cingit vitta capillos,
> tibi iactatur tristis Stygia
>   ramus ab unda,   805
> tibi nudato pectore maenas
> sacro feriam bracchia cultro.
> manet noster sanguis ad aras:
> assuesce, manus, stringere ferrum
> carosque pati posse cruores –   810
> sacrum laticem percussa dedi.

> For you, on the bloody turf,
> I offer the sacred gifts,
> for you the torch, snatched from the middle of a funerary pyre,
> fed the nocturnal fires,
> for you I move my head, twisting my neck,
> and chant,
> for you, worn in funerary manner,
> the band ties my loosened hair,
> for you is shaken the gloomy bough
> from the waters of Styx.
> For you, with my chest exposed, like a Maenad,
> I shall strike my forearms with the sacred knife.
> Let my blood flow on the altar:
> my hand, be accustomed to drawing out the knife,
> and to enduring your precious bleeding.
> I offer the sacred fluid, having struck myself!

The *sollemne sacrum* probably refers collectively to the strange items listed in lines 771–784 as customary offerings for Hecate. The reader visualizes the heroine raising

---

151 Reif 2016, 351–355 traces connections between Medea's ritualistic acts and acts described in the *PGM*.

a torch[152] while dancing ecstatically, moving her head and bending her neck.[153] Her disheveled hair is encircled with a headband, the characteristic *vitta* of the priestess.[154] At the same time, she is shaking a tree branch, probably yew,[155] as part of the ritual, and having exposed her breast,[156] she strikes her arm with a knife to let her blood drip on the altar.[157]

Even though this part of the ritual is gruesome in its entirety, emphasis is laid on the slashing of Medea's arm (807–811), which covers five verses compared to the approximately two-line description of every other action. The scene of self-mutilation would have reminded the reader of the rituals of Bellona and Isis, whose priests and priestesses were despised by the Romans for castrating and cutting themselves.[158] Seneca was critical of such excessive forms of worship as it is clear in a fragment from the *De Superstitione* which refers to the *Galli*, and the *Bellonarii*: *Ille -inquit- viriles sibi partes amputat, ille lacertos secat ... Dii autem nullo debent coli genere, si hoc volunt* (F68 Vottero). Therefore, by dramatizing an act which was despised by Romans even during official cult rites, he manages to ignite the disgust and indignation of his audience towards the heroine's magical practices.[159]

---

152 Reif 2016, 352–353 for torches as items often used in real magic.
153 Reif 2016, 353 for the connection between Medea's dance and the *PGM*.
154 Costa 1973, 145. Reif 2016, 353–354 links the headband with magic.
155 Boyle 2014, 329 proposes yew or cypress; Costa 1973, 145: yew. For the use of twigs in the *PGM* in connection to Medea's ritual see Reif 2016, 354.
156 Reif 2016, 355 notes the parallel with *PGM* IV 175, which requires the magician to be nude.
157 Reif 2016, 320 sees blood dripping as form of sympathetic magic: like Medea spills her blood, Creusa should spill hers. Even though human blood was never involved in indigenous Roman rituals, there are certain references of its use in magic: *PGM* IV 79–80 and IV 2207–2208 require the blood of a pregnant woman and that of a *biaiothanatos* respectively, to be used as ink; *PDM Suppl.* 60–101 instructs the spell operator to use blood from their thigh during the ritual; finally, *PGM* XCIII 1-6 details a ritual in honor of Hecate, which requires to pour blood in a vessel, and besprinkle it on the outside (with blood?) in order to acquire the goddess' favor. For detailed references to the use of blood in the *PGM* see Reif 2016, 158–159.
158 The connection between Medea's slashing of her hand and the mutilation of the *Bellonarii* was first noted in Costa 1973, 145.
159 Reif 2016, 339 notes the use of blood in magical papyri, but considers self-mutilation as unrealistic, arguing that it is Seneca's own invention meant to exaggerate the brutality of magic rituals.

Preces

The spell concludes with Medea's specific requests, indirectly providing the reader with information about other ingredients of the poison:[160]

> Tu nunc vestes tinge Creusae,
> quas cum primum sumpserit, imas
> urat serpens flamma medullas.
> Ignis fulvo clusus in auro   820
> latet obscurus, quem mihi caeli
> qui furta luit viscere feto
> dedit et docuit condere vires
> arte, Prometheus; dedit et tenui
> sulphure tectos Mulciber ignes,   825
> et vivacis fulgura flammae
> de cognato Phaethonte tuli.
> habeo mediae dona Chimaerae,
> habeo flammas usto tauri
>   gutture raptas,   830
> quas permixto felle Medusae
> tacitum iussi servare malum.
> Adde venenis stimulos, Hecate,
> donisque meis semina flammae
>   condita serva: 835
> fallant visus tactusque ferant,
> meet in pectus venasque calor,
> stillent artus ossaque fument
> vincatque suas flagrante coma
>   nova nupta faces.   840

> Now smear Creusa's garments,
> and as soon as she wears them,
> a creeping flame may burn the inner marrow of her bones.
> It remains concealed, shut in yellow gold,
> the fire which
> the one who atoned for his theft with his ever-growing liver gave me,
> and taught me to hide its powers
> with art, Prometheus; and Mulciber
> gave me the flames hidden in a pinch of sulphur,
> and I brought the sparks of living flame
> from my kinsman, Phaethon;
> I have the gifts of the middle part of Chimaera,

---

[160] Reif 2016, 346–347 surveys the links between Medea's concoction and those described in the *PGM*.

> I have the flames, seized from the
> burning throat of the bull,
> which, combined with Medusa's gall,
> I ordered to keep the poison concealed.
> Hecate, give power to my potion,
> and preserve the secret seeds of flame
> in my gifts:
> Let them trick the sight, and endure the contact,
> and let the heat travel up to the heart and veins,
> her limbs drip and bones smoke,
> and let the new bride outmatch her own
> torches with her blazing hair.

The first request has generated scholarly discussion as the task of smearing the clothes with poison seems to be too trivial to associate with any deity.[161] It might be more reasonable to view this as Medea's self-exhortation. More appropriate requests in the context of a prayer are the ones that follow: Hecate is asked to spur on the poison, make sure it remains undetected in the artifacts which Medea intends to donate to the bride, and boost its destructive power by affecting the victim's heart and veins, and by melting her limbs and bones.[162] Even though out of these requests only the last is attested in the *PGM*,[163] it is plausible that the magician could ask pretty much anything from the summoned deity or *paredros*.

The excerpt includes further information on the nature of the poison. Out of the ingredients mentioned (Prometheus' fire, the Vulcan's flame concealed in sulphur, the thunder of the flame of Phaethon, the fires of Chimaera and the Colchian bull, and the gall of Medusa),[164] the first one stands out as the most important. The central position of the specific ingredient can be justified if one takes into consideration that the Titan defied Zeus by stealing the fire from the Olympians and

---

161 Reif 2016, 329 believes it is addressed to the nurse. For other suggestions see Boyle 2014, 332.
162 Reif 2016, 291 notes the importance of magical *contagio* in the success of Medea's spell (i.e. passing the deadly magic to the objects through her touch).
163 Reif 2016, 341 points that the utter destruction of bones and limbs recalls the death which *PGM* XXXVI 231–255 intends to inflict on the victim (καταρρεῖ and ξηραίνεται).
164 We can certainly assume that Seneca again imitates the practice of encoding the materials used in magic. There is one ingredient that stands out, i.e. sulphur, whose fire-causing properties were well known in antiquity (Mart. 1.41.4–5, 10.3.3–4, 12.57.14; Stat. *Silv.* 1.6.74; Juv. 5.48). Mayor 2009, 227–228 and 289 n. 14 claims that in the first century CE, if not before, the Romans started speculating on the recipe used by Medea, with Pliny concluding that naphtha was among the secret ingredients (*HN* 2.235–236). She further suggests that the heroine might refer to a spontaneously igniting substance like the one described by the second century CE author Julius Africanus (*Kestoi* 2.11).

offered it to the humans (Hes. *Theog.* 565–566, *Op.* 50; Apollod. *Bibl.* 1.7.1) with the intent of helping mankind improve their lives. However, in this instance, Prometheus' fire is used for a reason that was never intended, that is, to cause harm, exemplifying in this manner the power of magic to reverse the beneficial aspects of a divine gift.

The list of ingredients in 820–832 probably elaborates on the materials alluded to, but never specified, at the beginning of the nurse's speech in 677–679:

> totas opes effundit et quidquid diu
> etiam ipsa timuit promit atque omnem explicat
> turbam malorum, arcana secreta abdita,

> She pours forth all the substances and brings out whatever
> herself feared for a long time, and displays the whole
> heap of evils, arcane, secret, concealed.

Before gathering the herbs and collecting snake poison, Medea brought out some ingredients she had stored. These the nurse describes as destructive (*turbam malorum*) but known only to few (*arcana*) — this agrees with their mythological origins —, kept separately and concealed. Since she claims that they remained hidden for quite some time (*diu*), it follows that Medea had obtained them in the past like the materials listed in 820–832 (*dedit ... dedit ... tuli ... raptas ... permixto*). The heroine's shrinking away from using them before (*timuit*) points to her earlier, benevolent character, and her revelation of them now is indicative of the shift in her depiction. The change is reinforced also by the characterization of Chimaera's fire as *dona*, which recalls and contrasts with Ovid's *munus* (*Met.* 7.296) for Medea's rejuvenating brew. Seneca thus links the heroine's past as a *pharmakos* with the present ritual, and by providing us with a list of these long-hidden, destructive materials, he emphasizes her change into an evil witch. From this perspective, the last three lines of the scene, which describe the barking of Hecate (840–841) and the lighting of the torch (842), confirm not only the successful conclusion of the ritual but also Medea's transformation.

1.7 Destruction on stage

In the last, fifth act, the reader witnesses the results of what Medea was 'building' throughout the play: Creon and Creusa have been burnt alive (880), the palace is in flames (885–886), and the fire will spread to the whole city (887). The subsequent murder of her children (970–971; 1019–1020) concludes the series of gruesome acts perpetrated by the heroine, completing her transformation.[165] All these events symbolize the destruction magic can cause on different levels (social, natural, and political). The family and the household, which are the core of society and the city, respectively, lie in ruins. Social continuity is disrupted because of the death of the children, both Medea's and Creon's. The latter's death and the destruction of the palace symbolize the destabilization of political order as the state is now headless. These circumstances can eventually lead to the city's total annihilation.

These images of death and destruction, the result of Medea's magic, sketch the heroine as a *monstrum* in accordance with Seneca's condemnation of the practice. The author, who took what was left from the heroine's long tradition as a beneficent *pharmakos* (166: *Medea superest*), manages to create an evil witch (910: *Medea nunc sum*) through an accurate, sinister and dark magic ritual (910: *crevit ingenium malis*) — *malum* here is used ambiguously: "my nature increased with my crimes" or "my nature increased with my magic". It is through the description of the gruesome magical details and ingredients (*malis*) that Seneca creates a unique visual impression that causes disgust and indignation, but mostly fear, to the reader which, in turn, can deter them from succumbing to superstition.

1.8 Conclusions

The *Medea*, like all Seneca's plays, is a multifaceted tragedy which, in its dealing with the theme of magic, draws thematic inspiration from contemporary life in the first century CE. In line with Stoic views on *superstitio*, whose negative features and impact are epitomized in magic, Seneca sketches the practice as a force that can destabilize the whole world. He presents the reader with a flat-out negative image of the witch, embellished with elements of societal prejudice to render the portrayal of Medea more realistic. Her wickedness is enhanced further by the sketching of her magical powers as thoroughly evil. From the very beginning, the reader witnesses the heroine uttering a curse full of sinister and subversive images which delineates the dreadful atmosphere that runs through the play but also reveals the irrationality of magic. The absurd character of such practices is underscored further through the contrast of Medea's curse with the prayer of the chorus, leading

---

[165] A disproportionate penalty for Jason's offenses and misdeeds, which underscores Medea's distorted idea of justice due to her uncontrolled *ira* (Guastella 2001, 197). Fischer 2008, 139 views the killing of the children as Medea's sacrifice which was removed from the ritualistic context, allowing Seneca to criticize gory crimes. Lefèvre 2002, 109–110 compares the ending of the *Medea* with Aeneas' killing of Turnus in Verg. *Aen.* 12.948–949 and concludes that Roman values and Stoic thinking are both distorted in the scene of the children's murder.

the reader to contemplate upon the heroine's triumph, the dominance of magic and the failure of religion. The depiction of the *ars magica* as a power that lays waste on the natural, social, and political order is complete in the scene of the ritual, where Seneca silences any beneficial aspects of Medea's magic found in earlier literature, most notably in Ovid's *Metamorphoses*, and presents it solely as an evil and destructive force. The realistic representation, effectuated through the imitation of structural elements and details recalling the *PGM*, essentially links the play with actual magical practices familiar to the reader. When Medea's crimes are finally revealed, the reader cannot help but feel horror and disgust at the results of magic, thus enhancing the 'apotropaic' role of the drama. Jason's exclamation at the very end of the play (1027: *testare nullos esse, qua veheris, deos*) is the Stoic *sententia* which distills the moral lesson of the whole play:[166] magic finds space in society through the human agent when normative religious ideas are suppressed — Lucan's epic, the *Bellum Civile*, famous for its suppression of the divine machinery,[167] also adheres to this principle with the depiction of Erichtho and her sinister practices, which are discussed in the next chapter.

---

[166] On the various interpretations proposed for the concluding verse of the *Medea* see Costa 1973, 159–160; Fitch and McElduff 2002, 20; Wiener 2006, 46; Fischer 2008, 163–164 and 177; Boyle 2014, 388; Reif 2016, 412–413.

[167] This issue, its causes, and results for Lucan's narrative are discussed in Feeney 1991, 250–301; for a brief overview see Roche 2019, 5–7.

2 Lucan, the Didactic Poet

Lucan's *Bellum Civile* has been often criticized for its macabre imagery and the author's love for gory violence. Among the narratives which cause the readers' chills and disgust is the Erichtho episode (6.413–830) on account of the witch's horrid depiction and the ritual she performs.[1] The inclusion of such a lengthy scene, which further encompasses a necromantic ritual, does not fit traditionally as well as structurally in the narrative of a historical epic. For years this 'unconventionality' has puzzled scholars, who attempted to assert the scene's function in the poem.[2]

As the witchcraft scene does not advance the plot nor influences the motives and actions of any character, its importance is sought from a non-narratological perspective.[3] It has been suggested that for Lucan magic offers a conceptual parallel to the civil war since both represent a violation of the natural order.[4] This idea, though correct, does not explain in full why Lucan devoted so many lines to the power of Thessalian magic or the extensive details of the necromantic ritual. Such length and accuracy can be justified if we accept that Lucan also intended to make a point specifically about magic, whose sweeping advent he witnessed during his lifetime.[5]

One need not assume that the author truly believed in the powers of magicians and witches but can accept that there were credulous people among his audience at whose edification he could have aimed.[6] The Erichtho scene, as I will show, serves as a vehicle for Lucan's criticism against magic as an anti-Stoic and anti-Roman practice. His disapproval takes different forms, and is channeled against the *ars magica*, its practitioners, as well as their clients, who believe in its powers. The extreme realism of the episode stimulates the reader to challenge contemporary claims about magic, and subsequently question its efficacy and moral value.

---

[1] Haskins 1887, lxxv; Morford 1967, 67; Fauth 1975, 332; Masters 1992, 179.
[2] Paoletti 1963, 11–26; Fauth 1975, 325–344; Ahl 1976, 130–149; Baldini Moscadi 1976, 191–192; Narducci 1979, 54–62; Martindale 1980, 367–377; Gordon 1987a, 231–241; Johnson 1987, 18–33; Tupet 1988, 419–427; Masters 1992, 179–215; Danese 1992; Reif 2016, 456–464.
[3] Le Bonniec 1970, 185 referring to the episode in its entirety: "… bien qu'elle soit strictement inutile a l'action, le consultant ne jouant aucun rôle dans l'épopée"; Ahl 1976, 146–147 notices that there is no other reference to the prophecy throughout the narrative.
[4] Fauth 1975, 338; Lugli 1987–1988, 96–97; Lapidge 1979, 368–369; Loupiac 1991, 261–262.
[5] Gordon 1987a, 234. Lucan's negative view of magic is noted in Pichon 1912, 196 and Le Bonniec 1970, 189.
[6] Both Pichon 1912, 193–197, and Le Bonniec 1970, 186–188 see a genuine interest in magic on Lucan's behalf, and an attempt to reconcile this belief with Stoic ideas. Morford 1967, 70 viewed the scene as a veiled criticism of Nero's superstitious character.

At first, Lucan presents us with the emotional turmoil and the motives of Sextus Pompey, which sketch him as a thoroughly anti-Stoic figure.[7] His decision to summon Erichtho exemplifies the Stoic idea that the existence of evil in the world is the result of human choice and action.[8] The reference to Sextus' deeds after the defeat of his father and the demise of the Republican cause emphasizes his anti-Roman character, but also allows for a connection, at the end of the episode, between Sextus, magic, and the continuation of the civil conflict in the years of the second triumvirate. Thus, in the reader's mind the scene also transforms into an etiological explanation for a series of events which were part of the greatest evil that has ever afflicted Rome.

The digression on love magic, and the passage detailing the effects of magic on nature underscore the subversive power of the magical art.[9] But Lucan furthers his criticism beyond this archetypal image of reversal through the philosophical coloring of these passages. Anti-Stoic traits permeate these lines to illustrate the destructive effects of magic, from a Stoic perspective, on the social and natural order, respectively. The last section of the excursus deals with the witches' control over animals, and the 'Thessalian trick', both images familiar to contemporary Romans. By listing these common tricks among the feats of Thessalian witchcraft, Lucan guides the reader to debunk the alleged power of Thessalian witches and, by extension, regard magic as charlatanry.

The futility of magic, however, becomes clear in the juxtaposition of the witch Erichtho with her practices. Lucan creates a monstrous, unreal witch surpassing her literary predecessors, and who, despite her grotesqueness, performs an extremely realistic spell with great accuracy.[10] The verisimilitude of the ritual serves as an anchor between the scene and contemporary experience, but it also makes

---

7 Sextus' anti-Stoic character and attitude has been extensively discussed in Martindale 1977, 375–379, and Tesoriero 2002, 233–234.

8 Ahl 1976, 295–296 argued that, in abandoning the traditional machinery of the epic and making *Fortuna* the major deity of the poem, Lucan creates an environment insulated from divine influence, allowing the reader to evaluate human conduct from a moral and legal perspective. Thus, Lucan's protagonists have free will, and their actions are the cause of any outcome, whether positive or negative. Ahl's suggestion also agrees with Seneca's views on theodicy, who attributed evil's existence to human action. For the problem of theodicy in Seneca see Fischer 2008, 11–56; for Lucan see Wiener 2010.

9 Gordon 1987a, 237–239.

10 The resonances of the *PGM* in Lucan's ritual have been extensively discussed in scholarship. See, for example, Fahz 1904, Nock 1972, 185–187, Baldini Moscadi 1976, 140–199, Graf 1997a, 190–204. The most recent and detailed analysis of the links between the 'Erichtho scene' and real magic is Reif 2016, 420–455. That said, Lucan did not necessarily consult real witchcraft books to create his scene (Pichon 1912, 192).

the failure of witchcraft more blatant in the reader's mind, who is left to wonder about the power of magic and its human practitioners.

2.1 Sextus Pompey: an anti-Stoic and anti-Roman anti-hero

The son of Pompey the Great, Sextus, is sketched negatively throughout the narrative of the Erichtho episode. In the prelude of the necromancy scene Lucan makes sure to delineate early on his 'anti-Stoic' attitude:

> degeneres trepidant animi peioraque versant;
> ad dubios pauci praesumpto robore casus
> spemque metumque ferunt. turbae sed mixtus inerti
> Sextus erat, ...[11]   420

> Base souls tremble in fear and revolve worse thoughts;
> a few, gaining their confidence beforehand toward the uncertain events,
> endure both hope and fear. But mingled with the inert crowd
> was Sextus...[12]

In the eve of the battle, the situation in both camps is ambivalent: some soldiers gather their strength to face their fear and moderate their expectations for what is to come, while others tremble at the unknown.[13] Lucan lumps Sextus together with the latter (*turbae inerti*), who, contrary to the Stoic *sapiens*, hesitate to take the steep and unsafe path to virtue (Sen. *Prov.* 5.11: *Humilis et inertis est tuta sectari: per alta virtus it*; *V.B.* 20.5). The uncertainty about the future causes Sextus anxiety and fear, which in turn drive his decision to obtain prior knowledge of fate:[14]

> qui stimulante metu fati praenoscere cursus,
> inpatiensque morae venturisque omnibus aeger
>   423–424

> With fear inciting him to foreknow the course of fate,
> both impatient of delay and anxious of all that was coming.

---

11 The text of Lucan is cited from Housman's edition.
12 All translations included in the chapter are my own.
13 Martindale 1977, 375–376 correctly interprets lines 418–419 as reflecting the sage's attitude, who is ready to endure any positive or negative development. Besides, the sapiens knows neither fear nor hope (Sen. *Constant.* 9.2; *V.B.* 5.3).
14 Martindale 1977, 377.

Sextus' motive to act (*metus*) is particularly unstoic since it is one of the four cardinal passions of Stoicism. It interferes with one's ability to deal as reasonably as possible with the present situation, and thus it disturbs the course to the desired goal of the *animi tranquillitas*.[15] His characterization as *aeger*, a word ordinarily used in Seneca's philosophical treatises to describe anyone who is manipulated by their passions (Sen. *Ben.* 7.16.6; *Ep.* 15.1), also fits Sextus' anti-Stoic portrayal. Fear, along with the inability to bear the delay (*impatientia*) of learning the future through his own experience, leads Sextus to frenzy (434: *furorem*) and further distances him from the attainment of rationality (*bona mens*), which was one of the goals of the *proficiens* (Sen. *QNat.* 3 pf. 14: ... *optare, quod sine adversario optatur, bonam mentem*).[16] Thus, in resorting to divination Sextus acts on impulse, contrary to Stoic tenets which 1) intended to transform the *impetus animi* into *habitus animi* (Sen. *Ep.* 16.6), and 2) considered one's ability to face the current misfortunes more significant than foreknowledge of the future (Sen. *Ben.* 5.17.5).[17] Sextus explicitly opposes this Stoic idea in 596–598:

> mens dubiis perculsa pavet rursusque parata est
> certos ferre metus: hoc casibus eripe iuris,
> ne subiti caecique ruant.

> My mind, struck with uncertainty, is terrified; yet again, it is prepared
> to face inevitable fears: remove this power from misfortunes,
> so as not to fall upon me sudden and unforeseen.

This statement further distances Sextus from the orthodox Stoic conception of the sage, who remains unmoved by the possible changes of fortune because he is "secure in the knowledge of his own virtus".[18] The *sapiens* has proven their virtue through their fight with *fortuna* (Sen. *Brev. Vit.* 5.3; *Constant.* 15.3–5; *V.B.* 5.3), having faced the impediments (*Brev. Vit.* 5.3: *adversarum patiens*) that appear in their path to their moral transformation (Sen. *Helv.* 5.1; *Ep.* 71.30; *Ben.* 6.35.1).[19] The attitude of the Stoic sage toward *fortuna* is aptly exemplified in the *sententia Fortuna fortes*

---

15 Tesoriero 2002, 242 n. 27.
16 Tesoriero 2002, 233 has already noted the Stoic overtone of *aeger* in Sextus' description, and connected his *furor* with the inability to overcome his passions.
17 The αὐτάρκεια of the sage, who lives each day as if it was his last, has been noted and discussed in contrast to Sextus' anti-Stoicism in Martindale 1977, 377–378.
18 Martindale 1977, 377.
19 For the role of *fortuna* in Seneca as a test for men to prove their virtue see Fischer 2008, 38–51 and Setaioli 2014, 399.

metuit, ignavos premit (Sen. *Med.* 159), an attitude which both Sextus and his companions lack, since they are characterized as *ignavi* (589, and 666).

Sextus fails to realize that what seems to people as unconnected, accidental events, are actually part of the preordained plan (*fata*) which governs the whole universe (Sen. *Ben.* 4.32.1; Cic. *Div.* 2.18–19).[20] Therefore, his request from Erichtho to undermine the powers of *fortuna*, which goes against the Stoic belief of the immutability of fate, is destined to fail. As Erichtho herself will later admit, she is powerless to change the final outcome set by destiny (611–615), and is only able to influence the course by, e.g., protracting life or accelerating death (607–610).

Sextus' unstoic mentality as well as his motives aptly illustrate that he is an example of a person who yields to *superstitio*.[21] He is an *animus impatiens*, a person *qui nullum ferre possit malum*, according to Seneca's definition (Sen. *Ep.* 9.2–3). This *impatientia* deprives him of the *pura mens*, one that is free from all evils (*V.B.* 5.3), and a prerequisite for the man's interaction with the God in Stoicism (F88 Vottero). His belief that celestial gods have only limited knowledge (433–434) is reprehensible as it implicitly underscores Sextus' lack of faith, a quality which was considered essential in the proper worship of the divine (Sen. *Ep.* 95.50: *primus est deorum cultus deos credere*). These traits, along with Sextus' excessive fear and desire to learn his own fate (600–601) are two of the roots of *superstitio* in Senecan theory (*Ep.* 22.15; 121.4).[22] The sketching of Sextus as a thoroughly anti-Stoic individual, but especially his *superstitio*, foreshadows his subsequent resorting to divination, not that of conventional oracles which were partially accepted by the Stoics, but the illicit practice of necromancy.[23] Most importantly, it provides the reader with a negative example of human conduct from a philosophical perspective.

Sextus is not only a notably anti-Stoic figure, but also an infamously anti-Roman persona. Lines 421–422 downgrade him to the status of an alien by referring to his alleged exploits during the time of the second triumvirate after the defeat of the republican forces:

> cui mox Scyllaeis exul grassatus in undis
> polluit aequoreos Siculus pirata triumphos.

---

20 Martindale 1977, 378.
21 Martindale 1977, 379.
22 Vottero 1998, 50–52. For Seneca's views on the proper worship of the divine see Setaioli 2014, 394–397; for his views on *superstitio* see Vottero 1998, 47–57 and 301–318 as well as De Biasi, Ferrero, Malaspina, and Vottero 2009, 683–685 and 776–787.
23 For the role of divination in the Stoic deterministic world see Sambursky 1987, 65–71 and Bobzien 1998, 87–96. Faraone 2005, 272 notes that Lucan places Erichtho's ritual against the acceptable types of divination listed in 6.425–430.

> who later, scourging the waters of Scylla as an exile,
> tarnished the naval victories of his father as a Sicilian pirate.

Sextus lived in exile scourging the seas as a pirate. This information, which is confirmed by various historical narratives (e.g. Cass. Dio 48.17.3–5, 48.20.2; Vell. Pat. 2.73), has certain implications for Sextus' depiction as the 'other'. More specifically, piracy was traditionally associated with Rome's archenemies, especially Phoenicians (Cic. *Rep.* 2.9), while Romans generally considered pirates dishonorable and barbarous people (Cic. *Rosc. Am.* 146; Quint. *Inst.* 3.8.44).[24] By referring to his subsequent activities as a pirate, not only does Lucan attribute these negative characteristics to Sextus, but also sketches him as a foreigner, and an enemy of the state.[25] The use of the word *exul* to describe Sextus' future situation drives the point home in a more compelling manner since Pompey's son was not actually exiled; but Lucan does link Sextus' status with that of people who were banished: just as they *de iure* ceased to be Roman citizens, Sextus will *de facto* cease to be Roman by conducting himself unbecomingly to the religious customs of Rome. For Lucan's readers the characterization *exul*, along with the necromancy, would have also recalled the events in the aftermath of the conspiracy of Scribonius Libo Drusus when Tiberius passed a law that forbade Roman citizens to practice any form of magic under threat of exile (Tac. *Ann.* 2.32; Cass. Dio 57.15.8–9).[26] This conceptual link further enhances Sextus' depiction as an enemy of Rome, and a lawbreaker who engages in an illegal form of divination (necromancy).[27]

Lucan's portrayal of Sextus opens the window for the reader to contemplate upon the emotions that lead to his spasmodic reaction. The exposure of the character's inner thoughts and fears triggers the mechanism of self-recognition, thus transforming Sextus into an anti-example of those who put faith in the power of magic;[28] and from the perspective of a Roman, his decision to resort to necromancy, in analogy to his post-civil war deeds, is implicitly presented as incompatible with the *mos maiorum*.

---

24 De Souza 1999, 150.
25 Tesoriero 2002, 232: "The depiction of Sextus as a Sicilian pirate ... reduced his role to that of a criminal whose activities posed a threat to Rome ...".
26 Tesoriero 2002, 230 has brought in the foreground a tenuous connection with Libo Drusus as a descendant of Sextus, whose relatives were continuously linked with magic.
27 Various forms of magic were prohibited by Roman law. For further details see page 12 n. 51.
28 Marti 1945a, 367 was the first to consider Cato and Caesar as representations of the Stoic moral poles, and Pompey as the Stoic *proficiens*. Minor characters also exhibit personal traits and behaviors which either contradict or befit the attitude of the Stoic sage, functioning as moral *exempla* (See the discussion on Domitius Ahenobarbus, Vulteius, and Scaeva in D' Alessandro Behr 2007, 65, 36–45, and 45–53 respectively).

2.2 Magic as anti-Stoic practice

After the introduction of Sextus, Lucan continues with a long digression about Thessaly, the capital *par excellence* of magic (Plin. *HN* 30.6), and the powers of Thessalian witches (6.434–506). This narrative contextualizes the Erichtho scene, serving as a prequel for her appearance, and a point of reference amplifying the powers of Lucan's witch.[29] In accordance with Lucan's presentation of Sextus, it also sketches magic as a practice that contradicts the tenets of Stoicism, and traditional Roman values.

In 440–441, commenting on the natural products of Thessaly, i.e. the herbs and rocks, the narrator claims that they have the power to conquer the gods. Since nature is assimilated with the Stoic supreme god and, in turn, the deities of Graeco-Roman religion are individual manifestations of his powers (Sen. *Ben.* 4.8), the idea that nature can create anything material that restrains gods goes against the belief that the only restriction the supreme god has placed upon himself is the orders of *fata* (Sen. *Prov.* 5.8). Lucan's characterization of Thessalian *carmina* as *inpia* (443) underscores his generally negative view of magic, further condemning its practitioners from a Stoic perspective as their spells are never uttered with *pietas*, the feeling Seneca considered essential in human worship of the divine (Sen. *Ep.* 90.3; 115.5; *Ben.* 1.6.3). But *pietas* was also a cardinal value in Roman thought, encompassing, among other relations, the correct attitude of men toward gods.[30] Therefore, the incantations of Thessalian witchcraft appear simultaneously hostile to Stoic principles and Roman religious values. This becomes clear in subsequent lines when the narrator claims that not only do these spells reach divine ears (444), contrary to the Stoic belief that ill-uttered prayers are not heard by the God (Sen. *Ep.* 95.2–3), but they also exercise coercion over deities (446 and 451), thus reversing the proper relationship between gods and humans.[31] The compulsive power of Thessalian spells, which is affirmed in a set of rhetorical questions (492–499),[32] enhances the anti-Roman character of magic through the implicit comparison with the *pietas* of Aeneas: in the broader context of the destruction of Rome's greatness in the civil war, the ideal Roman's reverence and

---

[29] Morford 1967, 70; Gordon 1987a, 237–239; Danese 1992, 217–219.
[30] For *pietas* in Roman religious thought see Scheid 2003, 26–28.
[31] Danese 1992, 204–211.
[32] As Le Bonniec 1970, 187 points out, Lucan has already ruled that gods are forced to obey the witches, and the questions pointing to different explanations in 6.495 are purely formulaic (*contra* Nock 1972, 190 who recognizes some type of *pietas* in magic). On anti-Stoic ideas in lines 492–494 see Fischer 2008, 175–176.

religious dutifulness has been replaced by the sacrilegious aggression of the witches, and Sextus' impiety.[33]

Immediately after this brief description of the two components of magic (materials and incantations), Lucan elaborates on the alleged powers of Thessalian spells. This exposition (452–506) shows the broad range of their purposes, but also reveals an essential difference between magical materials and words in Lucan's thought, which can be explained based on Stoic premises: the phrase *mens hausti nulla sanie polluta veneni | excantata perit* (457–458) — it refers only to cases of love magic, but it could easily apply to any type of magic — illustrates the poet's belief that potions and poisons are not as harmful as the incantations themselves. From a Stoic perspective, poison can cause physical harm, which would be judged as a non-preferred indifferent, that is an event or condition without moral significance one normally avoids. Spells, however, have the power to inflict passions on the human mind (Sen. *Ep.* 94.53), leading the victim to lose their rationality, and subsequently their ability to discern between what is morally good, bad, and indifferent (Cic. *Tusc.* 4.38–39).

The main body of the Thessalian digression is a catalogue of the various categories of spells which range from love charms (452–460), spells which reverse and exercise control over the natural world (461–491) as well as the famous Thessalian trick (499–506). As Tesoriero observed, the section on erotic magic (452–460) has more parallels with the *PGM* than the one detailing the effects of witchcraft on nature (461–491), and this discrepancy can be explained on the requirement of the *PGM* to have spells with realistic aims, which is not necessary in literature.[34] On the other hand, the reversal of the natural order as an effect of magic is central in literary depictions of witchcraft (e.g. Ov. *Met.* 7.199–209, *Am.* 1.8.5–10; Tib. 1.2.41–52; Ap. Rhod. *Argon.* 3.528–533; Sen. *Med.* 752–769). Together they serve the scene's didactic purpose by showing the destruction magic can cause in social relations and nature.

The first part focuses on love spells, a form of magic which was closer to reality and practiced more frequently than any other type of witchcraft. The passage is filled with anti-Stoic overtones in accordance with the poet's general view of magic:

---

[33] Danese 1992, 201–202; Tesoriero 2000, 101 and 2002, 239. For Sextus as an anti-Aeneas see Masters 1992, 181. For his affinities with the personality of Julius Caesar that render him a 'Caesar-like' figure see Tesoriero 2002, 233–236.
[34] Tesoriero 2000, 84; Graf 1997a, 200 for the idea that real spells need to have a link with reality and its experiences.

carmine Thessalidum dura in praecordia fluxit
non fatis adductus amor, flammisque severi
inlicitis arsere senes. nec noxia tantum
pocula proficiunt aut cum turgentia suco   455
frontis amaturae subducunt pignora fetae:
mens hausti nulla sanie polluta veneni
excantata perit. quos non concordia mixti
alligat ulla tori blandaeque potentia formae
traxerunt torti magica vertigine fili.   460

By the spell of Thessalian witches love not dictated by fate
is instilled in insensible hearts, and with illicit flames, stern
old men burn. Not only are their harmful potions so
effective or when they steal the pledge of love, swollen with juice
on the forehead, from the loving mother:
the mind, unpolluted by the venom of drained poison,
charmed by incantations, is destroyed. Those whom no union
of joined wedding and no power of charming looks binds,
they drag with the magical turning of the twisted thread.

Lucan claims that the sole purpose of love magic is to induce *amor* to the victim (452). However, this view is only partially confirmed by the evidence. Although many love spells intended to cause uncontrollable lust to the targeted individual, there were also spells which simply aimed to preserve or increase the already existing affection (*philia*) between lovers or married couples.[35] Faraone uses this distinction to form the basic taxonomy of ancient love spells: one category includes *philtra* and *charitesia*, while the other consists of *iugges, agogai, empura, agrupnetika*, and *philtrokatadesmoi*.[36] Lucan either ignores the first category or places these spells along with the more violent types of love magic of the second category, on which the excerpt focuses through direct references and allusions to specific subtypes: the *noxia pocula* is a type of *philtrokatadesmos*, a hybrid combination of a love spell (*philtron*) and a binding spell (*katadesmos*);[37] the *turgentia suco frontis*

---

[35] Following Faraone 1999, 28 who considers "spells for inducing *erōs*" and "spells for inducing *philia*" as two separate categories. Edmonds 2019, 94 also recognizes the existence of love spells which intended to strengthen love in an existing relationship.

[36] For this taxonomy and the characteristics of each spell type, see Faraone 1999, 27–29. The first, less violent category, includes spells inscribed on talismans and rings, threads, ointments, and elixirs. The second consists of incantations written on bound effigies, abused animals, burning materials, or apples.

[37] For the definition of *philtrokatadesmos* see Faraone 1999, 177. Examples of such spells include *PGM* IV 296–466, and VIII 1–63 as well as *DT* 111–112, 222, 241, and 271.

refers to the *hippomanes*, a common ingredient in aphrodisiacs;[38] the *torti...vertigine fili* alludes to the *iunx*, a type of *agoge* spell which, in Roman times, was performed with the use of a spinning top;[39] finally, the *flammis inlicitis* and *arsere* might be a cryptic allusion to the *empura*, "a type of *agoge* that requires the burning of herbs or *ousia* in a fire to force the victim (usually female) out by means of sympathetic or persuasive analogy".[40]

Lucan's exclusively negative depiction of love spells reveals his alignment with the views of the Stoics, who considered uncontrollable emotions, such as lust or love induced by magic, a passion which the *sage* avoids.[41] Their disapproval of love when it is a passion, like that which magic supposedly creates, is further supported through an excerpt from *Ben.* 6.25.2, where Seneca criticizes people's distorted sense of gratitude by comparing it to the state of mind of a lover in distress, who wishes harm for the subject of their desire:

> Quorum animus simillimus est pravo amore flagrantibus, qui amicae suae optant exilium, ut desertam fugientemque comitentur, optant inopiam, ut magis desideranti donent, optant morbum, ut adsideant, et, quidquid inimicus optaret, amantes vovent.[42]

> Their soul is identical to those burning with tainted love, who wish exile for their mistress so that they might escort her as she is abandoned and a fugitive, who wish poverty so as to provide for her when she is in greater need, who wish sickness so as to stand by her, and, in short, the lovers long for whatever her enemy would wish for.

These lines also recall the various forms of punishment against the target of a curse, such as exile (*CIL* II 172),[43] loss of property (*DTM* 1; *DTM* 6; Gager 101), sickness and

---

[38] Korenjak 1996, 121–122. There are three different definitions for the *hippomanes*: 1) a dark, fleshy mass that grows on the head of a newborn horse, 2) secretions of a mare, and 3) the apple-thorn plant (see Arist. *Hist. an.* 572a30–b4 and 577a10–15; Theophr. fr. 175; Ael. *NA* 3.17 and 14.18; Theoc. *Id.* 2.48).

[39] Baldini Moscadi 1976, 193–199. The Greek word (*rhombos*) for the *iunx* appears in *PGM* IV 2296, and 2336. For an elaborate discussion on the *iunx*, with emphasis on Greek love magic see Faraone 1999, 55–68.

[40] For the definition of the *empura* see Faraone 1999, 175. Examples include *PGM* IV 1496–1595, XXXVI 68–101, 102–133, 295–311, 333–360, LXI 39–71.

[41] Gill 2013, 148–149. The proverb of Hecaton of Rhodes provides evidence for the Stoic attitude specifically towards love magic (Sen. *Ep.* 9.6: *Ego tibi monstrabo amatorium sine medicamento, sine herba, sine ullius veneficae carmine: si vis amari, ama* [Gummere's text]) , "I will teach you a love spell without need of drugs, herbs, or any sorceress' incantation: if you desire to be loved, you must love".

[42] The text is cited from Haase's 1862 edition.

[43] This is the oath to Caligula which closes with a conditional self-imprecation that includes the penalty of exile. See note 42 on page 10.

physical harm (*DT* 51; 74; 75 A; 135), making more profound the connection between love induced by magic and Stoic passions.[44] Lucan's stance agrees with the orthodox Stoic views as we also infer from 10.70 (*vaesani ... amoris*) and 10.363 (*obscaenum ... amorem*) where he refers, respectively, to Antony's and Caesar's love for Cleopatra.[45] Both generals were seduced by the Egyptian queen by means of magic, according to the tradition created by the Octavianic propaganda.[46] Especially in the case of Caesar, the link between magic and lust is explicit (10.360 and 363: *expugnare senem potuit Cleopatra venenis ... hauserit obscaenum titulo pietatis amorem*), thus affirming Lucan's denunciation of magically induced *amor*.[47]

The Stoic negative view of love magic can be also explained on the basis of the school's views on family and society. Zeno and his followers despised adultery (DL 7.131), an act which magic spells supposedly can facilitate, while they considered procreation a social duty of the *sapiens* (DL 7.121). These beliefs probably led him to formulate the idea that women should be held in common among the sages (DL 7.33). The views of earlier Stoics appear to have shifted at least by the time of Cicero, when marriage also became a social duty of the *sapiens* (Cic. *Fin.* 3.68). Similarly, Seneca recognized love in general as the force which holds society together (Sen. *De Ira* 2.31.7), and that between husband and wife as its productive force.[48] Lucan alludes to the Stoic view on wedding as the binding force of society in 458 (*quos non concordia mixti alligat ulla tori*), and his use of *alligat* to describe the marriage union is quite interesting since the verb is also used in the *defixiones* to denote the act of binding someone through magic (see *DT* 217, 218, 277, 279, 283, 284, 303). Perhaps Lucan intended to use this ambiguity to underline the subversive power of love spells. From the Stoic perspective, which placed family at the core of social structure, magic is a force that destroys social bonds by creating relations outside the family which did not serve the purpose of procreation (454: *flammisque inlicitis...arsere senes*). Thus, it has the power to overturn the social order, and by extension violate natural order (453: *non fatis adductus amor*).[49] The central point of the excerpt, however, is love magic's influence on the human *mens*. And just like

---

[44] For the injuries that could befall the target of a curse see: Kagarow 1929, 55–58; Watson 1991, 30–38 (especially for literary curses); Collins 2008, 78–88.
[45] Tesoriero 2000, 77.
[46] Suda s.v. ἴυγξ reports that Cleopatra attempted to seduce all three Roman leaders (Antony, Caesar, Octavian) by means of magic, but eventually failed.
[47] Notice also the characterization of Caesar as *senex* (10.360) and the *arsere senes* in 6.454.
[48] Seneca's views on marriage are extensively discussed in Gloyn 2017, 78–106 who also includes a brief reference to the views of earlier Stoics in 78–79.
[49] My discussion is indebted to Tesoriero 2000, 77 who has already noted Lucan's negative depiction of love spells in connection to his Stoic inclinations.

love magic inflicts madness to people, by analogy magic in general has the power to upset the *mens* of the universe, the immanent causal principle that created the cosmos and governs everything within.

Lucan expands on this topic immediately after, describing the influence of magic on the natural order: Witches can incite, reverse, and stop natural phenomena (461–484). Such lists of *adynata* are central in literary descriptions of magic, functioning as an introduction to the witch's powers.[50] Lucan's catalogue, however, is much longer than those of earlier poets in an effort to emphasize the superiority of Thessalian witchcraft compared to other forms of magic, a point already made clear in 449–451, where he claims that Haemonian witches have the power to snatch the *paredros* summoned by Persian and Egyptian *magi*, the inventors of the *ars magica*.[51]

The passage has been interpreted as a parallel of the Stoic *ekpyrosis*, the cosmic dissolution which marks the end of one cosmic cycle and the beginning of another. This idea can be further affirmed by the use of words with philosophical flavor. The excerpt refers to the four Stoic elements out of which the cosmos and everything that exists within consists of: fire (462: *aether*), air (467: *caelum*), water (469: *aequor*), and earth (481: *terra*).[52] The *cessavere vices rerum* (461) reflects the idea that during the conflagration the world comes to a halt (Sen. *Ep.* 9.16), which is exactly the image presented to the reader in the next lines (462–469: *haesit...dies, torpuit...mundus,... non ire polos,...ventis cessantibus*). But this *ekpyrosis* is not the result of providence and divine plan since the sun, who activates the conflagration (Alexander of Lycopolis [Migne, *PG* 18, 428 C]; *SVF* 1.510), lies hidden in the clouds (466), and Jupiter, the *ratio* of the cosmos, is unaware of the natural events (464–465: *Iuppiter...miratur*; 467: *ignaro...Jove*). These changes occur due to the witches' spells, and there is no hint that the cosmos will be restored back to its original form. The *ekpyrosis* thus transforms into an anti-Stoic image of destruction caused by magic.[53]

---

50 In the *Medea* the protagonist refers to these magical feats as part of her argument to convince Hecate to assist her. Lists of *adynata* appear also in papyri (e.g. *PGM* I 120–125, IV 191–192, IV 1355–1372, XII 248–252, XIII 871–876, XXIX), but some of them might be excerpts from literary works.
51 Tesoriero 2000, 83.
52 Lapidge 1979, 368–369.
53 Sklenář 2003, 6 referring to the image of cosmic dissolution in 1.67–80: "Lucan has reversed the significance of *ekpyrosis*, transmuting it into a terrifying vision of the fire at the end of time (*suprema hora*). Nowhere does he suggest that this stage will be followed by a restoration of cosmic order ... thereby pressing his Stoic imagery into the service of an explicitly anti-Stoic position". On the contrary, Wiener 2006, 179–190 reasserts the Stoic character of Lucan's imagery of dissolution, and claims that for Lucan the civil war, like all historical events, was preordained by fate, and that

2.3 Magic as charlatanry

Apart from its anti-Stoic character, magic is also presented as charlatanry through allusions to tricks of contemporary magicians which Lucan's reader would be able to recognize. The image of Thessalian witches taming beasts, specifically the tiger and the lion (487–488) recalls that of wandering magicians who were able to train wild animals so as to fawn upon their master and anyone approaching them as a performance to gain money:

> has avidae tigres et nobilis ira leonum
> ore fovent blando;

> Hungry tigers and the wrath of noble lions
> fawn upon them with a gentle mouth.

The educated readers were probably aware that these animals could be trained (Sen. *Ep.* 85.41) as one can also infer from their use in the circus (*Ep.* 7.4 and *Brev. Vit.* 13.6). This knowledge is enough for the reader to debunk the supernatural aspect of this ability of Thessalian witches.

The excerpt which discusses the effects of Thessalian incantations on snakes also causes the same effect:

> ... gelidos his explicat orbes
> inque pruinoso coluber distenditur arvo;
> viperei coeunt abrupto corpore nodi,   490
> humanoque cadit serpens adflata veneno.

> ... for them the snake unfolds its frozen orbs
> and stretches itself on the frosty plain;
> though their body was torn, serpentine knots are joined together,
> and the snake dies when touched by human poison.

These lines present the witches of Thessaly as having control over serpents. Lines 488–489 allude to the charming of snakes, an ability that reflects the popular belief that certain peoples (e.g. Ophiogenes, Marsi, and the Psylloi) could hypnotize and handle them without getting harmed.[54] But the reference to the frosty field implies that the snake is in brumation, and the reader would have been aware that serpents can be handled safely in this condition (Sen. *Ep.* 42.4).

---

the *ekpyrosis* was among the causes of Rome's downfall as part of the inevitable cycle of creation and destruction.

54 For these three 'snake-master' races, and their alleged powers see Ogden 2013, 209–214.

Lucan next presents the reader with the inversion of a beneficial spell which was credited to the Marsi, and which caused snakes to explode (Lucil. fr. 575–576 Marx; Verg. *Ecl.* 8.71; *PGM* XIII 261–264 is a spell which can cause a snake to break open). The powers of these indigenous Italian peoples were proverbial in the age of Augustus as we can infer from Ovid's reference to their magical songs (*Ars Am.* 2.102), and Vergil's description of a Marsic priest who knew how to make poisonous snakes fall asleep, ease their anger, and relieve the symptoms of their bite with his incantations and touch (*Aen.* 7.750–760). Lucan creates a negative image of the Thessalian witch, whose supremacy over other witches even allows her to overturn the beneficial effect of the Marsic spell by reanimating dead snakes.[55] The section on animals closes with another odd ability of Thessalian witches which allows them to kill a snake with their saliva. This image has no connection to reality, and it is probably based on the folk belief that a specific type of snake would bite itself to death if spat upon (Lucr. 4.638–639). However, the transformation of human saliva, known to have natural healing properties (e.g. Plin. *HN* 28.37–38), into poison fits conveniently the broader Lucanian pattern of magic as a destructive reversal of nature.

Lucan concludes his digression with the description of another famous spell, the so-called 'Thessalian trick':

> ... illis et sidera primum
> praecipiti deducta polo, Phoebeque serena   500
> non aliter diris verborum obsessa venenis
> palluit et nigris terrenisque ignibus arsit,
> quam si fraterna prohiberet imagine tellus
> insereretque suas flammis caelestibus umbras;
> et patitur tantos cantu depressa labores   505
> donec suppositas propior despumet in herbas.

> By them, both the stars were first
> brought down from the highest sky, and bright Phoebe,
> similarly possessed by the dreadful poison of spells,
> grew pale and blazed with dark and terrestrial fires,
> just as if the earth kept her away from the face of her brother,
> and cast its shadow on the heavenly flames;
> and drawn down by the spell, she endures such great toils,
> until froth drips off, more closely, to the herbs below.

---

55 Tesoriero 2000, 100.

One of the most famous feats of Thessalian magic was the alleged power to draw down the moon and the stars.[56] Hill, rejecting the suggestion that the 'Thessalian trick' describes the astronomical phenomenon of eclipse, asserts that it should be some form of optical illusion performed by the witches at their will. To further support his argument, he cites a passage from Hippolytus (*Haer.* 4.37) which describes in detail how those who performed the trick used candles, mirrors, and pulleys to create an image of the moon which afterwards they pretended to draw down.[57] Lucan also seems to regard the process of drawing down the moon as something completely different from the eclipse, which he uses in 503–504 as a simile to describe the effects of the 'Thessalian trick'.[58] In any case, since authors from the fourth century BCE onwards questioned the supernatural aspect of drawing down the moon (e.g. Hippoc. *Morb. Sacr.* 4.17–19), it is not wrong to assume that the educated readers of the first century CE would also be aware of the rational explanations behind the trick.

Up to this point, Lucan's criticism of magic manifests itself in several statements and images which emphasize the anti-Stoic and anti-Roman essence of Thessalian witchcraft. His narrative depicts magic simultaneously as thoroughly evil and without real power. This contradiction culminates in the necromancy scene, in which the author presents a hellish witch with virtually unlimited powers who, however, eventually fails to procure the information Sextus is so desperate to obtain.[59]

2.4 Erichtho, the all-powerful superwitch

How does Lucan create his superwitch? In his sketching of Erichtho he combines an unprecedented number of elements from various sources, ranging from earlier depictions of witches to folkloric monsters, the Furies, and other literary figures. Similarities with literary stereotypes, especially Horace's Canidia, bring Erichtho's portrayal closer to popular conceptions of the witch in the Imperial times than their

---

56 Edmonds 2019, 19–28 discusses multiple passages which refer to this famous magic trick and its connection to witchcraft rituals. Scholars have tried to explain what exactly the expressions *lunam (de)ducere*, *lunam (de)trahere*, καθαιρεῖν or κατάγειν τὴν σελήνην might mean, with some arguing that they describe the astronomical phenomenon of lunar eclipse (see Hill 1973, 227–229 with the relevant notes).
57 Hill 1973, 224–225 who rejects the idea on the principle that 1) stars cannot suffer eclipse, and 2) it would have been extremely difficult to predict the exact date of a lunar eclipse so as to choose to perform the trick on that specific day.
58 Hill 1973, 236.
59 Gordon 1987b, 70.

Greek mythological counterparts of Circe and Medea, providing the reader with a conceptually credible figure of the *saga*.[60] This is as close as Erichtho's figure gets to the image of a contemporary witch.

The similarities with Lamia, who was the nightmarish monster terrorizing the Hellenistic mind, distance her portrayal from reality.[61] Contrary to the ordinary witch of the Roman times who dwells among the people, Erichtho is not even allowed to live in a city inhabited solely by witches (510–511), and especially in Thessaly, the capital *par excellence* of magic. Instead, like Lamia, she is forced to have her home among caves and ruins (511–512: *desertaque busta*; 642: *caecis ... cavernis*), completely isolated from human contact.[62] To sustain herself, she scavenges tombs and cannibalizes corpses (538–553, 564–569), but also drinks the blood of recently murdered people (555–557), thus recalling the vampiric aspect of Lamia, who feasts by sucking the blood out of both the living and the dead. Erichtho's imitation of animal sounds (688–690) might allude to Lamia's ability to change her form and to the shapeshifting skills of the *strix*.[63] Even though the murder of children, especially young boys (562–563), was both a *locus communis* in literary descriptions of magic as well as a popular belief among Romans, the even more abominable act of killing babies and fetuses (558–559) points to a direct influence of Lamia on Erichtho's sketching.[64]

But the most important modifications on the figure of the witch come with the adoption of elements from the depiction of Allecto in *Aeneid* 7 as well as Ovid's Invidia in *Metamorphoses* 2. Even though some of the physical characteristics of the Furies (e.g. snakes for hair, ugliness) had become stock features in literary depictions of witches, Erichtho's flogging of the corpse (726–727) is heavily inspired by Allecto's attack on Turnus (7.451) in the *Aeneid*.[65] Similarly, the descriptions of Erichtho's physical appearance, her actions, and dwelling recall details in the account

---

[60] Gordon 1987b, 71. For the literary models of Lucan's Erichtho see Morford 1967, 67–68; Korenjak 1996, 22 with notes on the same page.
[61] For a detailed discussion on child-killing monsters in the Graeco-Roman world (Lamia, Gello, Mormo, Empousa) see Johnston 1995, 361–387.
[62] Ager 2022, 170–171 notes that the cave is filled with a foul odor of decay that both Erichtho and her surroundings emit, and which makes her dwelling indistinguishable from Tartarus; the putrid smell functions as a "mental model" for witchcraft, reflecting the stereotypical impurity of the witch.
[63] Danese 1995, 432–433.
[64] These similarities between Lamia and Erichtho have been already highlighted in Gordon 1987a, 240–241. My discussion is greatly indebted to his.
[65] Hardie 1993, 86.

of Ovid's Invidia (*Met.* 2.760–794).⁶⁶ The modelling of Lucan's witch after Allecto, whose name literally means "implacable anger", and Invidia (jealousy) suggests that Erichtho is the personification of these two Stoic passions, adding a philosophical perspective to her portrayal. The connections with these literary figures bring Erichtho in complete accord with Seneca's description of personified anger in *De Ira* 2.35:⁶⁷

> qualia poetae inferna monstra finxerunt succincta serpentibus et igneo flatu, quales ad bella excitanda discordiamque in populos dividendam ... deae taeterrimae inferum exeunt, talem nobis iram figuremus, flamma lumina ardentia, sibilo mugituque et gemitu et stridore ... torvam cruentamque et cicatricosam ... offusam multa caligine, ... vastantem ... si aliter nocere non possit, terras maria caelum ruere cupientem ....⁶⁸

> Like the infernal monsters poets sketched out, girded with serpents and with fiery breath, like those most hideous goddesses who leave hell ... to excite wars and cause discord among the people, let us imagine anger as such, with eyes glowing in flame, hissing, groaning, roaring, rattling ... grim by the blood and full of wounds ... surrounded by great mist ... laying waste ... if she cannot cause harm in other ways, willing to upset the earth, sea and sky ....

The Senecan passage calls to mind *Aeneid* 7 when Juno summons Allecto from the Furies' seat (324: *dirarum ab sede dearum*) in the darkness of Hell (325: *infernisque ciet tenebris*). The Tartarean *monstrum* (328) rejoices with war and anger (325–326: *cui tristia bella | iraeque ... cordi*) and can stir fraternal strife (335: *unanimos armare in proelia fratres*). Her eyes are glowing with fire (448–449: *flammea ... lumina*), she has snakes for hair (450: *crinibus anguis*), and hisses (447: *sibilat*). Other details resemble those found in Ovid's description of Invidia, who groans (774: *ingemuit*) at the sight of Minerva; she might not be hissing, but her tongue is full of venom like a snake's (777: *lingua est suffusa veneno*); mist surrounds her dwelling (764: *caligine semper abundet*), and follows her wherever she goes (790: *adopertaque nubibus atris quacumque ingreditur*), laying waste to everything around her (791–794).

The similarities of Erichtho with Allecto and Invidia, and in turn with Seneca's personification of *ira*, suggest that Lucan's witch is the embodiment of the Stoic passions of anger and jealousy.⁶⁹ Thus, her escorting of Sextus back to the camp (827–828) can be viewed metaphorically as a 'demonic possession', through which

---

66 Independently argued in Baldini Moscadi 1976, 159–160 (with relevant notes), and Martindale 1977, 380–382.
67 Tesoriero 2004, 202 n. 59 noted the link between Seneca's *homo iratus* (*De Ira* 2.35–36) and Erichtho's portrayal.
68 The text is from Hermes' 1923 edition with minor changes.
69 Tesoriero 2000, 8 notes that the similarities with Seneca's *homo iratus* suggest "a philosophical element in her depiction: she is the personification of *ira*, a key motivating force behind the civil war".

Erichtho infects him with anger and envy,[70] two traits that 1) justify philosophically the historical continuation of the civil conflict between Sextus and Octavian, and 2) appear in later, propagandistic works hostile to him.[71]

Lucan has managed to present the reader with an all-powerful and abominable witch with philosophical taste, whose influence impacts events outside the narrative. Even her admission that she is unable to change fate, and that fortune is more powerful than Thessalian witches (611–614) does not undermine her power in the reader's eyes.[72] The statement adheres both to the traditional limitations of gods in literature and ancient thought as well as to Stoic principles. Her claim that she has the power to alter *fata minora*, albeit with difficulty (605–606), and the subsequent arrogant statement that it is easy for her to learn the future (616) would theoretically place her at the same level as the gods of conventional religion and literature. This conceptual equation with traditional deities, along with Erichtho's savage and ghoulish portrayal, set up the expectation for a successful necromancy, which is further enhanced by the graphic and accurate representation of her ritual.

2.5 Erichtho's necromancy

Lucan's choice to present the reader with a necromancy fits his general view of magic as an anti-Roman practice since this type of ritual never lost its barbarous character.[73] Since the rite entails the ascent of the dead soul to the realm of the living — an inversion of the traditional epic motif of the *katabasis* —, it is also, in and of itself, transgressive. Thus, necromancy incorporates those aspects of magic that a Roman and a Stoic would despise, and the conceptual link between magic, necromancy, and civil war becomes itself part of the criticism against witchcraft.

The spells of the *PGM* attest to two different types of necromancy, those involving only the summoning of the soul of the deceased (*PGM* IV 1928–2005 and IV 2006–2125),

---

[70] Tesoriero 2000, 272; Fratantuono 2012, 242 also notes that Erichtho inflicts Sextus with madness.
[71] Vell. Pat. 2.72.2: *hic adulescens erat studiis rudis, sermone barbarus, impetu strenuus, manu promptus, cogitatione celer, fide patri dissimillimus, libertorum suorum libertus, servorum servus, speciosis invidens ut pareret humillimis* (Shipley's 1961 text); "this young man was rough in his preoccupations, barbaric in his mode of speaking, restless and impulsive, shift at laying hands, quick in thought, different than his father with regards to loyalty, a freedman to his freedmen, a slave to his slaves, jealous of respectable people to the point that he would obey the most wretched".
[72] Pichon 1912, 195 and Le Bonniec 1970, 188 see this as Lucan's effort to reconcile the contradiction between magic and his belief in destiny.
[73] Pichon 1912 192: "Il (i.e. Lucan) a voulu présenter à ses lecteurs ce qu'il pouvait concevoir de plus violemment sacrilège, afin de porter au maximum l'effet d'angoisse et d'horreur". For Graeco-Roman attitudes toward necromancy see Ogden 2001, 263–268.

and those which intended also for the reanimation of their body (*PGM* IV 2140–2144 and XIII 277–283).[74] Erichtho's ritual, which belongs to the second category, is faithful to real spells, adhering to the two-tiered structure found in the *PGM* consisting of *logos* (the magical utterances urging the celestial and infernal powers to do the witch's bidding) and *praxis* (the acts and ritualistic moves accompanying the *logos*):[75] it begins with the material preparation necessary for her spell (667–684); it continues with the description of the *voces magicae* (685–693), followed by the spell proper (693–718); when the first spell fails, she lashes the corpse and utters another one (730–749), the content of which is abusive and threatening so as to compel the invoked deities to comply with her requests; after the successful reanimation of the corpse, she gives him proper instructions for the prophecy (762–774); finally, after the ritual has been completed she has to utter a last spell to dismiss the spirit of the dead soldier (822). Structurally, therefore, Erichtho's spell exhibits all the necessary parts to succeed.

2.5.1 The preparatory ritual

Erichtho searches among the dead soldiers to find the main ingredient for her spell, a well-preserved cadaver.[76] By underscoring the condition of the body (630: *pulmonis rigidi stantis sine volnere fibras*), Lucan adheres to the belief that certain ingredients should meet specific requirements in order to be suitable for magical use to guarantee the success of a spell.[77] He also complies with the typical idea that the dead used in witchcraft should belong to one of the following categories: those who died prematurely (ἄωροι), those who died a violent death (βιαιοθάνατοι), and those who remained unburied (ἄταφοι or ἀτέλεστοι).[78] Lucan's dead soldier (717: *militis*

---

74 Reif 2016, 452–454 discusses in detail some of the necromantic spells in relation to the Erichtho scene.
75 Martinez 1991, 8.
76 Masters 1992, 197 argues that the preparatory ritual begins with the selection of the body. Graf 1997a, 191 asserts that the ritual begins at line 624, and Reif 2016, 441 sees the line as an echo of *PGM* IV 2295; Baldini Moscadi 1976, 170 begins the discussion on Erichtho's ritual from 667.
77 The suitability of materials is a prerequisite also in rituals of conventional religion (e.g. haruspicy). *PGM* IV 2125–2139 is a spell that purports to stop the use of skulls which were inappropriate for magical divination.
78 For the categories of the dead exploited in magic see Massoneau 1934, 39–46, Tupet 1976, 82–91, Bremmer 1983, 101–108, and Ogden 1999, 15–23. Greeks and Romans shared the conviction that the souls of these individuals lingered between the two worlds, and their restlessness rendered them more prone to magical compulsion, but also reliable in predicting the future.

umbra) exemplifies simultaneously all three categories since, as a warrior, he suffered an untimely and brutal death, while he was also denied the proper burial rights (626: *corpora caesorum, tumuli proiecta negatis*). His body, therefore, is the ideal ingredient for necromancy.

The ritual continues with the preparation of the soldier's body:

> pectora tum primum ferventi sanguine supplet
> volneribus laxata novis taboque medullas
> abluit et virus large lunare ministrat.
> huc quidquid fetu genuit natura sinistro   670
> miscetur: non spuma canum quibus unda timori est,
> viscera non lyncis, non durae nodus hyaenae
> defuit et cervi pastae serpente medullae,
> non puppem retinens Euro tendente rudentis
> in mediis echenais aquis oculique draconum   675
> quaeque sonant feta tepefacta sub alite saxa,
> non Arabum volucer serpens innataque rubris
> aequoribus custos pretiosae vipera conchae
> aut viventis adhuc Libyci membrana cerastae
> aut cinis Eoa positi phoenicis in ara.   680
> quo postquam viles et habentis nomina pestis
> contulit, infando saturatas carmine frondis
> et, quibus os dirum nascentibus inspuit, herbas
> addidit et quidquid mundo dedit ipsa veneni.

> Then, she first fills the breast, expanded with new incisions,
> with hot blood and washes the inside from
> the gore and applies lunar potion in large quantities.
> In it, whatever nature brings forth by sinister production,
> is mixed: neither the foamy saliva of dogs, to which water causes fear,
> nor the innards of the lynx, nor the node of wild hyena
> is lacking, and neither the marrow of the serpent-fed stag,
> nor the echenais, which halts the ship as the east wind stretches
> the ropes amidst the sea, nor the eyes of snakes
> and the rocks which rattle, warmed under the breeding bird,
> nor the winged serpent of Arabia and the Red Sea-born
> viper, guardian of the precious pearl-oyster,
> nor the slough of the Libyan Cerastes, cast when alive,
> nor the ashes of a Phoenix that is placed on the eastern altar.
> To this, after she gathered vile and named banes, she
> added leafy garlands charmed with unspeakable spells,

and herbs which her dreadful mouth spat upon[79] when sprang, and whatever poison she gave to the world herself.

The witch first cleans the corpse internally by applying 'fresh blood' through the new holes she opens, thus adhering to the common act of purifying the materials to be used in magic rituals.[80] The *ferventi sanguine* could be a code name for a red-colored solution of pulverized hematite with some liquid, probably water, which was used as a cleaning agent in ancient medicine.[81] But this mineral was also known for its powers of attraction,[82] and therefore, it is suitable for a necromancy, which entails the luring of the soul back to the body.

Erichtho then fills the corpse with the *virus lunare* (669) along with some poisons and herbs (681–684).[83] Contrary to Tesoriero who claims that the materials enumerated in lines 671–684 are placed separately in the chest cavity, I believe that the description comprises the recipe for the concoction (*huc misceatur*) of Lucan's *virus lunare*, realistically expanding the literary model (Ov. *Met.* 7.262–284).[84] This mysterious substance has been identified with the σεληνιακὸν χρῖσμα (*PGM* VII 874), whose composition is unknown, but presumably had a slimy texture like that of an ointment.[85] Each of the alleged ingredients that Lucan puts forward are attested in

---

[79] Reif 2016, 443 views Erichtho's spitting on the herbs as part of the ritual such as the one described in *PGM* III 420–422.

[80] The *novis volneribus* are incisions Erichtho makes on the cadaver, a view further supported by the phrase *pectus apertum* in 722. As Tesoriero 2000, 220 points out, the verb *aperire* has a technical meaning "to make an incision" (*TLL* 2.0.214.78–215.19) in medical texts. The spirit is also meant to enter the body through these holes as line 722 indicates. Even though the purification of the body is not attested in any necromantic spells, there are a few instances in the *PGM* where the magician must cleanse the artifacts before their use in the ritual (e.g. *PGM* II 150–152, IV 172–212, 2880–2890, XII 193–201, *PDM* xiv 515).

[81] Plin. *HN* 36.129: *haematites magnes sanguinei coloris sanguinem reddens si teratur*; 36.146: *reddere enim sucum sanguinem*; Celsus *Med.* 5.5: *Purgant aerugo, auripigmentum, … lapis hematites …*

[82] Ps. Dios. *Lap.* 21.2: <Λίθος μαγνήτης> εἴτε <ἡρακλείας>· Ἄφροι <χαζαρμές>· παραπλησίαν ἔχει δύναμιν τῷ αἱματίτῃ, ξηραντικὴν καὶ ῥυπτικὴν καὶ ἑλκτικήν, ψυχρὰν τῆς β' τάξεως.

[83] Tupet 1988, 425 and Korenjak 1996, 186 note that the whole procedure is highly evocative of Aeson's rejuvenation in Ovid, where Medea drains his blood and replaces it with her magical juice (*Met.* 7.285–287). See also Baldini Moscadi 1976, 171 n. 5, and Ogden 2002b, 259–260. Volpilhac 1978, 278–279 claims that the procedure Erichtho performs on the body alludes to the Egyptian practice of mummification, arguing that the substances described in 671–684 are codified names for ingredients used in embalmment.

[84] Tesoriero 2000, 192 takes *huc* as referring to the cadaver as a vessel. My assumption is that *huc* points back to the *virus lunare*, especially if Lucan models the preparatory ritual after Ov. *Met.* 7.262–284 (see the previous note).

[85] Reif 2016, 426–427 with relevant bibliography, and 442 for the connection with the σεληνιακὸν χρῖσμα. Edmonds 2019, 23–24 identifies the *virus lunare* with the *aphroselenon* (moonfoam).

magical texts and/or in recipes of popular medicine, thus adding authenticity to the concoction: the foam of the saliva of rabid dogs;[86] the *viscera* of the lynx;[87] the *nodus hyaenae*;[88] the stag's marrow;[89] the *echenais*;[90] the eyes of the *draco*;[91] the ἀετίτης λίθος or gagites;[92] various snakes, and the slough of the Libyan Cerastes;[93] the ashes of a phoenix.[94] Lucan's list of ingredients is not a simple, dry imitation of magical recipes, but reveals a deeper understanding of the mechanisms of magic as several

---

86 Used as a preventive drug for rabies in humans (Plin. *HN* 29.99). The use of dog blood, secretions, and excrements are often encountered in magical texts (e.g. *PGM* IV 2578: οὐσία [νεκροῦ] κυνός; 2690, 2875: οὐσίαν κυνός; XIa 2: αἵματι κυνὸς μέλανος; XIII 240–241: ἀνφώδευμα κυνός).
87 Baldini Moscadi 1976, 171 considers the *viscera lyncis* a cryptic reference to *lyncourion*, a stone created by the urine of the animal, and which was used both in magic and popular medicine. Tesoriero 2000, 193 rejects the idea on the grounds that *viscera* cannot denote anything else than the organs. His suggestion also fits the general use of animal organs in magic (e.g. *PGM* II 45–50, VII 181–182, XII 434–439, XIII 1064–1069, *PDM* xiv 82–83, 1042–1045), and the specific feline's medico-magical powers, which were known to the people of the first century CE (Plin. *HN* 28.122).
88 The first cervical vertebra of the animal, which, as Pliny informs us, was used as a remedy for epilepsy (*HN* 28.99). Its appropriateness in magic rituals is inferred by Pliny's claim that the Magi had attributed to hyenas magical skills (*HN* 28.92, 93, and 99), and is further affirmed by the text of the *PGM* which attests to the use of certain parts of the animal in witchcraft (*PGM* VII 203–205 and 206–207: skin; CXXIII a-f 69–71: tooth; *PDM* xiv 82–83: heart; xiv 1194–1195: excrement).
89 The potency of animal marrow is well-attested in recipes of popular medicine (*HN* 28.145, and *passim* in the book for different animal marrows and their uses). The stag's marrow was known for its restorative properties (*HN* 28.185; 235; 241) and protective powers against reptiles (*HN* 28.150).
90 The *echenais* or *remora* was a small fish which could slow down ships by attaching to their hull, and delay birth by stopping the fluxes of women (Plin. *HN* 32.1). Due to its binding powers, it also functioned as a love-charm and a spell to hinder litigation in court (Plin. *HN* 9.79). For its uses in magic see Watson 2010, 639–646 and Faraone 2022, 277–286 (also discusses its use in obstetrics).
91 For the use of animal eyes in spells see, for example, *PGM* I 223 (eyes of a night-owl); 285 (of a wolf); IV 2943–2944 (of a bat). The eye of the *draco* appears in a recipe for an ointment with the power to nullify nightmares (*HN* 29.20) and delirium (*HN* 30.24).
92 For the identification of the *saxa* with the *aetites lithos*/gagites, see Baldini Moscadi 1976 171. A hollow rock filled with pebbles which caused it to rattle, this stone was said to have various medical properties (Plin. *HN* 10.12), especially in the area of obstetrics (Ael. *NA* 1.35; Plin. *NH* 36.39).
93 Snakes were considered the primordial manifestation of gods, and as such they are addressed in magical invocations (e.g. *PGM* III 670–671, IV 939, 1638, 1655–1656, 2613–2614, VIII 11, XII 89). Their skin and blood were frequently used in magical recipes (e.g. *PGM* III 703, IV 2004–2005, XII 160, XXXVI 178–187), while the figure of the *ouroboros*, the snake swallowing its own tail, was often carved on amulets and tablets in the course of a magical ritual (e.g. *PGM* I 145–146, VII 579–590, XII 201–269, XII 270–350, XXXVI 178–187).
94 The phoenix was a legendary bird of oriental and Egyptian origin, known for its alleged power to be reborn from its ashes. It was considered the manifestation of the Sun god (see *PGM* XII 231, XIII 881), and its nest and ashes were said to possess medicinal properties (Plin. *HN* 29.29). For the origins and importance of the bird in Graeco-Roman religion see Lecocq 2016, 449–478.

of these materials possess properties that appear suitable for necromancy. The stag and the snake, known for the annual shedding and regrowing of, respectively, their antlers and slough, epitomize the circle of death and rebirth. Similarly, the phoenix, a legendary bird which is reborn from its ashes is a powerful symbol of reincarnation. The *echenais* is included because of its binding powers: just as it can delay a sailing ship, it can also keep the summoned soul attached to the body.[95]

2.5.2 The spell proper

The preparation of the body (*praxis*) is followed by Erictho's first incantation (*logos*), which in turn is divided into two parts. The first part, lines 685–693, describes the *murmura* (686) of the witch, such as dog barking (688: *latratus…canum*), the howling of wolves (688: *gemitusque luporum*), the cries of owls (689: *quod trepidus bubo, quod strix nocturna queruntur*), the shriek and wailing of wild beasts (690: *quod strident ululantque ferae*), the serpents' hiss (690: *quod sibilat anguis*) as well as the noises of waves, forests, and thunders (691–692: *planctus inlisae cautibus undae | silvarumque sonum fractaeque tonitrua nubis*). The reference to a witch's strange, inarticulate sounds is a *locus communis* in literary accounts of magic (see Hor. *Sat.* 1.8.24–25; Ov. *Met.* 7.190–191), but animal noises in particular are only found in real spells.[96] Lucan's list alludes clearly to the *voces magicae* of the *PGM*, which were usually transliterated names of Egyptian and oriental deities.[97] This description, which aestheticizes the non-sensical utterances found in the *PGM*, brings Erichtho's incantation even closer to real spells. At the same time, the combination of animal sounds and noises of natural phenomena underline the threatening

---

95 The suitability of these materials for Erictho's necromancy has been noted by Korenjak 1996, 189–190 and Tesoriero 2000, 194–195 and 197.
96 See, for example: *PGM* IV 560–561 hissing; 929 and 1006–1007 barking; VII 767–774: popping sound, hissing, groaning, and others; XIII 84–88, 598–602: among others, birdglyphic, baboonic, and falconic. The link between the *voces magicae* in Erichtho's spell and *PGM* has been noted in Nock 1972, 185 and Volpilhac 1978, 273–276; for an elaborate discussion see Reif 2016, 443–445 who traces the connections with *PGM* XIII 442–471, VII 765–779, and IV 1459–1469.
97 This can be said with certainty only in instances where the magical words are understandable (Graf 1991, 191–194, and 210 n. 27); for a list of *voces magicae* that occur in *PGM*, and their possible interpretations, see Brashear 1995, 3429–3438 and 3576–3603 as well as Gager 1992, 265–269. Suggested origins include the *ephesia grammata* as well as 'gibberish' from Egyptian spells (Brashear 1995, 3429 n. 235). See also the discussion in Versnel 2002, 105–158.

aspects of magic by appealing to the reader's 'unconscious' since wild animals and natural phenomena are permanent threats for humans.[98]

Erichtho continues with the articulate part of her spell, which is a prayer to the deities of the Underworld adhering, as Graf points out, to the common tripartite structure of Graeco-Roman prayers, including magical ones. Lines 695–706 constitute the *invocatio*, 707–711 the *narratio*, and 712–718 are the *preces*:[99]

> Eumenides Stygiumque nefas Poenaeque nocentum   695
> et Chaos innumeros avidum confundere mundos
> et rector terrae, quem longa in saecula torquet
> mors dilata deum; Styx et quos nulla meretur
> Thessalis Elysios; caelum matremque perosa
> Persephone, nostraeque Hecates pars ultima, per quam 700
> manibus et mihi sunt tacitae commercia linguae,
> ianitor et sedis laxae, qui viscera saevo
> spargis nostra cani, repetitaque fila sorores
> tracturae, tuque o flagrantis portitor undae,
> iam lassate senex ad me redeuntibus umbris,   705
> exaudite preces ...

> O Furies, abominations of the Styx and punishments for the criminals,
> and you, Chaos, ready to confuse innumerable worlds,
> and you, lord of the earth, whom the unnecessarily protracted death
> of the gods tortures endlessly; you, Styx, and the Elysian fields,
> of which no witch is worthy; the one who hates the sky and her mother,
> Persephone, and you, underworld manifestation of our Hecate, through whom
> the spirits and I communicate without talking,
> and you, guardian of the spacious residence, who feeds
> our intestines to the ferocious dog, and you, sisters, who will spin
> again the thread of life, and you, ferryman of the burning waves,
> already old and weary of returning the souls back to me,
> hear my prayer....

Erichtho's invocation of each deity is followed by an epithet or descriptive clause, thus affirming the formulaic affiliation with real prayers.[100] Similarly to the invocations found in the *PGM* and the *defixiones*, which address the deities whose favor or aid the magician seeks for the success of the spell, Erichtho invokes almost all the deities and infernal demons whose assistance was essential in both real and

---
98 Graf 1997a, 201.
99 See page 5 n. 18; Reif 2016, 440.
100 For the structure and formulas of religious prayers see Hickson 1993, 9–11.

literary necromancies:[101] the *Eumenides*, the underworld demons of vengeance who hindered the souls of the dead;[102] *Chaos*, which is appropriately invoked because the soldier's resurrection evidently leads to the mixing of the upper and lower worlds, an innate quality of chaos;[103] the *rector terrae*, Pluto, who has complete oversight over the Underworld and the dead;[104] the *Styx*, which functions as the boundary between the two worlds, allows the souls to cross back to the realm of the living;[105] the Elysian fields;[106] Pluto's consort, *Persephone*, who is able to annually travel to and from the Underworld;[107] *Hecate*, the patroness of witchcraft and the ἄωροι (*pars ultima*) to not only assent to the reanimation of the body, but also guarantee the success of the ritual;[108] the *ianitor sedis laxae*, whose identity is concealed, but whose importance in the context of the necromancy lies in his control over the

---

101 For a list of the gods invoked in necromancies see Fahz 1904, 10–15. But see Faraone 2005, 273 on the differences between Erichtho's necromantic spell and those of 'King Pitys' (*PGM* IV 1928–2144) as well as 281 for a possible explanation.

102 The Derveni Papyrus Col. VI refers to the Eumenides as evil spirits hindering the souls (δαίμονες ἐμπο[δών εισι | ψυχαῖς ἐχθροί) and as an example of the demons that the sorcerers attempt to appease or drive away with their spells. They are often addressed or mentioned in magical utterances (e.g. *PGM* IV 1418, 2798, 2860, and *DT* 22, 24, 26, 29–33, 35).

103 Tesoriero 2000, 205–206. Chaos is sometimes referred to or invoked in magical incantations (*PGM* I 316, IV 443, 1459, 2535, 2859; *DT* 251).

104 Its Greek equivalent, ἡγεμονῆα γαίης, is found in *PGM* IV 1963–1964; a prominent deity in magical utterances as we infer from the text of the *defixiones*, where he is addressed with various names and titles which underline his sovereignty over the dead (Πλούτων/*Pluto*: *DT* 1, 22, 24, 26, 29, 38, 111, and *PGM* IV 1462; χθονιθαρχωθ: *DT* 18; φθιμένων βασιλεὺς: 198; Ὅρκος: 161, 163; *Dis*: 191, 139; δόμινους: 231).

105 This function of the Styx is evident from *PGM* IV 1460–1470, in which the spell caster asks from various infernal deities, including Styx, to send up the ghosts of the dead to perform a service.

106 The invocation to the Elysian fields occurs nowhere in the *PGM*. Perhaps it functions as a substitute for the address to Erebos (e.g. *PGM* VII 348–358; Erichtho also mentions it in line 731 of her *epanankos*) to underscore the virtually limitless power of Erichtho, who appears to be able to summon souls that are destined for the Elysian fields. For Erebos as the place that holds the souls of virtuous people before they undergo purification see Serv. ad *Aen*. 6.404.

107 She is invoked either along with Pluto or separately, with different names and designations, such as Περσεφόνη (*DT* 74, 75), Φερσεφόνη (*DT* 50, 81), *Persefina* (*DT* 268), or Κόρη (*DT* 3, 9, 10, 13), *regina tenebrarum* (*DT* 288, 289), and δόμινα (*DT* 269).

108 Tesoriero 2000, 208; Hecate is another goddess called upon in magic rituals, either in her triple or chthonic form: Ἑκάτη χθονία (*DT* 22, 24, 26, 29–33, 35, and *PGM* III 47, IV 1443–1445), Κούρα τριώνυμος (*DT* 22–24, 26, 29–32) ῥηξίχθων (*DT* 38), Εἰνοδία (*DT* 41), ἀκρουροβόρη Σελήνη (*DT* 41), and Ἑκάτη τρίμορφος (*DT* 242). For her required assent and co-operation in magic rituals see Johnston 1990, 144–147.

access point between the two worlds;[109] the Fates (*fila sorores | tracturae*), who must re-spin the thread of the soldier's life for Erichtho's spell to succeed;[110] Charon (*portitor undae*), who transported the dead to the Underworld, continuously providing the witch with souls for her spells.[111] The length of the list lends greater force to the incantation, especially since Erichtho has asked for the favor of each and every god who functions as an intermediary between the netherworld and the world of the living.[112] The exclusively chthonic character of these deities represents the popular belief that the easiest and quickest way to achieve anything was through these powers.[113]

The first section of the prayer closes with the witch's *verba precandi* (706: *exaudite preces*).[114] The use of the imperative to express the devotee's intention to make a request is rare in real religious prayers, where the subjunctive was preferable as it reflects the human submission to the divine. In magical prayers, especially in the *defixiones*, the respectful address is more than often substituted with commands to emphasize the utterer's control over gods.[115] Erichtho's imperative of the forceful verb *exaudire*, instead of the milder *audire*, reflects her "imperious power over the gods."[116] The peremptory demand is renewed at 711 (*parete precandi*), further emphasizing the shift in proper attitude toward the gods.

---

109 Ancient scholiasts suggest either Charon or Cerberus (Usener *ad loc.*), but this is unlikely since the former is invoked separately in lines 704–705, while the latter is fed by the *ianitor* (702–703), and therefore it cannot be the same character. Bourgery 1928, 310 identified the figure as Aeacus (he is addressed once as the gate-keeper of the Underworld in *PGM* IV 1464). Haskins 1887, 221 suggests Hermes, and Korenjak 1996, 199 Anubis through religious syncretism. Tesoriero 2000, 209 proposed that Lucan intentionally avoids naming the god, alluding to the obscure deities invoked in magic spells, such as *Mathureuphramenos*, Σισοχωρ, and Στερξερξ (mentioned in *DT* 22, 24, 26, 28–35, 37). Hermanubis, who is mentioned in *PGM* IV 3140, is another possible identification. On depictions of Anubis holding the keys to the Underworld see Wortmann 1968, 70, and Morenz 1975, 510–520.
110 Korenjak 1996, 199. On this popular image of Fates see Dietrich 1965, 61, 64–66, 72–74, and 289–294. They were prominent in spells (see, for example, *PGM* II 100, IV 1455, IV 1463, 2859), and although they are invoked only once in a necromantic incantation (*PGM* IV 1455 and 1463) their powers would have been considered ideal for such rituals.
111 Charon is invoked in *PGM* IV 1452.
112 Reif 2016, 445–446 finds echoes of *PGM* IV 442–447 and 1459–1469 in Erichtho's invocation.
113 On the conviction, shared among the ancients, concerning the power of infernal gods and spirits in bringing one's aims into fruition, see page 17 n. 71. They are especially prevalent in curses and vindictive prayers given their binding powers and role as agents of punishment for a perceived injustice or injury.
114 For petitionary formulas in literary prayers see Hickson 1993, 45–51.
115 Johnston 2004, 367.
116 Tesoriero 2000, 211.

The prayer continues with the *narratio*/argument, which served the purpose of convincing the deities why the current prayer merits a favorable response:

> ... si vos satis ore nefando
> pollutoque voco, si numquam haec carmina fibris
> humanis ieiuna cano, si pectora plena
> saepe deo lavi calido prosecta cerebro,
> si quisquis vestris caput extaque lancibus infans   710
> inposuit victurus erat, parete precanti.

> ... If with a mouth blasphemous
> and polluted enough I address you, if I never cast these spells
> while hungry for human flesh, if I have often cut off god-filled
> breasts, and washed them with warm brains,
> if any child placed its head and inwards on your plates,
> and was going to survive, obey my prayer.

Using the literary device of anaphora, Erichtho lists a number of her past devotions in consecutive conditional clauses (*si voco...si cano...si lavi... si inposuit*), which was a regular way of expression in the *narratio* of literary prayers.[117] But contrary to the pious deeds of the petitioner in real prayers of magic, she recounts atrocious and impious actions: blasphemy (706–707), cannibalism (707–708), human sacrifice (708–709), and child murder (710–711).[118] Even though these acts, which have no precedent in authentic magical prayers, were deemed unforgivable sins, and completely offensive acts toward the gods, they reflect social stereotypes that emphasize the danger witches posed to society.[119] In doing so, Lucan manages to link Erichtho with the worst aspects of the witch as it was conceived in popular thought, guiding the reader to condemn her practices and, by extension, Sextus who sought her aid.[120]

---

[117] Hickson 1993, 11.
[118] Korenjak 1996, 200 observes that these acts are not found in real spells, which more than often required the magician's purity through abstinence from spilling blood, eating meat, and having sexual intercourse (e.g. *PGM* I 41–42, 54–56, IV 52–55, 734–736). The only instances where acts like those of Erichtho are referred to can be found in the διαβολαί, which intended to cause divine wrath against a person by attributing to them various sacrilegious actions (see, for example, *PGM* IV 2474–2484, 2571–2599, 2654–2661, VII 605–610, XXXVI 138–144, *DT* 155, 188, 295). For human sacrifice in magic see page 18 n. 73.
[119] Korenjak 1996, 200; for the image of the witch in ancient popular thought see Graf 1997a, 61–88.
[120] Tesoriero 2000, 212.

The last part (*preces*) defines further Erichtho's requests to the gods of the Underworld:

> non in Tartareo latitantem poscimus antro
> adsuetamque diu tenebris, modo luce fugata
> descendentem animam; primo pallentis hiatu
> haeret adhuc Orci, licet has exaudiat herbas,   715
> ad manes ventura semel. ducis omnia nato
> Pompeiana canat nostri modo militis umbra,
> si bene de vobis civilia bella merentur.

> I do not ask for a soul hiding in the hollows of Tartarus,
> and who is long accustomed to the darkness, but one that left the light behind,
> and now is descending; especially one that still lingers at the chasm
> of pale Hades, and though obeying these charms,
> will travel to the shades a single time. To the son of the leader,
> let the Pompeian ghost of the soldier, among us until lately, foretell everything
> if civil wars are worthy of your gratitude.

Erichtho asks for a single soul (*animam*) of a person who has not yet entered the Underworld (*non in Tartareo latitantem*) to foretell the future to Pompey's son (*omnia ... Pompeiana canat*).[121] In making the request, Erichtho switches to first person plural (*poscimus*), which is a very unusual change especially in prayers offered by one devotee. Tesoriero claimed that the switch is warranted since Erichtho addresses the gods also on behalf of Sextus.[122] This interpretation is in accord with the didactic aspect of the *Bellum Civile* as it further reinforces Sextus' complicity in the necromancy. By pointing to his responsibility, the poet indirectly shows to the reader that those who resort to magic are equally guilty as the person who performs the spells.

2.5.3 The second spell

The first spell ends only with partial success since the spirit has been summoned but refuses to enter the 'embalmed' body (720–723). This enrages Erichtho, who

---

[121] Instances of future prediction by means of necromancy are well attested in the *PGM* (see, for example, IV 154–285, 1928–2005, 2006–2125, 2125–2139, and the discussion in Faraone 2005).
[122] Tesoriero 2000, 217.

lashes the corpse (*praxis*: 726–727), and immediately utters a second, more powerful incantation (*logos*: 730–749):[123]

> Tisiphone vocisque meae secura Megaera, 730
> non agitis saevis Erebi per inane flagellis
> infelicem animam? iam vos ego nomine vero
> eliciam Stygiasque canes in luce superna
> destituam; per busta sequar per funera custos,
> expellam tumulis, abigam vos omnibus urnis. 735
> teque deis, ad quos alio procedere voltu
> ficta soles, Hecate pallenti tabida forma,
> ostendam faciemque Erebi mutare vetabo.
> eloquar inmenso terrae sub pondere quae te
> contineant, Hennaea, dapes, quo foedere maestum 740
> regem noctis ames, quae te contagia passam
> noluerit revocare Ceres. tibi, pessime mundi
> arbiter, inmittam ruptis Titana cavernis,
> et subito feriere die. paretis, an ille
> conpellandus erit, quo numquam terra vocato 745
> non concussa tremit, qui Gorgona cernit apertam
> verberibusque suis trepidam castigat Erinyn,
> indespecta tenet vobis qui Tartara, cuius
> vos estis superi, Stygias qui perierat undas?

> Tisiphone, and Megaera undisturbed by my voice,
> are you not leading with your cruel floggings this wretched soul
> through the emptiness of Erebus? Soon I will call you forth
> by your true name, and abandon you, Stygian dogs, in the celestial
> light. Through pyres and funerals I will hunt you down like a guard,
> I will expel you from the tombs and drive you away from urns.
> And I will reveal you to the gods, whom you are accustomed to visiting,
> disguised with a different countenance, Hecate, pale and wasted,
> and I will forbid you alter your hellish face.
> I will openly state what meals confine you beneath the earth's immense
> weight, Proserpina, through which bond you
> love the gloomy king of night, what pollution you suffered
> and Ceres does not want to call you back. Against you, worst ruler of the
> world, I will send the sun to the open hollows,
> and you shall be punished by the sudden light. Do you obey, or

---

[123] Repeating a spell until it succeeds or casting a different one after the initial had failed seems to have been standard practice in witchcraft as we infer from the magical papyri (e.g. *PGM* II 45–64, 144–166, IV 1035–1046, 1435–1495, 1904, 2096–2098, 2901–2939, 3087–3091, 3227–3245, LXII 32–38). Reif 2016, 446–447 discusses some of the texts which call for the repetition or the utterance of another spell as soon as the first spell fails.

> must he be invoked, at whose name the earth always
> trembles and shakes, who looks upon the uncovered Gorgon
> and with his lashes punishes the trepid Erinys,
> who lives in Tartarus out of your sight, for whom
> you are the gods above, and who had passed through the Stygian waters?

The purpose of such incantations which are termed *logoi epanankoi* was to compel divine assistants to comply with the requests of the spell caster in cases where they were either unwilling to obey or delaying the spell's completion. Although all the *logoi epanankoi* aimed essentially at the same result, it is possible to distinguish between two subcategories: some have a more friendly tone (e.g. *PGM* IV 1035–1047, LXII 32–36), while others include abusive language and various threats against the *paredros*, such as revelations of a secret, physical violence and torture (e.g. *PGM* II 54–55) as well as disturbances of the natural order (e.g. *PGM* IV 2312–2330, V 283–285).[124]

Lucan's second spell is less faithful to real *logoi epanankoi* since there is no repetition of the invocation, and no restatement of the original request — either would have been redundant in literary framework.[125] Its content, however, is in line with the general concept of this type of incantations as Erichtho directs her wrath toward the same deities who were invoked in the first spell: *Tisiphone* and *Megaera* (Eumenides); *Hecate*; *Hennaea* (Persephone); *pessime mundi arbiter* (Pluto). The threats of revealing a deity's true names (against Eumenides),[126] real face and form (towards Hecate),[127] and certain shameful information (concerning Persephone),[128] as well as the threat of exposing Hades to light,[129] all have parallels in the *PGM*. A final, great threat is made collectively against all the gods, whom Erichtho warns that, if they do not submit to her requests, she will summon a super-powerful entity who can compel them, as she implies, to do her bidding.[130] As he does in the case of

---

124 For these characteristics of *logoi epanankoi* see Graf 1997a, 202.
125 For the relationship between Lucan's text and these spells see Bourgery 1928, 310–311, Nock 1972, 186–187, Baldini Moscadi 1976, 179–184, and Reif 2016, 446–451.
126 E.g. *PGM* IV 277–280; XXXVI 260–263 with Reif 2016, 447–448.
127 E.g. *PGM* III 498–501, VIII 9–11 with Reif 2016, 448.
128 E.g. *PGM* IV 2476–2494 with Reif 2016, 449.
129 Korenjak 1996, 210 notes the similarity with the threat in *PGM* LXII 28–31.
130 Erichtho does not explicitly name who this deity might be, and scholars have made various assumptions: Haskins 1887, 223, and Pichon 1912, 192 n. 3 argued that this mysterious figure is Demiurgus/Demogorgon; Bourgery 1928, 312 identified him with Hermes Trismegistus, and Rose 1913, li–lii with the Semitic Ahriman; Baldini Moscadi 1976, 180–184 maintains that Lucan refers to another Semitic deity, Iao/Iahweh, whose name frequently comes up in the *PGM*. However, both Demiurgus and Hermes Trismegistos should be ruled out because they were considered benevolent

love magic (452–460), Lucan intentionally ignores here the less offensive or less violent types of such spells with the intent to underscore the sacrilegious character of magic.

The second spell proves effective as the soul enters its vessel, and eventually the corpse is reanimated (750–757). The initial failure was only a brief obstacle which Erichtho surpasses immediately (750: *protinus*) and with little effort as she utters the *epanankos* only once, contrary to real spells, which sometimes were repeated multiple times. The short pause adds to the reader's thrill, increasing their certainty that nothing else can go wrong which Erichtho is unable to fix.

2.5.4 The instructions

The witch then utters a brief speech addressing the reanimated corpse (762–774). As expected in this part of the spell, Erichtho restates her requests in a more detailed manner: she commands the soldier to speak the truth (762–763: *dic … vera locutum*), to include names and places in his response (773–774: *da nomina rebus, | da loca*), and reveal fate's plan (*da vocem qua mecum fata loquantur*). The position of this excerpt immediately after the coercive spell as well as its instructive content alludes to certain formulas found in the *PGM*. More specifically, it recalls instructions given by the magician to the summoned *paredros* such as those in III 626–632, and IV 1848–1858.[131] These lines conclude technically the ritual of reanimation, which is now complete. The necromancy, built up for almost a hundred lines, reaches its culmination and the reader's expectations are to the highest point.

---

deities, and therefore Lucan's account contradicts their true nature. The Semitic alternatives might fit better to the profile of an evil, omnipotent god, but their use as models is probably a more distant possibility than that of another, more popular figure, namely Typhon/ Seth (Korenjak 1996, 210). Although most of the powers described in lines 745–749 are probably the poet's invention to underline the superiority of this deity to all the other gods, they closely resemble the powers attributed to Typhon in the *PGM* (see IV 179–201, 243–247, and 264–274). The deity's depiction as an inhabitant of Tartarus (*indespecta tenet Tartara*) further supports his identification with Typhon, who was incarcerated there after his defeat by Zeus (Hes. *Theog.* 868; Pind. *Pyth.* 1.15–28). In the magical papyri, he is often assimilated with the Egyptian god Seth (e.g. *PGM* VII 964, XII 138, 373–375, XIV 20, XXXVI 317–320, CXVI 1–17), a development that has its origins probably back to the Classical period, but became standard during Roman times as we infer from Plutarch's *De Iside et Osiride* 351 F.

131 Reif 2016, 452.

2.6 Is it even possible? The failure of Erichtho

Lucan meticulously creates the illusion of an upcoming successful divination by employing different techniques: the abominable and anti-human description of Erichtho; the amplification of her powers through the implicit comparison with those of regular Thessalian witches; the realistic and accurate ritual she performs; her own statements about her powers and the validity of necromancy *passim* in the narrative (e.g. 615–616, 771–773, 621–623).[132] All these elements lead the reader to anticipate a clear and truthful prophecy, which will include specific events and names, contrary to the ambiguity of conventional oracles (770–771). But Sextus' and, by extension, the reader's anticipation is wholly denied, despite the corpses last-minute assurances for a comprehensive prophecy (783–784).[133]

The soldier neither reveals the exact "course of fate" (423), nor responds to the protagonist's inquiries concerning the general outcome of the war (592–593), any unforeseen events during its course (597–598), as well as the deaths of himself and his companions (601). Each and every promise of the witch vanishes into thin air, like our expectations, as the prophecy is vague and utterly cryptic. It is difficult for Sextus even to guess the outcome of the war since the initial impression left by the description of the mourning *Latii* and the exalting *diversi* (782–799) is contradicted immediately after by the prophesied death of the winner (799–802), while the inclusion of Marcus Junius Brutus (792), whose homonymous descendant is a proponent of the republican cause, among the rejoicing party creates even more confusion.[134] Likewise, Sextus' question regarding his own fate remains unanswered as the corpse forbids him to inquire about his death (812). The only information it provides is that one day he will die (803–805) — indeed, a necessity of life according to the Stoics (Sen. *Ep.* 77.19) — which, without details of the place and time of the inevitable, renders the necromancy more useless than conventional oracles, given the much-emphasized potency of the rite.[135]

---

[132] Masters 1992, 197–198 has already analyzed how Erichtho's statements throughout the episode influence the reader. See also Gordon 1987a, 232.
[133] Tupet 1988, 426 claims that the utterance of the corpse is hardly a prophecy. *Contra* Makowski 1977 and Gordon 1987a, 233 who consider the necromancy successful. Dick 1963 sees an implicit success in the prodigies and prophecies of the poem, which emphasize the idea that "knowledge of the future annihilates hope. Prodigies burden mankind, magically induced prophecies portend death, and dreams presage annihilation for the dreamer" (49).
[134] Korenjak 1996, 226.
[135] The inadequacy of divination in Lucan has been discussed in Masters 1992, 141–149, and more recently in Santangelo 2015.

The failure of necromancy is not unexpected in view of Lucan's philosophical inclinations. The Stoics scorned death (Sen. *Ep.* 30.5–10; 82.16) and considered it an indifferent (Sen. *Ep.* 82.10–13, 17; *Marc.* 19.5). As such and taking into account the principle that one should be ready to face the inevitable at any moment (*Ep.* 15.11; 30.16–17; 91.16), it is only reasonable to infer that foreknowledge of death was both useless and reprehensible in Stoic eyes (Sen. *Ep.* 70.4–5; 85.22–23). This idea is reflected in the corpse's statement prohibiting Sextus to inquire about his fate (812), further instructing him that the only way to know is through experience (812–813) and not by any means of divination — even the prophecy by his father, Pompeius Magnus, will not be enlightening (814–815).

Instead of clear predictions, the corpse offers the Stoic advice (802: *solacia*) regarding the proper attitude to death.[136] Since death makes no exceptions (Sen. *Ep.* 77.11–13; 66.42–43; 71.15) and both leaders of the factions will eventually meet their doom (811), it urges Sextus to die, without consideration for his glory (807–809). The paraenesis echoes the belief that an honorable death has more value than a dishonorable life (Sen. *Ep.* 77.6; 70.7). In the reader's mind, who knows that Caesar will eventually win the war and establish his dictatorship, the statement also points to the Stoic idea of death as appropriate form of opposition to tyranny (Sen. *De Ira* 3.15.3–4). The rejection of the necromancy (as a form of divination), and the corpse's proffered advice — it functions as the author's mouthpiece — echo the views of Cato, Lucan's Stoic sage, in Book 9.[137]

2.7 Conclusions

Like his uncle Seneca, Lucan's attitude toward magic is highly critical. The Erichtho episode becomes the vehicle for his attacks against people who resort to magic as clients, magicians and witches, but also the practice itself in various ways. From the perspective of a Stoic and a Roman, Lucan passes a negative judgment on the motives of Sextus Pompey to summon Erichtho, conforming to the Stoic idea that evil — here it appears in the form of Erichtho — exists only due to human will and action. The anti-Stoic character of the *ars magica* is further underscored in the digression on Thessalian witchcraft, which describes in philosophical terms how magic has the power to upset the natural and social order. The section ends with a reference to common magical tricks such as the magicians' alleged control over wild animals and snakes, and the famous optical illusion of the 'Thessalian trick',

---

[136] Tesoriero 2000, 262.
[137] Cato's attitude toward divination is discussed in Santangelo 2015, 185–186.

which allow the educated reader to view the practice as charlatanry. The futility of magic, however, becomes apparent through the juxtaposition between the gruesome and horrific portrayal of Erichtho and the failure of her magic ritual, despite the witch's meticulousness and accuracy. The extreme realism of the ritual, which recalls features from spells of the *PGM* and the *DT*, serves as an anchor between the scene and contemporary experience, but it also makes the failure of magic more deafening for the reader, who is led to question the claims of magicians as well as the efficacy and moral value of their practices in real life.

3 Petronius: Parody of Literature, Mockery of Magic

The *Satyrica* is a fascinating work which has been considered an artistically enhanced, and often exaggerated representation of low-class life in the Neronian period.[1] As such, the depiction of popular superstitions which are found throughout the narrative is anchored in reality: for instance, entering the *triclinium* with the right foot because the opposite will bring misfortunes upon the host (30), the connection of the cock's crow with the imminent death of someone close by (74), or the spitting on one's own bosom to avert bad luck (74). Such unfounded convictions, some of which are encountered even in modern day Italy, reflect contemporary Neronian superstition.[2]

But as has been already observed, in the *Satyrica*, superstition manifests not only in the beliefs of low-life characters, but also in the rituals witnessed herein. Making an example out of Quartilla's *nocturnas religiones* (17.9), Šterbenc Erker has convincingly argued that the rites which are characterized by obscenity and ridiculousness are parodies of proper religious rituals.[3] She further asserted that the lewd element reflects the common elitist prejudice against the religious practices of the lower classes which considered them a danger for the chastity of both men and women. In other words, the highly sexualized nature of Quartilla's initiation

---

[1] Freudenburg 2017, 116–117; Martin 1988 considers the matter of Petronius' realism "un faux problème" (238), further claiming that reality is depicted through "le prisme d'une imagination puissante" (241) which alienates contemporary readers. Scholars have recognized different degrees of realism in the *Satyrica*: Auerbach 1953, 30–31 argues that Petronius' novel reaches the narrow limit of ancient realism by recreating the daily life of the freedmen, with the characters using the everyday, non-artificial language of the lower classes; Sullivan 1967, 76 considers the *Satyrica* a work of "limited realism" which he associates with Petronius' satirical trope (75); Bakhtin 1981, 221–224 claims that the 'Story of the widow of Ephesus' combines the elements of the "ancient complex" into a compound event that reflects real life; Schmeling 1996, 28–29 denies that realism exists in the *Satyrica*; Conte 1996, 175–176 postulates that individual parts appear realistic, but not the whole; Courtney 2001, 221 argues that Petronius mixes realism (as it was conceived by Auerbach) with imagination; Panayotakis 1995, 194 views Petronius' realism as the result of the influence of mimic plays on the *Satyrica*. Studying the language of the freedmen in the *Satyrica*, Boyce 1991 and Jones 1991 are led to different conclusions about the novel's realism (for and against, respectively).

[2] Rini 1929 discusses some superstitions encountered during the *Cena* and finds evidence of their existence in modern-day Italy. For a more recent study of popular superstitions in the *Cena* see Grondona 1980.

[3] An assessment that appears invariably in analyses of the Quartilla episode: see, for example, Cosci 1980, and Panoussi 2019, 68–69 (parody of initiation rites); Pinna 1978, 225–238 (parody of oriental mysteries).

https://doi.org/10.1515/9783111429441-003

rite exemplifies for Šterbenc Erker the false religion and superstition of the masses from the perspective of the upper class, while revealing an implicit promulgation of the elite's morality.[4]

Her interpretation thus aptly responds to another question of Petronian scholarship, that is, whether the *Satyrica* is a work of moral didacticism, or simply a piece of entertainment.[5] Choosing one option over the other does not do any good to the novel since these alternatives are not mutually exclusive. With regards to its content, the *Satyrica* has often been seen as a parody, and parodies can produce an edifying effect — of course not all do, and not for everyone.[6]

My reading of Petronius is based on and expands upon Šterbenc Erker conclusions by showing that in the cultural environment of the first century CE, when magic and superstition have become a trend in literature, certain episodes of the *Satyrica* can be read also as a parody of the respective literary motif.[7] Such ridicule of the literary *topos* also functions, in and of itself, as a criticism of the life conditions upon which the motif is modelled. In other words, the all-humorous context of the novel transforms the descriptions of superstition and *quasi*-magical rituals into social criticism of magic in the first century CE. This twofold function is of course expected in a work written by someone who allegedly held the position of Nero's *arbiter*

---

4 Šterbenc Erker 2013, 130.
5 The moralizing tendencies of Petronius have been accepted by Highet 1941, Bacon 1958, and Arrowsmith 1966, each one arguing from a different perspective. The 'anti-moralist' school, which considers the *Satyrica* to be mere entertainment, is represented by: Perry 1925, 25–26; Sullivan 1967; Schmeling 1969, 49–50 and 64; Walsh 1974, 185 ("bawdy entertainment", a view followed by Panagiotakis 1995, 195 who links it to the innate purpose of mimic plays); Slater 1990, 3; Lawall 1995, iv; Schmeling 1996, 483–484. Courtney 2001, 124 claims that the technique of first-person narrative by a low-life character (Encolpius) impedes our view of the author as a strict moralist. That said, he still maintained that a moralistic evaluation of first century social life underlies the novel's narrative. A middle road, what Schmeling and Setaioli 2011, xxxvi termed the 'neo-moral' interpretation, was put forward in Zeitlin 1971, arguing that the anarchy and confusion in the *Satyrica* reflect the author's view of the real world (633), and that the ironic style is, in and of itself, a form of criticism (680); Rimell 2002, 5 also argues that the view of the *Satyrica* as pure entertainment is the result of the fragmentary condition of the text as well as of "not reading the *Satyricon* from a distance".
6 Schmeling and Setaioli 2011, xxxiii–xxxiv mention some of the scholarly views proposed about the "inner form" of the *Satyrica*. The following list offers some examples but is in no way exhaustive: parody of the ideal novel (Heinze 1899); parody of wandering epics, such as the *Aeneid* and the *Odyssey* (Klebs 1899); satire (Highet 1941); non-traditional satire (Sandy 1969); comedy (Slater 1990); portrayal of an anarchical world (Zeitlin 1971); Encolpius' "confession" of his life with the purpose of entertaining the reader (Schmeling 1996, 486); Menippean satire (Jensson 2004).
7 An observation already made in Sullivan 1963, 87 and Panayotakis 1995, 171 (who further claims that Petronius designed the Oenothea episode after mimic *exodia*).

elegantiae (Tac. *Ann.* 16.18) and may have been responsible for judging virtually everything, from artistic taste to social morality.[8]

The first section analyzes the inset narratives of the werewolf (62) and the *strigae* (63) and shows how Petronius infuses legends and folktales, circulating at the time, with contemporary stereotypes about magic to create new stories, whose veracity, however, is unquestionable only in the imagination of low-life characters of the novel's exaggerated world. This is further affirmed by the freedmen's statements as well as their subsequent ritualistic actions which reveal their credulity. But for the educated reader,[9] these stories are merely horror comedies ridiculing the clichés about witches and magic, just as the 1984 film *Ghostbusters* parodies modern beliefs about ghosts and monsters.[10]

The second part of the discussion focuses on the healing rituals of Proselenos and Oenothea as burlesque representations of magic. Recipes of folk medicine, partially similar to those executed in practice by the two priapic priestesses, were often seen as *quasi*-magical, and Petronius validates this view using various methods. He predisposes the reader about the magical nature of these rituals through the sparse statements concerning the cause of Encolpius' impotence, and the description of the priestesses which brings their figures closer to witches. Both rituals are a pastiche of earlier literary sources, while they also bear features that reflect those found in the *PGM*, and which enhance further their realism as well as their magical nature in the reader's eyes. The ridiculous and highly sexualized character of these rites as well as their eventual failure provoke the reader's laughter and reveal a latent critical attitude toward magic.[11]

---

8 An obscure figure in the history of the period and the life of the court, our information for Petronius comes mainly from three sources: a brief reference in Plin. *HN* 37.20, two extensive passages in Tac. *Ann.* 16.17–20, and a reference in Plut. *Mor.* 60 d-e. For the identification of the author of the *Satyrica* with the Tacitean Petronius see: Sullivan 1968a, 27–33; Walsh 1970, 67–70; Rose 1971, 38–59; Schmeling 1996, 457–460; Courtney 2001, 5–11; Schmeling and Setaioli 2011, xiii–xvii. For a detailed discussion of Petronius' portrayal in Tacitus see Rankin 1971, 88–99.
9 Agreeing with Sullivan 1985, 160–161 on the matter of the *Satyrica*'s readership.
10 Ogden 2021, 1 characterizes them as "campfire horror stories". Horsfall 1989, 194–195 places both tales in the context of the long tradition of storytelling during dinners as a popular form of entertainment. Boyce 1991, 87 discusses the similes used throughout Niceros' tale and considers them the storyteller's 'tools of the trade'.
11 McMahon 1998, 207 n. 103 referring to the ritual of Oenothea: "The entire episode about the attempts to cure Encolpius's impotence is, in fact, a thematic criticism of belief in superstition".

3.1 Popular horror stories: the werewolf in Petronius

Petronius' inset narrative in 62 is considered an iconic werewolf tale that served as a model for subsequent representations of the beast in literature and art.[12] Although relying on existing myths and legends about Lycaon, the Anthidai family, and the Nervian tribe, this account is unique in its mixing of these traditions with new elements.[13] In other words, Petronius creates a pastiche by crystallizing these stories into a new tale, infusing it further with details of magical and/or medical nature. By doing so, he creates an account of the metamorphic sorcerer which is detached from its literary models and closer to popular superstitions of his time.

After Encolpius, Ascyltus, and Giton join the dinner at Trimalchio's villa, and having enjoyed several dishes, the host asks Niceros, one of his frequent guests and friend, to tell a story. The tale which functions intranarratively as a form of entertainment for the banqueteers is a personal recollection of the freedman's experience from the time he was a slave in Capua (62):

> erat autem miles, fortis tamquam Orcus. apoculamus nos circa gallicinia, luna lucebat tamquam meridie. venimus inter monimenta: homo meus coepit ad stelas facere, sed ego <pergo> cantabundus et stelas numero. deinde ut respexi ad comitem, ille exuit se et omnia vestimenta secundum viam posuit. mihi [in] anima in naso esse, stabam tamquam mortuus. at ille circumminxit vestimenta sua, et subito lupus factus est. nolite me iocari putare; ut mentiar, nullius patrimonium tanti facio. sed, quod coeperam dicere, postquam lupus factus est, ululare coepit et in silvas fugit. ego primitus nesciebam ubi essem, deinde accessi, ut vestimenta eius tollerem: illa autem lapidea facta sunt. qui mori timore nisi ego? gladium tamen strinxi et †matavitatau† umbras cecidi, donec ad villam amicae meae pervenirem. [...] "lupus enim villam intravit et omnia pecora...: tamquam lanius sanguinem illis misit. nec tamen derisit, etiam si fugit; servus enim noster lancea collum eius traiecit." haec ut audivi, operire oculos amplius non potui, sed luce clara †hac nostri† domum fugi tamquam copo compilatus, et postquam veni in illum locum in quo lapidea vestimenta erant facta, nihil inveni nisi sanguinem. ut vero domum veni, iacebat miles meus in lecto tamquam bovis, et collum illius medicus curabat. intellexi illum versipellem esse, nec postea cum illo panem gustare potui, non si me occidisses. viderint alii quid de hoc exopinissent; ego si mentior, genios vestros iratos habeam.[14]

---

12 Frost 2003, 51 notes that werewolf tales in subsequent literary works incorporate features which are first encountered in Petronius. Boyce 1991, 86: "...Niceros' lycanthrope is a constitutional werewolf".
13 The possible sources of inspiration for Petronius's werewolf tale have been discussed exhaustively in earlier scholarship. See, for instance, Schuster 1930, 158–162; Tupet 1976, 74–75; Baldwin 1986, 9; Veenstra 2002, 139–143; Gordon 2015, 34–46. Panayotakis 1995, 92–93 notes similarities with Novius' *Fullones Feriati*, an atellan farce.
14 The text is cited from Müller 2009.

So, there was a soldier, hell of a brave man. We departed around cockcrow while the moon was shining as if it was noon. We went to the cemetery: my lad started peeing around the tombstones, but I kept singing while counting them. When I finally looked towards my lad, he undressed himself of all his clothes and placed them by the street. My soul reached my nose, and I stood like a dead man. But he urinated around his garments and, out of the blue, transformed into a wolf. Do not think that I am joking; no one's fortune is enough for me to lie. But, as I was saying, after he became a wolf, he started howling, and fled to the forest. At first, I did not know where I was, and eventually I approached to pick up his clothes: however, they turned into stone. Who would be scared to death, if not me? Nonetheless, I drew out my sword and –'swish!'– I slayed shadows, until I arrived at the farm of a friend of mine. [...] "For a wolf entered the house and all the cattle...: like a butcher it drained the blood out of them. However, it did not trick us, even if it fled; for a slave of ours pierced its throat with a spear." When I heard this, I could not sleep anymore, but at dawn I ran back to the house like a robbed tradesman, and after I reached the place where the garments had become stone, I found nothing except for blood. As soon as I arrived at the house, my soldier was lying in bed like an ox, and a doctor was treating the wounds on his neck. I figured out he was a werewolf, and from that time onward I could not snack next to him, even if you had killed me. The rest may see what they think about this; if I am lying, may the wrath of your guardian spirits fall upon me.[15]

The story has several connections with the Arcadian myth of Lycaon in Ovid (*Met.* 1.216–239) and the legend of the Anthidai in Pliny (*HN* 8.81). The soldier, after he undergoes the metamorphosis, vanishes from the scene (*fugit*), attacks the cattle in a nearby farm, and slaughters all the animals (*omnia pecora*), spilling their blood (*sanguinem illis misit*) like a butcher (*tamquam lanius*). These actions echo Ovid's description (*Met.* 1.232–235) of a transformed Lycaon fleeing his house (*ipse fugit*), attacking neighboring cattle (*vertitur in pecudes*) driven by his bloodthirst (*cupidine caedis*), and rejoicing in the blood of the dead animals (*sanguine gaudet*). Neither possesses anymore the ability to articulate themselves, and their effort to speak results in howling (Lycaon *exululat* and the soldier *ululare coepit*). The influence of the Anthidai legend may be traced in the soldier's divesting and recovery of his clothes, before and after the transformation, respectively.[16] Just as the members of this Arcadian family must strip themselves (Plin. *HN* 8.81: *vestituque...suspenso*) before swimming across the lake and being transformed into wolves, similarly the Petronian character also needs to remove his garments (*exuit se ... vestimenta secundum viam posuit*). And just as they must pick up those very same clothes (Plin. *HN* 8.81: *eandem recipere vestem*) after they assume their previous form, the soldier also gets back his own garments. Even though it is not mentioned explicitly, the recovery of the clothes seems a prerequisite for the werewolf to return to its earlier form, which justifies the petrification of the soldier's garments while he was

---

15 All translations included in this chapter are my own, unless noted otherwise.
16 Veenstra 2002, 142.

in wolf shape, but when Niceros went back to check the area where they were previously located, he found nothing.[17]

Apart from the influence of these Arcadian tales, in which wolf-transformation is involuntary, the soldier's willing transformation in Petronius recalls the description of the Nervians who, according to Pomponius Mela (*De situ orbis* 2.14), can turn into wolves at their own will (*si velint*).[18] While discussing the life and customs of this tribe of northern Europe, Herodotus (4.105) claims that the Nervians run the risk of being branded as 'sorcerers' (κινδυνεύουσι δὲ οἱ ἄνθρωποι οὗτοι γόητες εἶναι), pointing to an implicit connection between magic and shapeshifting in ancient thought.[19] Pomponius' reference to the practice of human sacrifice (*hominesque pro victumis feriunt*) among the Nervians, which would have been considered both barbaric and foreign to Roman custom, also facilitates their assimilation with foreign magicians.[20]

All these legends point to a connection between 'the other,' witchcraft, and lycanthropy in Graeco-Roman thought, which became even more solid in Augustan literature. In Vergil's *Eclogue* 8, Moeris can change his shape into that of a wolf by means of potions (95: *venena*). Although not explicitly stated, Moeris is apparently a magician as we infer from the description of his powers to summon the dead and charm the crops (8.95–99),[21] while his name indicates that he is probably Egyptian, thus also representing the 'other'.[22] The second example of this triple link is

---

[17] Veenstra 2002, 139 n. 12. Already argued in Schuster 1930, 162 who further thinks of the petrification as a variant of concealing the werewolf's garments under stones; Smith 1975, 173 sees the urination and subsequent petrification of the clothes as a protective mechanism; Gordon 2015, 59 n. 137 considers it a "comical way of preventing their theft".

[18] The distinction between 'voluntary' transformation, and metamorphosis as a result of external intervention (e.g. divine punishment or curse) has been discussed in earlier scholarship. For the distinction between the two, and its implications, see Veenstra 2002, 134 n. 2. An exhaustive list of primary sources on werewolf voluntary and involuntary transformation with detailed comments can be found in Ogden 2021, 18–54.

[19] Ogden 2021, 25; Gordon 2015, 40–41 claims that the element of magic is introduced in the account of the Nervians' transformation by Herodotus to suggest how these rumors might be explained.

[20] Ogden 2021, 25–26. Just as the Arcadians represent the "internal other" among the Greeks (Gordon 2015, 39 drawing upon the conclusions of Bonnechere 1994, 86), the Nervians, might have occupied a similar position among Romans. For human sacrifice as a stereotype in magic see page 18 n. 73.

[21] The enchantment of crops was considered one of the powers of magicians as we infer from early Roman laws which prohibited the use of incantations with the purpose of stealing someone's agricultural production (Plin. *HN* 28.17–18: *non et legum ipsarum in duodecim tabulis verba sunt: qui fruges excantassit...*). See also Tupet 1976, 181–187; Graf 1997a, 62–65; Ogden 2002a, 277–278.

[22] Ogden 2021, 26 and n. 34 on the same page, has already noted the Egyptian etymology of the name. "Moeris" is the Greek adaptation of the Egyptian name *Mu-ur* which means "great water" or *Mer-ur* which means "great canal" (Wallis Budge 1902, 48).

Propertius' infamous *lena* Acanthis, who possesses multiple supernatural powers (4.5.5–18), including the ability to transform into a nocturnal wolf (4.5.14: *sua nocturno fallere terga lupo*), and whose name strongly suggests that she is non-Roman. In both Augustan authors, wolf transformation is not the result of a curse, like in the Anthidai story, or a form of punishment, as it is the case with Lycaon, but a magical process undertaken willingly by the subjects.[23] Evidently, Petronius presents the reader with a new story which, although it is based on existing myths and legends, borrows, and expands upon, the literary models of the Augustan era.[24]

3.1.1 Adding more magic to the legend

The place and time of the soldier's metamorphosis are admittedly elements peculiar to Petronius' account which reinforce its connections to magic.[25] The transformation happens in a cemetery, a place closely linked with sorcery in Graeco-Roman thought and literature as it was a favorite spot for witches to perform their debased rituals mainly for two reasons: first, burial grounds were regarded as liminal spaces between the Underworld and the world of the living, thus providing easier access to demons and evil spirits (*paredroi*) summoned in magic rites; second, they were the ideal place to collect many of the necessary objects and ingredients used in witchcraft.[26] Of course, these popular views trace their origins in reality as the practice of burying curse tablets inside or around tombs to put the spell into effect aptly proves.[27] In addition, some spells of the *PGM* corpus instruct the magician to

---

[23] Gordon 2015, 46 discusses these passages and concludes correctly that the transformation is "contextualized as magic". On similarities with Moeris and Acanthis see also Bronzini 1988, 168.

[24] Gordon 2015, 46 notes that like Moeris, who hides in the woods after being transformed into a wolf, the soldier also runs to the forest.

[25] Though Tib. 1.5.47–60 has been seen as alluding to a connection between werewolf transformation and cemeteries (Ogden 2021, 38 citing Schmeling and Setaioli 2011, 256–257).

[26] E.g. in *Sat.* 1.8 Horace narrates the rituals of two witches that take place in a garden situated on top of an old burial ground, and in the *Bellum Civile* 6.511–513 Lucan describes how Erichtho makes her home near deserted tombs, allowing her to gather in copious amounts what she needs for her rituals. Smith 1975, 172 argues, based on Tib. 1.5.54, that Romans thought of cemeteries as places haunted by werewolves.

[27] The practice of depositing binding spells in graves had been common at least since the classical period (see Pl. *Leg.* 11.933d with Gager 1992, 250). For the different places where people would bury a *defixio* see McKie 2022, 49 table 3.1.

perform an action in or close to graves,[28] while others require the use of materials exclusively or easily found in graveyards.[29]

The time of the shapeshifting process is also an addition inspired by contemporary beliefs about witchcraft that enhances the story's magical aspect. The transformation takes place around two o'clock at night as the phrase *circa gallicinia* indicates.[30] Strikingly, Niceros uses a second expression of time (*luna lucebat tamquam meridie*) which, however, does not further narrow down the hour defined by *circa gallicinia* and, therefore, seems redundant. This pleonasm can be explained since Petronius' intention is to underscore the magical aspect of the soldier's transformation, which is now reinforced through the moon's association with magic.[31] Apart from this profound link, the expression recalls the use of planetary phases to define the exact hour in spells. More specifically, the phrase *luna lucebat tamquam meridie*, which points to the full moon, when the earth's natural satellite is diametrically opposed to the sun, seems to be conceptually equivalent to the expression σελήνης οὔσης διαμέτρου ἡλίου, which is found in *PGM* IV 2220–2221.[32]

---

28 *PGM* III 24–26 instructs the spell caster to bury the body of a dead cat in a grave or burial place (ἐν μνή[μ]ατι [ἢ ἐν ǀ ᵃτ]ῷ τόπῳ [τοῦ]ᵇ τά[φου]), IV 2215–2216 to bury an inscribed tablet in the tomb of a *biaiothanatos* (ἐπὶ ἀώρου θήκην), IV 2218–2221 to place a seashell in the tomb of a *biaiothanatos* (εἰς ἀώρου μνῆμα), and XII 211 to dig an offering pit in a sanctified grave (ἐν σήματι).
29 For instance, *PDM* xiv 428–450 lists seven grains of barley from a tomb among the ingredients for a potion; *PGM* IV 2871–2877 requires the use of *ousia* of a virgin who died prematurely as an offering during the spell; necromantic spells, such as *PGM* IV 1928–2005, almost always necessitate the use of a human skull (σκύφος) or a whole body (e.g., *PDM* xiv 1070–1077: place an inscribed reed leaf in an embalmed body's mouth). For examples of surviving materials (*ousia*) which were rolled up in curse tablets see Jordan 1985, 251. For a discussion on *ousia*, which usually comprised parts of the human body, such as hair, fingernails, bones as well as garments and personal items, see Hopfner 1921, 401–408. For the social criticism against the exploitation of corpses in modern Greece for magical purposes see Versnel 1991, 63; Bernand 1991, 364–369 argues that the punishment for desecrating a tomb was meant to stop the swapping of corpses rather than their exploitation in magic rituals. However, digging out bodies in order to use their parts in witchcraft was not a literary invention since Ammianus Marcellinus claims that the capital punishment was enforced in cases where someone would desecrate a tomb for such purposes (19.12.14).
30 On the interpretation of this expression of time see Schmeling and Setaioli 2011, 256.
31 Schmeling and Setaioli 2011, 256 on the connection between the moonlight and magic.
32 See, for example, *PGM* II 43: ἀπὸ ζ´ τῆς σελήνης; III 338: εἰς τὴν ἀνατολὴν τῆς σελήνης τριακονθήμερον; III: 455–456 τῆς σελήνης οὔσης δευτέρας; IV 57: σελήνης δὲ πληρωθε[ίσης]. For a study of the lunar phases in the *PGM*, and their particular connections with the effectiveness of different types of spells see Martín Hernández 2024, especially 93 and 98–100.

The most important insertion in Petronius' werewolf tale is the soldier's urination around his garments.[33] In general, this liquid by-product of human metabolism had many uses, with some being characterized as popular medicine at best (Plin. *HN* 28.65–67), while others as magical.[34] Especially its confining and protective powers, which seem most relevant here, are attested in both literature and encyclopedic works: in Apul. *Met.* 1.13.8 the witches urinate on Aristomenes to stop him from leaving the place;[35] according to Pliny (*HN* 28.69), Osthanes, the Persian Magus who followed Xerxes throughout his military campaign, maintained that drops of urine on someone's foot in the morning functioned as protection against evil enchantments. Although to ward off evil, and to confine something or someone are seemingly opposite actions, the core idea is basically the same: urine creates an unseen boundary which cannot be violated.[36] Under this light, the divestment and recovery of the clothes, which harbors a symbolic meaning,[37] is furnished with ritualistic importance when the soldier urinates around them as a form of protection.[38]

3.1.2 A story only for credulous lads?

In non-fictional works, stories about werewolves have another thing in common: their veracity is frequently questioned by the author, who indirectly reproves the

---

[33] Baldwin 1986, 9 thinks of the urination around the clothes as a comic version of the tale in Plin. *HN* 8.81. Smith 1975, 173 following Schuster 1930, 161–162 also recognizes Petronius' parodic intentions. Bronzini 1988, 161 sees the soldier's urination as a reaction to the deathly atmosphere of the cemetery.
[34] For magical aspects of ancient medicine see: Edelstein 1937, 201–246; Renehan 1992; Edmonds 2019, 116–148, Faraone 2018 (focusing mostly on healing amulets), and Cordovana 2020, especially 71–73. Galen (*De simpl. med. fac.* 10.2.15) discusses several medical uses of urine. *PDM* xiv 636–669 lists urine as an ingredient in a spell of attraction; in *PDM* xiv 956–960 urine functions as an indicator of female fertility.
[35] Scobie 1975, 109 claims that urinating on a person intends to hinder them from leaving a specific place. Perhaps it was the bad odor that led people to assume that urine had such powers.
[36] Watson 2004, 652–653 argues that the shape of circle (*circum-*) and the urination operate together to produce this effect. See also Bronzini 1988, 166 who places the emphasis on the shape of the circle rather than the act of urination itself.
[37] Veenstra 2002, 143: "For a moment the garment of civilization is removed, and the skin of a different, more savage life is put on in answer to a call from a brutal past, that still has to be morally vanquished."
[38] Smith 1975, 173 also adds that the soldier's urination around the clothes plays no role towards the transformation itself.

credulity of certain groups.[39] Herodotus (4.105), for instance, completely rejected the rumors about the Nervians' transformation as falsehoods (ἐμὲ μέν νυν ταῦτα λέγοντες οὐ πείθουσι), despite people who were spreading the story swearing the opposite (ὀμνύουσι δὲ [ταῦτα] λέγοντες).[40] Pliny also showed the same disbelief, arguing that not only should all werewolf tales be regarded as untrue (*HN* 8.80: *falsum esse confidenter existimare debemus*) and shameless lies (*HN* 8.82: *nullum tam inpudens mendacium est*), but also that anyone who believed in them should be considered gullible. More specifically, he directs his criticism toward the naïveté of the Greeks (*HN* 8.82: *mirum est quo procedat Graeca credulitas!*) and the masses (*HN* 8.81: *unde tamen ista vulgo infixa s<i>t fama in tantum*).[41] Pausanias also passes a judgment on the credibility of the Lycaon myth in a lengthy argument (8.2.4–8.2.5). He claims that the transformation of the Arcadian king seems plausible to him (ἐμέ γ' ὁ λόγος οὗτος πείθει) due to the myth's antiquity (ἐκ παλαιοῦ) and probability (τὸ εἰκὸς). To explain the latter, he resorts to a comparison between the time of Lycaon and his own era. He argues that back then, the pious and just would be often visited by the gods and be rewarded for their personal qualities by being elevated to divine or semi-divine status, while the sinners would be instantly punished, citing as an example Niobe, who was punished by being turned into a rock. In his own time, however, when sin and injustice had reached their peak only tyrants and despots became gods or demi-gods in the people's mind, and divine punishment was reserved for the afterlife. Strangely, despite his eagerness to believe the truthfulness of Lycaon's transformation, Pausanias rejects the legend of Damarchus as a tale spread by charlatans (6.8.2: οὔ μοι πιστὰ ἦν πέρα γε τῆς ἐν Ὀλυμπίᾳ νίκης ὁπόσα ἄλλα ἀνδρῶν ἀλαζόνων ἐστὶν εἰρημένα), arguing that neither the Arcadians nor the dedicatory inscription in Olympia recount the transformation. If the story was true, he concludes, it would have been recorded there along with his victory.[42] These references may allow for the assumption that, with some exceptions which can be justified on the grounds of personal beliefs, much of the educated elite considered werewolf tales purely fictional.

Similarly, the credibility of the story in Petronius is a perplexing issue which, however, reveals the ridicule of such supernatural tales through the tension

---

39 Gordon 2015, 40 notes that "for the educated elite, the point of recounting such stories was to illustrate the credulousness of others — for Pausanias, as a Greek, that of the Arcadians; for Pliny, as a Roman *eques*, that of 'the Greeks'". The credulity of the Greeks was proverbial even during the time of the Republic as we infer from Cic. *Flac*. 4.
40 Gordon 2015, 40–41.
41 Veenstra 2002, 142; Gordon 2015, 39–40.
42 This analysis of Pausanias' argument is greatly indebted to Veenstra 2002, 140 and Gordon 2015, 37–39.

created between the credulity of the freedmen and the possible reaction of the educated reader.[43] Niceros' fear of being mocked by *istos scholasticos* (61.4) and his subsequent comments *passim* concerning the veracity of his narrative are indicative of these two different attitudes.[44] The truthfulness of the werewolf tale is asserted first by Niceros himself, who states that he is not joking and that he would not lie about his experience even for a great sum of money (62.6: *nolite me iocari putare; ut mentiar, nullius patrimonium tanti facio*).[45] Given that freedmen based their social status on their fortune and not on their ancestry, the claim is quite compelling for his audience, which mostly consists of members of this social class.[46] Finally, when he concludes the story, Niceros utters a conditional self-imprecation asking to suffer the wrath of the audience's *genii* if he is lying (62.14: *ego si mentior, genios vestros iratos habeam*). Even though swearing to one's own honesty is a common rhetorical trope to avoid objections from the audience,[47] the latter's social status, in this case being freedmen and low-class individuals, allows the assumption that Niceros would not have expected any negative reactions. Indeed, the reaction of his audience (63.1: *attonitis admiratione universis*) and Trimalchio's comments immediately after the end of the werewolf tale (63.1–2: *Salvo [...] tuo sermone [...] si qua fides est, ut mihi pili inhorruerunt, quia scio Niceronem nihil nugarum narrare: immo certus est et minime linguosus*) prove that the other freedmen considered the account truthful.[48] Thus, the comments are meant to enhance the story's realism in the eyes of the credulous freedmen, who would not hesitate to believe such wildly outlandish tales.

These same comments, however, have a different impact on the educated reader. What draws the attention of the naïve, intranarrative audience and aims at convincing them about the story's veracity, simultaneously induces suspicion in Petronius' readers as it explicitly opens the possibility that the story is an outrageous

---

43 Bronzini 1988, 156: "La separazione tra mitico e reale non era unanimemente ammessa, per cui il racconto di Nicerote era o appariva 'favola' per le persone colte, mentre per il narratore e per il suo pubblico era un pezzo di storia di vita, vero o verosimile, da immaginario contadino".
44 Boyce 1991, 85 claims that the phrase reveals Niceros' own sense of inferiority, which is rooted in his freedman status. See also Plaza 2000, 147 whose distinction between satirical and theatrical laughter, *ridere* and *deridere* (61.4), reflects exactly these two attitudes.
45 Bronzini 1988, 168 claims that since the connection between urination and transformation is not explicitly drawn, Niceros necessarily makes this comment to enhance the credibility of the story.
46 Schmeling and Setaioli 2011, 257. On the power and status of the freedmen relating to their wealth, see Mouritsen 2011, 109–119.
47 Schmeling and Setaioli 2011, 259.
48 Bronzini 1988, 174; Conte 1996, 176; Schmeling and Setaioli 2011, 260.

lie.⁴⁹ The probability of a negative reaction increases dramatically since the very same additions which enhance the magical character of the story also recall the description of the mental disease of lycanthropy:⁵⁰

οἱ τῇ λεγομένῃ κυνανθρωπίᾳ ἤτοι λυκανθρωπίᾳ νόσῳ κατεχόμενοι κατὰ τὸν Φευρουάριον μῆνα νυκτὸς ἐξίασι τὰ πάντα μιμούμενοι λύκους ἢ κύνας καὶ μέχρις ἡμέρας περὶ τὰ μνήματα μάλιστα διατρίβουσι.⁵¹

Those afflicted by the so-called cynanthropy, that is lycanthropy, go out at night during February imitating, in all aspects, wolves or dogs, and they spend their time especially in cemeteries, until dawn.

The onset of the symptoms occurs at night, which is the time when the soldier and Niceros happen to roam in the graveyard. They subside at dawn, exactly before Niceros goes back to the place where the clothes were left, only to find out that they are gone. The cemetery as the place of the metamorphosis is also significant because people suffering from lycanthropy are often found there.⁵² Finally, the soldier's urination in public space is an action that dogs usually perform, and thus it can be linked to a patient's behavior imitating a canine.⁵³ These similarities offer a stronger anchor for the educated reader to question the veracity of the werewolf tale by providing a rational, and more specifically medical explanation for its core elements. In other words, what Niceros' audience considers a truthful account of supernatural transformation, Petronius' reader views it as a superstitious belief imposed upon the freedmen due to their credulity and lack of medical knowledge.

---

49 Bronzini 1988, 174 recognizes the ambiguous function.
50 The extant medical works which describe the onset of the disease, its symptoms, and possible cures are dated to late antiquity and the early Byzantine times. However, this does not mean that lycanthropy was unknown to earlier physicians. According to the *Suda* (μ 205), Marcellus of Side, the doctor who was born at the end of the first century CE and flourished under the emperors Hadrian and Antonius Pius, had composed a didactic epic on lycanthropy. Although the poem does not survive, a prose form of his account was included in the entries of medical encyclopedias on this disease, and the physician Aëtius (6.11) explicitly attributes the information he provides to Marcellus (Περὶ λυκανθρωπίας ἤτοι κυνανθρωπίας Μαρκέλλου). It is safe to assume that, even if lycanthropy and its symptoms were not medically described until some decades after Nero's reign, they at least would have been known through practical observation.
51 The text is from *CMG* VIII.2, 151 Olivieri.
52 Gordon 2015, 46 for the cemetery as a novel setting of the Petronian tale which recalls medical descriptions of lycanthropy, specifically, Marcellus of Side.
53 Gordon 2015, 59 n. 137.

3.2 Popular horror stories: the witches of Trimalchio

Trimalchio embarks on narrating a personal recollection from his youth. The incident, which involves the snatching of a corpse by two witches as well as the sudden, unexplained death of an otherwise healthy Cappadocian slave after encountering them, is also meant to entertain Trimalchio's guests:

> Cum ergo illum mater misella plangeret et nostrum plures in tristimonio essemus, subito strigae stridere coeperunt; putares canem leporem persequi. Habebamus tunc hominem Cappadocem, longum, valde audaculum et qui valebat: poterat bovem iratum tollere. Hic audacter stricto gladio extra ostium procucurrit, involuta sinistra manu curiose, et mulierem tamquam hoc loco —salvum sit, quod tango—mediam traiecit. Audimus gemitum, et—plane non mentiar—ipsas non vidimus. Baro autem noster introversus se proiecit in lectum, et corpus totum lividum habebat quasi flagellis caesus, quia scilicet illum tetigerat mala manus. Nos cluso ostio redimus iterum ad officium, sed dum mater amplexaret corpus filii sui, tangit et videt manuciolum de stramentis factum. Non cor habebat, non intestina, non quicquam: scilicet iam puerum strigae involaverant et supposuerant stramenticium vavatonem. Rogo vos, oportet credatis, sunt mulieres plussciae, sunt nocturnae, et quod sursum est, deorsum faciunt. Ceterum baro ille longus post hoc factum numquam coloris sui fuit, immo post paucos dies phreneticus periit.

> So, when his wretched mother was lamenting him, and many of us were in sorrow, the witches suddenly began: you would think that a dog was chasing a hare. We had a Cappadocian lad, a tall fellow, certainly a little bold, who was also strong: he could raise an angry ox into the air. He boldly run outside with his sword drawn out, having covered his left arm with care, and pierced the woman amidst her body, just right here — may this part of my body remain safe. We heard a cry of pain and — obviously I am not lying — we did not catch a glimpse of the witches. Our muttonhead though, came back inside and fell ill on the bed, and he had a bluish body, as if he was beaten with a whip, because the evil hand had evidently touched him. After the door was shut, we returned to our posts, but as soon as the mother embraced her son's body, she touched it and realized that it was a small bundle made of straw. It did not have a heart, or intestines, or anything: evidently, the witches had already snatched the boy and replaced it with a doll of straw. I beg you, you must believe me, wise women exist, also witches that can turn the world upside-down. As for the rest, that tall muttonhead never regained his color after this incident; on the contrary, few days later he died in delirium.

The passage is another variation of the popular tale about the metamorphic witch.[54] Even though the ability of magicians and demon-like creatures to shape-shift had already been established in popular thought and literature before Petronius' time (e.g. Lamia, Ovid's Dipsas, and Propertius' Acanthis), the idea of the transformation

---

[54] Bronzini 1988, 174–175 and Ogden 2021, 30 aptly pair Trimalchio's story with the preceding werewolf tale. Admittingly, the term *versipellis*, which is used for the werewolf in 62 was used broadly for shapeshifters (Bronzini 1988, 175; Ogden 2021, 5–7).

into a screech-owl was probably developed in the first century CE.[55] In both Republican and Augustan literature, *strix* is consistently used to denote only the ominous bird.[56] The connection with the shape-shifting witch first occurs in the *Fasti*, where Ovid expresses the possibility of the *strix* being in fact an old hag who assumed this form by means of incantation (6.141–142: *sive igitur nascuntur aves, seu carmine fiunt | neniaque in volucres Marsa figurat anus*).[57] Even if we assume that the idea of a woman being able to transform into a screech-owl had been circulating for a while among the common people, it is Ovid's literary attestation that solidifies it, creating a universal model for subsequent authors.[58] Petronius confirms the assumption of Ovid by creating a story about the shapeshifting witch, and by adopting a distinctive linguistic term for her description (*striga*).[59]

Petronius' *strigae* bear many of the bird's qualities, such as its characteristic shriek (*stridere*), its appearance during the night (*nocturnas*), and a preference to prey on children (*puerum*).[60] But their portrayal is further embroidered with popular stereotypes about witches: they are wise (*plussciae*) and have the power to upset the natural order (*quod sursum est, deorsum faciunt*), like Seneca's Medea, and

---

[55] Constantini 2016, 6. On shapeshifters in Roman literature and popular thought see Ogden 2021, 28–41. On stories about human-*strix* transformation see also Scobie 1978, 76–80.

[56] See, for example, Plaut. *Pseud.* 820; Tib. 1.5.52; Ov. *Met.* 7.269; Prop. 3.6.29, 4.5.17. The earliest occurrence of the word *strix* in Latin is found in Plautus' *Pseudolus* in a passage where the cook disparages his rivals by claiming that they put in their dishes *striges*, which rip the intestines of those who eat their food. The vile nature of this bird is also underlined in Serenus Sammonicus' *Liber Medicinalis* 1035, in which the poet, citing Titinius, mentions that the *strix* would make a baby suckle her breast milk which was in fact poison. In the realm of witchcraft, parts of this bird were used as ingredients for magic charms and potions, such as the one Canidia prepares in Hor. *Epod.* 5.19–20 or Medea in Sen. *Med.* 733–734. As a bird of ill-omen, and a bird of Hell (Sen. *HF* 686–688; Hyg. *Fab.* 28), it figured prominently also in curses. For a detailed discussion on the nature of the *strix*, an analysis of the passages which refer to it as well as the transformation of the legend, see Oliphant 1913, 133–149 and 1914, 49–63.

[57] In *Am.* 1.8.13–14, Ovid suspects that Dipsas can change into a bird (*hanc ego nocturnas versam volitare per umbras | suspicor, et plumis corpus anile tegi*) without, however, mentioning specifically the *strix*.

[58] Ogden 2021, 29.

[59] Constantini 2016, 7–8.

[60] Oliphant 1913, 134–135 on the universal features of the *strix* legend, and 144–145 for the modifications and additions of Petronius. Their habit of preying on children and young people brings the *strigae* close to the image of popular child-killing demons such as Gello and Lamia (Ogden 2021, 32; for a detailed study on these monsters as well as the figure of the *strix* see Johnston 1995).

Lucan's Erichtho.[61] The snatching of the corpse alludes to the use of human bodies in magic, attested both in literary depictions of witchcraft (Apul. *Met.* 2.30; Luc. 6.667–669)[62] and in real spells.[63] Especially the description of the *vavato*, with which the *strigae* replace the stolen body, and which lays emphasis on the absence of the heart and intestines, alludes to the use of human organs in magic rituals, and specifically the heart of an untimely dead.[64] Finally, Petronius' elaborate description of the fate of the Cappadocian is also an addition which draws his sketching of the *striga* closer to the popular image of the witch in Rome.[65] The brave slave falls ill immediately after his encounter with the witches, and within a few days he dies of an unknown illness in delirium (*phreneticus periit*). Causing harm, either with a single touch (*mala manus*) or by means of poison and incantation was the quintessential power of witches.[66]

---

61 See also Schmeling and Setaioli 2011, 263. Stanley Spaeth 2010 examines the features of liminality and inversion in the depiction of witches to conclude that such stories reflect anxieties of men losing their active role (and subsequently their masculinity), also serving to enhance the control of proper sexual roles by means of laughter.

62 This seems to be the reason for the *anus cantatrix*'s attempt to steal the corpse which ends up with Thelyphron's mutilation in Apuleius (Apul. *Met.* 2.30). Bronzini 1988, 177 connects the stealing of the body to necrophagy.

63 See, for instance, *PGM* IV 2125–2139, 2140–2144, 2577–2578; XIII 275–285; XIXa 49.

64 *PGM* IV 2577–2578 (καρδίαν ἀώρου); IV 2646 (καρδίαν παιδὸς νέου). We are also aware of the Graeco-Roman belief that witches killed men, especially young boys, for their rituals because their livers were used as ingredients in love potions, their entrails in divination, and their bodies, just as that of any other human being, in necromancy rituals (see Dickie 2001, 133 who also notes that this was exactly the accusation that Cicero brought against Vatinius, trying to convince the audience that his opponent consulted the spirits of young boys who had been ritually sacrificed [Cic. *Vat.* 14]). This might also be the insinuation underlying the descriptions of Sextus Pompey practicing black magic (*Anth. Lat.* 402). Ogden 2021, 31 wonders if the witches have snatched the corpse and replaced it with a straw doll or if they have ripped its heart and intestines and placed straws in the body cavities; Schuster 1930, 174–176 claims that the witches have only removed the intestines, leaving the rest of the body intact.

65 Cherubini 2009, 148 shows that in Ovid's *Fasti* 6.147–150, the attack of the *striges* on a child and its results (e.g. scratches on the body, pallid color) appear similar to those suffered by the Cappadocian. See also Bronzini 1988, 178.

66 For the *mala manus* in the context of witchcraft see Cherubini 2009, 145–151; Schmeling and Setaioli 2011, 262 citing primary sources and bibliography.

3.2.1 Another story for the credulous?

Contrary to the werewolf story where the criticism of magic is somewhat playful and well-supported, in Trimalchio's tale it appears 'raw'. Since there is no point of comparison leaving an open window even for a partially rational explanation of the *strigae* story, as it is the case with Nicero's tale, the educated reader would have rejected it as outrageous solely on the grounds of its implausibility.

Before his narration Trimalchio claims (63.2) that the story is supernatural (*rem horribilem*), and the narrated events difficult to believe (*asinus in tegulis*).[67] These statements, as well as his in-advance apology (63.1: *si qua fides es*), help him respectively draw the attention of his freedmen audience and achieve the *captatio benevolentiae*.[68] Trimalchio's exclamation (63.6: *salvum sit, quod tango*) in the middle of the tale, apparently accompanied by a hand gesture, reveals his own superstitiousness but also forms a powerful combination of sound and image that imposes fear upon the other freedmen.[69] Like Niceros, Trimalchio also insists on the truthfulness of his story, giving simultaneously a warning to his guests: *Rogo vos, oportet credatis, sunt mulieres plussciae, sunt nocturnae, et quod sursum est, deorsum faciunt* (63.9). The comment concerns more the existence and powers of witches rather than the specifics of the tale. This broad statement urges Trimalchio's audience to consider real all stories involving witches, including his, implying by extension that magic is also real.

The successful impact of his words on the intranarrative audience is illustrated in 64.1: Encolpius, echoing Trimalchio's exhortation, describes how the banqueteers were astonished, but at the same time they showed no disbelief of what they just heard (*miramur nos et pariter credimus*); almost simultaneously, they perform a quick ritual to ward off the witches, which affirms not only their credulity but also their superstitiousness — they kiss the table while uttering a wish that the *strigae* stay away from them (*osculatique mensam rogamus Nocturnas ut suis se teneant, dum redimus a cena*).[70] This combination of action and speech seems to

---

[67] On the meaning of this expression and its origin see Rose 1922; Smith 1975, 175; Schmeling and Setaioli 2011, 260.
[68] Schmeling and Setaioli 2011, 260.
[69] Smith 1975, 177 considers the phrase an apotropaic formula. See also Schmeling and Setaioli 2011, 262. In any case a superstitious gesture since it reveals a belief in a magical connection between the person who touches, the one who gets touched, and anyone who repeats the same act (Cherubini 2009, 146).
[70] Smith 1975, 178; Bronzini 1988, 178; Schmeling and Setaioli 2011, 264.

comprise a domestic ritual, which took place regularly at banquets.[71] According to *Serv. Dan.* (ad Verg. *Aen.* 1.730), there was a time of repose between the first two courses of a dinner, followed by a libation to the hearth and a boy proclaiming *Dii propitii*:

> apud Romanos etiam cena edita sublatisque mensis primis silentium fieri solebat, quoad ea quae de cena libata fuerant ad focum ferrentur et in ignem darentur, ac puer deos propitios nuntiasset...[72]

> Even among Romans, after the dinner was served and the first course was cleared, there used to be a time of repose, until the offerings from the dinner were brought to the hearth and burned, and a boy had proclaimed the gods propitious...

In the *Satyrica*, the ritual occurs after the banqueteers finished the main course, and before the servants bring out the *secundae mensae* in 68–69.[73] Due to the ubiquity and legitimacy of table rituals, whose function was based on the assimilation of the table with altars and its role as the *ara* of the *Lares* and *Genii*, most Romans would regard the kissing of the table as a religious rather than a magical rite.[74] However, the performance of the ritual for the purpose of warding off a possible attack by witches rebrands the ritual in the eyes of the educated reader as magical since it reflects a belief in the power of ritual-like actions and special artifacts to protect against evil spirits, which was neither strange nor uncommon among Petronius' contemporaries.

Trimalchio's statement that the story is unbelievable (63.1: *asinus in tegulis*), and his subsequent efforts to convince the intranarrative audience produce the opposite result for the educated reader. The initial claim introduces the element of suspicion regarding the veracity of the tale that follows, functioning similarly to Niceros' comments in the werewolf tale. Trimalchio's subsequent exhortations insisting on the truthfulness of the events only assist in enhancing the reader's negative predisposition toward the *strigae* story, and by extension toward magic itself.

What furthers the criticism of magic is the superstition of the freedmen, exemplified through Trimalchio's apotropaic gesture and the table rite. The reader of Petronius cannot help but laugh at the credulity and reactions of the freedmen, who not only believe in the existence of witches and the power of magic, but also in the

---

[71] The ritual appears quite similar to the one that takes place in 60, on which see Schmeling and Setaioli 2011, 250.
[72] The text is cited from Thilo's 1881 edition.
[73] For the arrival of the *secundae mensae* in 68–69, see Schmeling and Setaioli 2011, 250.
[74] Dölger 1930, 214; See also the discussion in Schmeling and Setaioli 2011, 264.

power of words and actions to ward off evil.[75] Placing themselves in the intranarrative audience's shoes invites any rational individual to recognize the freedmen's naïveté. This realization, in turn, ignites the readers' will to conceptually dissociate themselves from such behaviors by adopting a different, critical attitude toward such tales: they question their credibility and, by extension, real-life magic.

3.3 The rituals of Proselenos and Oenothea: priestesses or witches?

In the wake of Šterbenc Erker's view of Quartilla's *nocturnas religiones* as a distorted version of low-class rituals, this section focuses on applying the idea to the rites of Proselenos and Oenothea, and further show that Petronius' depiction brings them closer to magic. I chose not to discuss the Quartilla episode because, in my view, it exhibits no strong ties to real spells. On the contrary, the rituals performed by Oenothea and her assistant, Proselenos, bear many similarities to certain spells of the *PGM* which, along with the highly sexualized character of these scenes, assimilate them with magic. This is evident throughout the narrative of the Proselenos and Oenothea episodes as it will become clear soon. However, Petronius, using specific techniques, predisposes the reader to regard these rites as magical even before their performance: he emphasizes witchcraft as the probable cause of Encolpius' impotence, while his description of Proselenos and Oenothea resembles more that of a witch rather than a priestess. By doing so he encourages the reader to anticipate a cure of *quasi*-magical nature.[76]

After he experiences the first incident of impotence, Encolpius claims that his condition is the result of witchcraft (128.2: *veneficio contactus sum*).[77] In the reader's mind, the suspicion is confirmed indirectly by Chrysis, who reveals that such maladies often occur in the area which is inhabited by women who have the power to bring the moon down (129.10: *in hac civitate, in qua mulieres etiam lunam deducunt*), a common feat of witches in literary descriptions of magic.[78] When the first spell proves unsuccessful, Proselenos reinforces Encolpius' convictions by putting

---

[75] The ridiculous and comic nature of both Niceros' and Trimalchios' tale has been asserted by Bronzini 1988, 176.
[76] McMahon 1998, 83–86 and 205 also discusses the passages (134.1–2, 10–11, and 12; 138.7) which lead the reader to expect a magical treatment.
[77] See, for instance, *DT* 85a, with McMahon 1998, 10 n. 40; there are also recipes of popular medicine whose overdose could lead to impotence (Plin. *HN* 24.58; 26.94). For magic as cause of impotence see McMahon 1998, 75–86.
[78] On 'drawing down the moon' see page 58 with notes on the same page.

forward two alternative hypotheses as probable causes for his condition which point to witchcraft: either screech-owls have consumed his energy, or he accidentally stepped on feces or on a corpse while walking at a crossroad (134.1).[79] Even Proselenos' introduction of Encolpius to Oenothea points to witchcraft and the evil eye as the cause for his impotence since she claims that the hero's condition is the result of being *malo astro natus* (134.8). The phrase explains Encolpius' malady with recourse to astrology, a form of pseudo-science which, under certain conditions, could be considered magic.[80]

Apart from these sparse statements, the description of the two women successfully associates them with the figure of the witch as it was conceived in Roman thought. Both Proselenos and Oenothea are described as *aniculae* (Proselenos: 131.2, 131.7; Oenothea: 136.13, 138.2; collectively: 138.3), thus reflecting the stereotypical view of witches as old women,[81] while the latter is also described as ugly (133.4: *deformis*).[82] Moreover, they both exhibit a sexual thirst, which matches the lust of witches in popular Roman thought and literature:[83] Proselenos rubs Encolpius' erected phallus under the guise of showing both him and Chrysis that she cured his impotence — this would be obvious by sight, without need to touch him, which proves that Proselenos aims also at her own sexual pleasure, no matter how brief or of what sort; Oenothea appears more eager for sexual gratification by behaving

---

[79] Schmeling and Setaioli 2011, 518.
[80] McMahon 1998, 84. Astrology was not considered magic by itself since it was widely accepted as a legitimate art and practiced by reputable Romans, such as Lucius Tarutius Firmanus, Marcus Manilius, and Nigidius Figulus. However, a theoretical link was established between these two arts at least since the time of Pliny, who considers astrology, along with medicine, one of the source-disciplines of magic (*HN* 30.2). This connection was not only theoretical, but also practical, in cases where astrology was used illegally (e.g. to predict an emperor's death [Tac. *Ann.* 12.52.3 on the exile of Furius Scribonianus]). Therefore, astrology was not assimilated with magic, unless it was practiced by people who were reputedly magicians or witches or if it was associated with other rituals of witchcraft (for example, astral divination is recounted among the powers of witches in Philostr. *VA* 7.39, and in the story of Thessalus of Thralles in *De uirtutibus herbarum* 1–28 we read that magical potions are more effective if the herbs are collected when the planets are appropriately aligned); for the importance of the social position of the astrologer in characterizing their practice as magic, see Edmonds 2019, 262–263. For a general overview of astrology in Rome see Barton 1994, 32–63 and Edmonds 2019, 236–268; for astrology as a form of magical divination see Garosi 1976, 76; Edmonds 2019, 263–264.
[81] Rini 1929, 84. For the meanings and connotations of *anus/anicula* in Latin, including the links to magic see Schmeling and Setaioli 2011, 23.
[82] On ugliness and old age as a feature of witches in Roman literature see Stanley Spaeth 2014, 46–47. On similarities between Proselenos and Oenothea with the figure of procuress see Sullivan 1968a, 123–124.
[83] Stratton 2014, 162–163.

like a 'dominatrix' as she first penetrates Encolpius with a leather dildo and then beats him, supposedly as part of the healing ritual. The inversion of roles in sexual activities — Oenothea becomes the active partner and our hero the passive one — is another example of the reversal of nature, which was commonly attributed to witches.[84]

In the case of Oenothea, her sketching as a witch is supported further by the self-description of her powers.[85] She claims that she is the only one who can cure Encolpius' impotence, which she admits is a trivial task compared to what she is capable of. Her magical powers are detailed in the hexametric poem in 134.12:

> quicquid in orbe vides, paret mihi. florida tellus,
> cum volo, siccatis arescit languida sucis,
> cum volo, fundit opes, scopulique atque horrida saxa
> Niliacas iaculantur aquas. mihi pontus inertes
> submittit fluctus, zephyrique tacentia ponunt   5
> ante meos sua flabra pedes. mihi flumina parent
> Hyrcanaeque tigres et iussi stare dracones.
> quid leviora loquor? lunae descendit imago
> carminibus deducta meis, trepidusque furentes
> flectere Phoebus equos revoluto cogitur orbe.   10
> [tantum dicta valent. taurorum flamma quiescit
> virgineis extincta sacris, Phoebeia Circe
> carminibus magicis socios mutavit Ulixis,
> Proteus esse solet quicquid libet. his ego callens
> artibus Idaeos frutices in gurgite sistam   15
> et rursus fluvios in summo vertice ponam.]

Whatever you see in the world, obeys me. The blooming earth,
whenever I want, becomes sluggish and dry, with its juices exhausted,
whenever I desire, pours forth its treasures, and the crags and prickly rocks
spring forth the waters of the Nile. For me the sea restrains its sluggish
waves, and the winds lay their silent
blasts at my feet. The rivers and the Hyrcanian
tigers obey me, and I ordered the snakes to stand still.
Why talk about trivia things? The image of the moon descends,
drawn down by my spells, and the trepid Sun
is forced to turn around his raging horses, revolving his orb.

---

[84] Stanley Spaeth 2014, 45; Stanley Spaeth 2010, 239–244 on witches and the different manifestations of the inversion motif.
[85] Rini 1929, 84. Setaioli 2011, 287. For the purpose of predisposing the reader, it does not really matter whether these claims are made by Oenothea or are Encolpius' (as a narrator) expectations about the powers of a witch (Setaioli, 2011, 286–287).

> Magical words[86] have such great power. The flame of the bulls subsides,
> put out by the virgin's rituals; the daughter of the Sun, Circe,
> transformed the comrades of Odysseus with her magical songs;
> Proteus is used to turning into whatever he likes. I, skillful
> in these arts, will plant Idaean bushes in the sea,
> and set the rivers back to the highest peak.

Catalogues of a witch's powers are a *locus communis* in narratives of magic, and Oenothea's description has many similarities with such passages, most notably Verg. *Aen.* 4.487–491.[87] The poem refers to some of the most generic abilities attributed to witches, including control over nature and its elements (1–6), charming of animals, specifically tigers and snakes (7), drawing down the moon (8–9), manipulating planetary movement (9–10), and upsetting the natural order (14–16).[88] To further showcase her powers, Oenothea indirectly compares them with those of Medea and Circe (12–13), the archetypal witches of ancient literature, as well as with Proteus' shape-shifting skills (14). Especially her reference to the famous 'Thessalian trick' sketches her as a witch as it alludes both to Chrysis' statement (129.10: *in hac civitate, in qua mulieres etiam lunam deducunt*) and to several intertextual parallels.[89]

The characters' comments as well as the external and behavioral characteristics of Proselenos and Oenothea create an appropriate narrative environment for Petronius to present priapic rites as magic. At the same time, when pieced together, these features lead the reader to assimilate the two priestesses with witches and, along with the rituals' structure and specific details, impose upon the reader the view of the rites as magical.

3.3.1 Priapic rituals and magic: Proselenos

The first who attempts to treat Encolpius' impotence is Proselenos. Since the hero believes that his condition is the result of witchcraft (128.2: *veneficio contactus sum*) what could work better than a magical treatment, and especially one that aims at counteracting the magic that caused it? While bearing similarities with *quasi-*

---

[86] For the interpretation of *dicta* as 'incantations' see Setaioli 2011, 292.
[87] Setaioli 2011, 291–292; Schmeling and Setaioli 2011, 520 note the intertextual connection with the list of Dipsas' powers in Ov. *Am.* 1.8; see also Walsh 1974, 42. The excerpt also bears close resemblance with *PGM* XXXIV 1–24, which Dodds 1952, 133–137 considers a possible novel fragment.
[88] Setaioli 2011, 294–298 breaks the poem down to sections according to the 'unaturalness' of the events, showing also how they are listed in an ascending order.
[89] On the 'Thessalian trick' see pages 57–58 with notes.

magical recipes of popular medicine which promised to cure impotence or increase erection,[90] the ritual described in the *Satyrica* appears to be Petronius' own invention (131.4–7):[91]

> illa de sinu licium protulit varii coloris filis intortum cervicemque vinxit meam. mox turbatum sputo pulverem medio sustulit digito frontemque repugnantis signavit … hoc peracto carmine ter me iussit expuere terque lapillos conicere in sinum, quos ipsa praecantatos purpura involverat, admotisque manibus temptare coepit inguinum vires. dicto citius nervi paruerunt imperio manusque aniculae ingenti motu repleverunt. at illa gaudio exultans "vides" inquit "Chrysis mea, vides, quod aliis leporem excitavi?"

> She produced from her bosom a string of various colors with twisted threads and bound my neck. Then, she raised with her middle finger dirt mixed with saliva and marked my forehead, though I felt disgusted … after the incantation ended, she ordered me to spit thrice and drop three rocks in my bosom which, having chanted incantations on them, she had wrapped with a purple rag, and started testing the powers of my phallus. Faster than said, the sinews complied with her orders, and the hands of the little old lady were full of great movement. But she, jumping in joy, said: "do you see, my Chrysis, what hare I flushed out of its hole for others?"

Unfortunately, the fragmentary condition of the text poses a challenge to our full understanding of the scene. It is quite probable, however, that the ritual included a magical utterance, and thus the phrase *hoc peracto carmine* refers to some lost verses which would have aligned it with magic rites.[92] If this is the case, the ritual conforms to the two-tiered structure of the *PGM* consisting of *logos* and *praxis*.[93]

Structurally the scene can be divided into two parts: the preparatory ritual, and the ritual proper, which also includes the lost utterance.[94] During the first phase, Proselenos produces from her bosom a thread made of multi-colored sewing fibers, and binds it around the neck of Encolpius, an action recalling Aphrodite's removal of her *kestos himas* (Hom. *Il.* 14.214–215). The thread functions as magical material (*ousia*) necessary for the effectiveness of sympathetic magic, and Schmeling assumes that it must have had some connection to Circe.[95] Without doubt, it is meant

---

90 Schmeling and Setaioli 2011, 501 mention *PGM* VII 182–185. See also *PDM* lxi 58–62 and the recipes in Plin. *HN* 20.35 and 21.162.
91 Panayotakis 1995, 172–173.
92 Schmeling and Setaioli 2011, 500.
93 For this general observation on the structure of the spells in the *PGM*, see page 62, and n. 75.
94 Setaioli 2000, 159 divides the ritual in three parts.
95 Schmeling and Setaioli 2011, 499; since Encolpius and Circe cannot be bound to each other by marriage or the power of true love, Proselenos ties them with magical threads (which reminds us of Lucan's reference to the *iunx* in 6.458–460).

to tie Encolpius to his mistress, but since this is primarily a healing spell and the protagonist alleges that his impotence was inflicted by means of magic, the thread might also serve as an amulet to counteract the effects of a negative spell that might have caused the malady.[96] The use of amulets for the purpose of healing is well-attested in recipes of popular medicine (Plin. *HN* 28.45, 48, 91, 95, 211, 217; 32.52) and in the *PGM* (e.g. VII 260–271, which purports to stop the ascent of the uterus).[97]

The preparation continues with Proselenos spitting on the ground to form mud and then, using her middle finger, she marks Encolpius' forehead with it. Even though the mixing of saliva and mud to create a magical ointment is attested only in Petronius' *Satyrica* and in the *New Testament* (Jhn. 9.6), the beneficial properties of human saliva were well-known in antiquity as we infer from Pliny's discussion of its medical applications (e.g. *HN* 28.35–39).[98] However, there are uses which can be better described as superstitions rather than medical treatments (*HN* 28.38):

> inter amuleta est editae quemque urinae inspuere, similiter in calciamentum dextri pedis, priusquam induatur, item cum quis transeat locum, in quo aliquod periculum adierit.[99]

> It functions as an apotropaic act for a person to spit on their urine after relieving themselves and, likewise, on the right foot's shoe before wearing it, and while one crosses a place in which they have incurred some danger.

Pliny himself draws a distinction between the different uses of saliva, categorizing these apotropaic rituals against the Evil Eye as *amuleta*.

Likewise, the middle finger (*digitus medius*, *infamis* or *impudicus*) as a symbolic representation of the *membrum virile* also figured prominently in apotropaic acts as we surmise from Juvenal 10.52–53, the *Carmina Priapea* 56.1–2, and Martial

---

96 Weinreich 1909, 97 views the process as a healing ritual, while Panayotakis 1995, 173 wonders if it is destined to fail. Amulets (in Greek *periamma* or *periapton*, literally translating into "object tied around") in their simplest form consisted of a bunch of fibers twisted together. More elaborate talismans consisted of inscribed tablets, stones or voodoo dolls which were tied around various body parts, most notably the neck, with an enchanted thread. The practice is attested in both the text of the *PGM* (I 67–70; I 144–148; IV 1075–1085; VII 206–207) and in literature (Plin. *HN* 28.48; Verg. *Ecl.* 8.73–74; Ov. *Fast.* 2.575). For an overview of the different forms and functions of amulets, see Ogden 2002b, 261–274; Faraone 2018; Edmonds 2019, 119–148.

97 According to the instructions, the spell caster needs to engrave the magic formula on a tin leaf, and then hang it around their neck with a thread made of fibers of seven different colors.

98 For the similarities between the ritual of Proselenos and the specific *locus* in the *New Testament*, see Setaioli 2000, 159–172.

99 The text is cited from Pliny's 1963 Loeb edition (Rackham et al.).

2.28.1–2.[100] The closest parallel to Proselenos' ritual is found in Persius' *Satire* 2, in which the poet criticizes various aspects of the religious life of his contemporaries, most notably their *superstitio*.[101] In lines 31–34 he mocks older women who resort to apotropaic acts to protect their grandchildren, and his description bears some similarity with the ritual in Petronius: *Ecce avia aut metuens divum matertera cunis | exemit puerum, frontemque atque uda labella | infami digito et lustralibus ante salivis | expiat* ("Look, a grandmother or an aunt fearing the gods lifts the boy from the cradle and purifies his forehead and wet lips with the infamous finger and lustral saliva").[102] These intertextual parallels underscore the heavily apotropaic character of Proselenos' preparatory actions which, along with Encolpius certainty that he was bewitched, indicate that the first phase should be viewed as an effort to counteract the negative effects (impotence) of some type of magic that befell Encolpius.

The preparations were followed by a now-lost utterance (131.5: *hoc peracto carmine*) which, along with subsequent actions, comprise the second phase. Proselenos instructs Encolpius to spit thrice and throw three enchanted stones wrapped in purple clothing on his lap. According to the *scholia* on Theocritus, the action of spitting on an object or person for the purpose of protecting them from the Evil Eye was often accompanied by an incantation, thus suggesting a possible connection between the rites of Proselenos and real ones.[103] However, since an apotropaic use of saliva has been employed already by Proselenos, it is only reasonable to assume that Encolpius' spitting has a healing function, similar to that found in Hipponax fr. 78 W, where the person suffering from impotence must redden the head of his phallus with mulberry juice and then spit on it thrice.[104] In fact, the Petronius excerpt does not clearly state that Encolpius spat on his bosom, thus leaving open the possibility that he spits on his phallus.

---

[100] The power of phallus to avert the Evil Eye is well-documented through texts and archaeological findings. For a brief discussion on primary sources see Francese 2007, 194–195; Bernand 1991, 102 claims that the act of spitting and the *membrum virile* are employed together in a Roman mosaic portraying a phallus ejaculating into a disembodied eye (the Evil Eye). For a detailed discussion on the phallus and its connection to the Evil Eye, see Johns 1982, 61–76, and Clarke 2003, 94–113.
[101] Setaioli 2000, 161; Schmeling and Setaioli 2011, 500.
[102] The text is from Ramsay's 1957 edition.
[103] Schol. in Theocr. 7.127a and b; In *Id.* 6.39–40 and 7.126–127 Theocritus refers to spitting as a means to avert bad luck and connects it to rituals performed by an old woman (γραία). The apotropaic powers of saliva are further affirmed by Pliny's account of the popular superstition involving an infant's nurse spitting three times on the child if a stranger arrives or a sleeping infant is looked upon (*HN* 28.39).
[104] A similarity already noted in West 1974, 142–143.

What the text states explicitly is that he puts three enchanted pebbles wrapped in a purple rag on his breast. Even though no exact parallel exists elsewhere, several details connect Encolpius' action to magic: employing the number 'three' (thrice spitting, three pebbles), which was considered magical;[105] the use of stones whose powers were magically enhanced;[106] their wrapping in a piece of purple clothing.[107] The power of stones to heal various medical conditions, including impotence, has been well-documented in ancient literature, and was attributed to the nature of the stone[108] or to some mythological connection,[109] and they often became more potent and functional with the engraving of signs, words, and images upon them.[110] Encolpius recognition that the stones were already enchanted (131.5: *praecantatos*) indicates that these were not simple pebbles, but some type of gemstones. Their wrapping in a piece of clothing was meant to facilitate their amuletic function and effectuate their healing purpose.[111] If the aim of the first phase was to dispel the witchcraft, the second phase aimed at curing its effects (impotence). It thus becomes evident that the ritual in 131.4–5 should be viewed as an amalgam of literary tradition and magical *realia* of the first century CE.

The scene ends with the priestess testing Encolpius' *membrum virile* through prolonged touching (131.5: *temptare coepit*). Even though it is quite tempting to think of Proselenos' action as alluding to the rubbing of the penis found in magical recipes against impotence such as *PGM* VII 184–185 (Στ[ύ]ειν, ὅτε θέλεις· πέπερι μετὰ μέλιτος τρίψας χρῖέ σου τὸ πρᾶγμα) as well as *PDM* lxi 58–62, the act seems to be more of an aftermath of the ritual.[112] It allows Proselenos to take advantage of Encolpius sexually under the guise of checking the effectiveness of the spell, thus connecting it to the highly sexualized ritual of the priapic priestess Quartilla, and foreshadowing the nature of Oenothea's healing rite.

---

105 For the significance of number "three" in magic, see Lease 1919, and Laroche 1995, 570; for this connection as it appears in primary sources see Tavenner 1916, 117–143.
106 For the healing properties of stones and their use in magic see McMahon 1998, 156–173.
107 Could this action have been modelled after specific instructions such as those in *PGM* XCVII 1–6? for the purple color and its relation to magic see Weinreich 1909, 97–99.
108 McMahon 1998, 156.
109 McMahon 1998, 163.
110 McMahon 1998, 157.
111 McMahon 156–157.
112 McMahon 1998, 203 views the action as "manual stimulation" which underscores Encolpius' passive role in the ritual, further connecting the treatment of Proselenos with the Quartilla episode.

3.3.2 Priapic rituals and magic: Oenothea

The spell proves only temporarily successful, and Encolpius' illness recurs during his sexual encounter with Circe, leading Proselenos to openly wonder what evil has befallen him (134.1: *quae striges comederunt nervos tuos, aut quod purgamentum [in] nocte calcasti in trivio aut cadaver?*). The rhetorical question, although hinting at the failure of her own spell, does not cast any doubt on the power of magic intranarratively. On the contrary, it reinforces its value by implying that Encolpius is bound by greater charms, which need to be dealt with by a witch more powerful than herself. For this reason, she leads the protagonist into Oenothea's room, where the main priestess attempts a second, more invasive 'treatment' (138.1–2):

> profert Oenothea scorteum fascinum, quod ut oleo et minuto pipere atque urticae trito circumdedit semine, paulatim coepit inserere ano meo ...
> hoc crudelissima anus spargit subinde umore femina mea *
> nasturcii sucum cum habrotono miscet perfusisque inguinibus meis viridis urticae fascem comprehendit omniaque infra umbilicum coepit lenta manu caedere *
>
> Oenothea brought out a phallus made of leather, which she then anointed with oil and crushed pepper as well as ground seeds of nettle; little by little, she started pushing it up my anus ...
> The most cruel of old hags then sprinkled my loin with this juice
> She combined the sap of cress with southern-wood, and with my genitals having been drenched with it, she grasped a branch of fresh nettle, and started hitting me, with a gentle move of her hands, everywhere below my navel.

Again, the fragmentary condition of the text poses an obstacle for the full understanding of the scene. The excerpt is Petronius' unique creation, combining elements found in earlier literature, and real spells. Oenothea first manufactures a magical ointment consisting of oil, ground pepper, and nettle seeds, with which she first covers the leather dildo and then Encolpius' thighs. That these materials are combined and not applied separately on the *fascinum* is clear, as Encolpius seems to refer to them collectively (138.2: *hoc...spargit...umore femina mea*), and from real magic recipes, such as *PDM* xiv 1155–1162 ("hawk's dung; salt, reed, bele plant. Pound together. Anoint your phallus with it..."), *PDM* lxi 58–62 (spell for erection: "Woad plant [or corn flag?] grows in the oasis in abundance; it's both female and [male]. Boil these in a pot and grind them up [in wine with] pepper; smear it on [your] genitals"),[113] as well as *PGM* VII 184–185 (Στ[ύ]ειν, ὅτε θέλεις· πέπερι μετὰ

---

[113] Translations of the papyri are from Betz 1986.

μέλιτος τρίψας χρῖέ σου τὸ πρᾶγμα).[114] Each of these plant-based substances have natural qualities that appear appropriate for the healing of impotence.[115] She then dips the hero's genitals in a liquid made out of cress juice and southern wood, and continues with the abuse of Encolpius' *membrum virile* which recalls the treatment process in Hipponax 92W (and less the one which appears in Hipponax fr. 78W).[116]

3.3.3 Magic: Another failure

Despite Proselenos' trust in Oenothea's powers, and the latter's boastful self-description (134.12), the second ritual also fails as we infer from the hero fleeing the priapic temple while bleeding — apparently, he was sexually and physically abused under the guise of treatment — chased by the two women (138.3–4). Both failures are stunning, even when compared to the failed necromancy in Lucan, since Erichtho was at least able to reanimate the corpse and force it to speak, albeit with difficulty (Luc. 6.719–729). In contrast, Petronius' witches could not even successfully perform a healing spell, which is an admittedly easier task compared to necromancy, and one for which there were multiple conventional alternatives that the reader would know them to be effective.

The failure of Oenothea's ritual becomes even more remarkable in the face of her self-praise. In retrospect, the poem in 134.12 is vital for the realization of the parody of the motif of magic as it aligns the figure of Oenothea with literary witches, recalling similar, both generally and specifically, catalogues of the witches' powers:[117] Oenothea boasts that she can make Nile's water spring forth from rocks (vv. 3–4: *scopulique atque horrida saxa | Niliacas iaculantur aquas*), whereas the spells of Thessalian witches hinder the flooding of the Nile (Luc. 6.474: *Nilum non extulit aestas*); the sea calms its waves at her chant, and the winds subside (vv. 4–6: *pontus inertes | submittit fluctus, zephyrique tacentia ponunt | ante meos sua flabra pedes*), while Medea makes the waves resound and the sea swell, though the winds are silent (Sen. *Med.* 765–766: *sonuere fluctus, tumuit insanum mare | tacente vento*), just as Thessalian witches do (Luc. 6.469–470: *ventis cessantibus aequor | intumuit*); Oenothea's magic can dry the blooming earth (vv. 1–2: *florida tellus…arescit*) just as

---

114 Schmeling and Setaioli 2011, 535.
115 McMahon 1998, 208 with notes, citing also primary sources.
116 The similarity between Oenothea's ritual and Hipponax fr. 92 W has been noted in West 1974, 144–145.
117 Setaioli 2011, 298–299 for intertextual parallels. Connors 1998, 43 claims that Petronius assigns Circean magic to Oenothea in the context of fragmenting and re-combining epic with parodic intent.

Medea stuns it with her spell (Sen. *Med.* 760: *aestiva tellus horruit cantu meo*); Petronius' witch exercises control over Hyrcanian tigers and serpents (vv. 6–7: *parent | Hyrcanaeque tigres et iussi stare dracones*), thus recalling Lucan's description of Thessalian sorceresses, who charm wild tigers, lions (Luc. 6.487–488: *has avidae tigres et nobilis ira leonum | ore fovent blando*) and snakes (Luc. 6.488–489: *gelidos his explicat orbes | inque pruinoso coluber distenditur arvo*), as well as Medea's luring of snakes (Sen. *Med.* 705: *Postquam evocavit omne serpentum genus*); she can reverse the rivers' flow (v. 16: *et rursus fluvios in summon vertice ponam*), which is one of the *adynata* listed by Medea (Sen. *Med.* 762: *violenta Phasis vertit in fontem vada*) and occurs also in Lucan's catalogue (Luc. 6.473–474: *amnisque cucurrit | non qua pronus erat*); the Sun reverses its course at Oenothea's spell (vv. 9–10: *trepidusque furentes | flectere Phoebus equos revoluto cogitur orbe*), just as he submits to Medea (Sen. *Med.* 768: *die relicto Phoebus in medio stetit*); finally, like all witches, including Medea (Sen. *Med.* 770: *adesse sacris tempus est, Phoebe, tuis*) and her Thessalian counterparts (Luc. 6.505–506: *et patitur tantos cantu depressa labores | donec suppositas propior despumet in herbas* [sc. Phoebe]), Oenothea can draw the moon down (vv. 8–9: *lunae descendit imago | carminibus deducta meis*). Not only do these similarities sketch Oenothea as a witch, but they specifically parallel her to Medea, especially in light of the reference to the famous myth that the Colchian maiden rendered the bull's breath harmless for Jason by means of magic (vv. 11–12). However, since Oenothea boasts that her powers surpass those of Medea as well as the feats of Circe and Proteus (vv. 13–16), when the second healing ritual fails, the reader cannot help but laugh at these absurd and over-exaggerated claims. Thus, the literary motif of the *adynata*, which enhanced both Erichtho's and Medea's powers, and which was used to stir fear in the reader in a sinister and gloomy atmosphere, transforms into a source of laughter and ridicule in the *Satyrica*.

3.3.4 Magic as charlatanry

In the end, magic proves to be mere charlatanry, confirming the reader's expectation which Petronius had built gradually through various techniques.[118] Oenothea, an ugly old hag, promises to cure Encolpius on the condition that he spends the night with her (134.11). The requirement reveals her lust which ties well with the

---

[118] The presentation of magic as charlatanry is one of the forms of criticism against the practice in the Graeco-Roman world as Gordon 1987b, 65–66 has argued. Walsh 1970, 178 claims that, in the Quartilla episode, Petronius mocks religious characters of questionable value. The Oenothea episode as a mockery of 'religious charlatans' has been discussed in Panayotakis 2015, 36–45.

stereotypical image of the witch, but most importantly with the other female characters of the novel, specifically Quartilla and Proselenos. Thus, the reader is led to suspect correctly that what they are about to witness will not be any different from the rituals of Quartilla and Proselenos in terms of character and effectiveness.[119]

This suspicion becomes a certainty even before Oenothea's main rite. In 135.3–5 the reader sees the priestess/witch performing several actions: she places a table on the altar, and on top of it some burning charcoal; she then repairs a broken cup with black pitch, and fixes the nail that held the cup on the wall; finally, she brings out of her kettle a bag filled with an old pig's cheek and beans, instructing Encolpius to shell them.[120] The hero probably understands the task to be part of the ritual as the verb *iussit*, which recalls Proselenos' command in 131.5, indicates and proceeds to complete it, but his slowness angers Oenothea, who cleans the beans with her teeth. Encolpius obedience implies that he perceives all these actions as an early part of the healing ritual, misguided by the pretense of Oenothea and her boastful poem. For the reader, however, the same actions comprise a list of chores, an attempt to tidy up the place since Oenothea does not exhibit the expected, proper attitude toward sacred objects and materials.[121]

Even the hero has a scintillation of wit that momentarily aligns his views with those of Petronius' reader[122] when Oenothea resumes with her role-playing through the performance of a pretentious ritual in 137.10:

> infra manus meas camellam vini posuit, et cum digitos pariter extensos porris apioque lustrasset, avellanas nuces cum precatione mersit in vinum. et sive in summum redierant sive subsederant, ex hoc coniecturam ducebat. nec me fallebat inanes scilicet ac sine medulla [ventosas] nuces in summo umore consistere, graves autem et [plenas] integro fructu ad ima deferri *

> She placed below my hands a wine-goblet and, as soon as she had purified my stretched fingers altogether with scallion and parsley, she plunged some filberts in the wine while praying. And whether they had resurfaced or remained sunken, from this she made several

---

[119] Panayotakis 2015, 36–37 shows that Encolpius disregards multiple 'red flags' that would have led anyone — in fact they lead us, the reader — to see the similarities between the Quartilla and Oenothea episodes which reveal both characters as tricksters.
[120] McMahon 1998, 205 notes that the scene anticipates the invasion of magic in the episode.
[121] For Panayotakis 1995, 178 these details enhance the farcical character of the Oenothea episode. On the scene as a parody of Callimachean Hecale and Ovid's Baucis see Slater 1990, 131.
[122] And with his mature self, i.e. the narrator, who utters a poem in 137.9, which underscores the omnipotence of money (Setaioli 2011, 330 citing Beck), after he commits sacrilege against Priapus by accidentally killing the god's favorite goose, and successfully bribes Oenothea in order to spare him from punishment (137.6–7). For a full commentary on the poem, which is rightly viewed as passing a judgment on the personality of Oenothea (Slater 1990, 164) see Setaioli 2011, 329–344.

predictions. It did not slip my notice that, naturally, the empty ones and those without their kernel, full of air, remained on top, but the heavy ones and those full, with their core intact, were dragged to the bottom.

It is not clear whether these actions comprise some preparatory part of the healing ritual,[123] or an effort to cleanse Encolpius of the sacrilege. Scholars, however, rightly consider it as some type of fortune telling, and various elements throughout the text point to a specific category of spells, namely bowl divination.[124] Conforming to the structure of the *PGM* consisting of *logos* and *praxis*, the ritual begins with Oenothea purifying Encolpius' hands by rubbing them with scallions and parsley, both materials used in magic recipes.[125] She then puts some nuts in a cup filled with wine while uttering a prayer, perhaps addressing the god(s) whose presence is necessary for the success of the spell. She then proceeds with her predictions based on whether the nuts floated or sank in the cup.

Despite his naïveté, Encolpius recognizes the trick behind Oenothea's rite (the empty shells would float, and the rest would sink in the bottom of the cup), revealing momentarily the author behind the character to illustrate the skepticism with which educated people view magic. And even if the hero later hearkens to Oenothea's instructions and endures the abusive ritual,[126] the rational explanation behind the trick can only strengthen further the reader's critical attitude toward magic.

3.4 Conclusions

Realistic, yet excessive, Petronius' depictions present the reader with multiple facets of the life of the lower classes in the first century CE. Several parts of the *Satyrica*'s narrative betray a strong interest in superstition and magic, both trends in

---

[123] McMahon 1998, 207.
[124] Schmeling and Setaioli 2011, 534.
[125] The exact nature of *porrum* remains a mystery, but it was certainly a plant of the *genus Allium* (onion, shallot, scallion, leek, etc). The use of onion is attested in *PGM* IV 1340–1341, 2462–2463, 2584–2585, and 2650 as well as in IV 85, which suggests the existence of a specific ritual, in which this vegetable had a central position; finally, wine was widely used in magic as we infer from *PGM* XIII 357 (preparatory ritual), *PDM* xiv 772–804 (love potion), and xiv 917–919 (a potion to cause sleep). For the use of leek in magic rituals see the comment in Schmeling and Setaioli 2011, 534.
[126] McMahon 1998, 209: "His involvement, willing or not, in a belief system based on the efficacy of remedies drawn from the natural world and on their corresponding magical elements prompts his acknowledgement that his problem can be attributed to witchcraft". Eventually, even the hero perceives the charlatanry and flees from the hands of the two women (Slater 1990, 248).

Neronian everyday life and literature, while Petronius' parodic treatment of these topics reveals an implicit criticism of real-life beliefs. The inset narratives of the werewolf and the *strigae*, although based on oral tradition (old-time myths, legends, folktales) as well as earlier literature, exhibit a number of elements which recall certain features found in the *PGM*. Petronius' modifications to the archetypal stories enhance his tales' realism and underscore their magical aspect, simultaneously allowing the novel's educated reader to distance themselves from the intranarrative audience with regards to their respective reactions. In other words, what the freedmen consider truthful accounts of Niceros' and Trimalchio's life events, the reader rejects in disbelief as far-fetched stories ridiculing several clichés about witches and magic.

Moving from superstitious beliefs to action, Petronius sketches the healing rituals of Proselenos and Oenothea as burlesque representations of magic by connecting Encolpius' impotence with witchcraft and by incorporating stereotypes about witches in his descriptions of the two women. He further underscores the magical character of the rituals by alluding to earlier literary treatments of magic, and by emphasizing features which are also found in real spells. Individual details, which underline the magical aspect of Proselenos' and Oenothea's rites, provide an anchor with reality, but the element of ridicule and their highly sexualized character, as well as their eventual failure, provoke the reader's laughter and reveal the criticism of magic, which appears as nothing more than mere charlatanry.

4 Epilogue

Neronian literature, the product of an all-changing era, marks an emphatic change from the aesthetic norms established by Augustan authors. This shift, brought about partially by the developments in the institution of patronage during the last decades of Augustus' reign, finds its most imposing articulation in witchcraft scenes. As the multi-ethnic structure of the Roman Empire facilitated the cultural exchange among diverse groups, different traditions made their way to Rome. What was relatively new and came to be considered partially foreign, both aspects of magic, stirred people's curiosity, and caused anxiety to the followers of Roman traditions as well as to supporters of the established social, political, and religious order.

The detailed and accurate, to an obsessive degree, descriptions of magic in Seneca's *Medea*, Lucan's book 6, and Petronius' *Satyrica* reveal looming anxieties on behalf of these authors. The cross-generic examination of the motif of magic in their works substantiates that high-decree realism permeates Neronian descriptions of witchcraft. Such a detailed and accurate representation, emblematic of the period's literary production, is not merely a tool that differentiates these authors from their Augustan predecessors, but it has been transformed into an essential component in expressing strong disapproval for the saliency of magic in the first century CE. In all three authors, as I showed, realism functions as an interface between contemporary experience and literature, and becomes subordinate not only to the criticism of magic, but also to Lucan's and Seneca's Stoic worldview as well as Petronius' satiric taste.

Accepting the philosophical orientation of Senecan drama and its educational role, I examined the *Medea* as a play influenced also by Stoic ideas on superstition, whose most extreme form is magic. I argued that realism corroborates the moralizing value of the play, first by bringing Medea's mythological figure closer to the reader's conception of a witch, and then by emphasizing the contrast of her opening imprecation with the normative prayer of the chorus. In the play's central scene, realism validates Seneca's criticism of magic by essentially transforming the heroine's earlier, ambiguous portrayal as *pharmakos* into a Stoic *monstrum* that causes only harm and destruction within the narrative. The gruesome details that provoke the nurse's horrified reaction also arouse fear and disgust in the reader, and the realistic elements, which recall magical practices possibly known to them through experience or hearsay, facilitate the process of recognition, guiding their moral response to magic.

My analysis of Lucan's Erichtho scene also illustrates the author's critical stance toward magic from the perspective of a Stoic and a member of the elite. The anti-Stoic and anti-Roman character of the *ars magica* is immediately realized in the portrayal of Sextus and the description of the powers of Thessalian witchcraft — the latter also points to aspects of magic that reveal the practice as charlatanry in the reader's eyes. In sketching Erichtho as a powerful witch, unparalleled in Latin literature, who performs a realistic and accurate necromantic spell, Lucan plays with the psychology of the reader, guiding them to expect a successful completion of her ritual. Thus, the eventual failure of Erichtho to answer Sextus' questions regarding his future stuns the reader, underscores the futility of magic, and leads them to question its power and moral value.

In the *Satyrica*, the parodic treatment of the literary motif of witchcraft reveals the author's implicit criticism of magic. As I showed, the narratives of the werewolf and the *strigae*, although based on existing myths and legends, display features that recall real spells and reflect popular beliefs about magic. Petronius' modifications to these archetypal stories enhance their magical aspect in the intranarrative audience's eyes but, at the same time, allow the novel's educated reader to recognize the absurd and irrational claims of magic. Thus, realism, which serves to lend credence to the inset tales in the eyes of the freedmen, causes a different reaction from the reader, who rejects the tales in disbelief. The criticism of magic becomes more vigorous in the descriptions of the rites of Proselenos and Oenothea, who are sketched as witches rather than priapic priestesses. Confirming the reader's anticipation, their rituals resemble more the magical recipes of the *PGM* than mainstream healing rituals. The realistic features form the link between the novel's imaginary cosmos and the real world, and when the sexual and ridiculous aspect of the rites is revealed, the reader can only laugh at the antics of magic, while their eventual failure underscores magic as charlatanry.

Bibliography

Ager, B.K. (2022), *The Scent of Ancient Magic*, Ann Arbor.
Ahl, F. (1976), *Lucan: An Introduction*, Ithaca.
Andrikopoulos, G. (2009), *Magic and the Roman Emperors*, Ph.D. Diss., Exeter.
Arrowsmith, W. (1966), "Luxury and death in the *Satyricon*", in: *Arion* 5, 304–331.
Ashton, E. (2011), *Mixanthrôpoi: Animal-human Hybrid Deities in Greek Religion*, Liège.
Audollent, A. (1904), *Defixionum tabellae*, Paris.
Auerbach, E. (1953), *Mimesis: The Representation of Reality in Western Literature*, tr. W.R. Trask, Princeton.
Bacon, H.H. (1958), "The Sibyl in the bottle", in: *The Virginia Quarterly Review* 34.2, 262–276.
Bakhtin, M.M. (1981), *The Dialogic Imagination: Four Essays*, Texas.
Baldini Moscadi, L. (1976), "Osservazioni sull'episodio magico del libro VI della Farsaglia di Lucano", in: *SIFC* 48, 140–199.
Baldwin, B. (1986), "Why the Werewolf urinates?", in: *PSN* 16, 9.
Barton, T. (1994), *Ancient Astrology*, New York.
Bartsch, S. (2006), *The Mirror of the Self: Sexuality, Self-knowledge, and the Gaze in the Early Roman Empire*, Chicago.
Bartsch, S., Freudenburg K. and Littlewood, C.A.J. (eds.) (2017), *The Cambridge Companion to the Age of Nero*, Cambridge.
Bernand, A. (1991), *Sorciers Grecs*, Paris.
Betz, H.D. (1986), *The Greek Magical Papyri in Translation: Including the Demotic Spells*, Chicago.
Bobzien, S. (1998), *Determinism and Freedom in Stoic Philosophy*, Oxford.
Bonnechere, P. (1994), *Le sacrifice humain en Grèce ancienne*, Liège.
Bonner, C. (1950), *Studies in Magical Amulets, chiefly Graeco-Egyptian*, Ann Arbor.
Bourgery, A. (1928) "Lucain et la magie", in: *REL* 6, 299–313.
Boyce, B. (1991), *The Language of the Freedmen in Petronius' Cena Trimalchionis*, Leiden.
Boyle, A.J. (1997), *Tragic Seneca: An Essay in the Theatrical Tradition*, London.
Boyle, A.J. (2008), *Octavia: Attributed to Seneca*, Oxford.
Boyle, A.J. (2014), *Seneca: Medea*, Oxford.
Brashear, W.M. (1995), "The Greek *magical papyri*: an introduction and survey; Annotated Bibliography (1928-1994)", in: *ANRW* II.15.5, 3380–3684.
Bremmer, J.N. (1981), "Greek hymns", in: H.S. Versnel (ed.), *Faith, Hope, and Worship: Aspects of Religious Mentality in the Ancient World*, Leiden, 193–215.
Bremmer, J.N. (1983), *The Early Greek Concept of the Soul*, Princeton.
Bronzini, G.B. (1988), "Il lupo mannaro e le streghe di Petronio", in: *Lares* 54, 198–201.
Buckley, E. and Dinter, M. (eds.) (2013), *A Companion to the Neronian Age*, Malden MA.
Burriss, E.E. (1936), "The terminology of Witchcraft", in: *CPh* 31.2, 137–145.
Castagna, L. (2002), "Anticlassicismo Neroniano? Spunti per una verifica", in: L. Castagna and G. Vogt-Spira (eds.), ix–xix.
Castagna, L. and Vogt-Spira, G. (eds.) (2002), *Pervertere: Ästhetik der Verkehrung*, Leipzig.
Champlin, E. (2003), *Nero*, Cambridge MA.
Chaumartin, F.R. (2014), "Philosophical tragedy?", in: G. Damschen and A. Heil (eds.), 653–669.
Cherubini, L. (2009), "Scilicet illum tetigerat mala manus: inganni e disinganni delle streghe in Petr. 63", in: *QRO* 2, 143–155.
Cipriano, P. (1978), *Fas e nefas*, Roma.

Cizek, E. (1972), *L'époque de Néron et ses controverses idéologiques*, Leiden.
Clarke, J.R. (2003), *Roman Sex: 100 B.C. to 250 A.D.*, New York.
Clauss, J.J. and Johnston, S.I. (eds.) (1997), *Medea: Essays on Medea in Myth, Literature, Philosophy and Art*, Princeton.
Cleasby, H.L. (1907), "The Medea of Seneca", in: *HSPh* 18, 39–71.
Collins, D. (2008), *Magic in The Ancient Greek World*, Malden.
Connors, C. (1998), *Petronius the Poet: Verse and Literary Tradition in the Satyricon*, Cambridge.
Constantini, L. (2016), "Roman witchcraft: 'contaminations' between literature and reality", in: *Narrating Witchcraft: Agency, Discourse and Power*, 30 Jun - 01 Jul 2016, University of Erfurt, Germany, (unpublished conference paper).
Conte, G. (1996), *The Hidden Author*, Berkeley.
Cordovana, O.D. (2020), "Pliny the Elder: Between Magic and Medicine", in: A. Mastrocinque, J.E. Sanzo, and M. Scapini (eds.), *Ancient Magic: Then and Now*, Stuttgart, 61–80.
Cosci, P. (1980), "Quartilla e l'iniziazione ai misteri di Priapo (Satyricon 20,4)", in: *MD* 4, 199–201.
Costa, C.D.N. (1973), *Seneca Medea*, Oxford.
Courtney, E. (2001), *A Companion to Petronius*, Oxford.
D' Alessandro Behr, F. (2007), *Feeling History: Lucan, Stoicism, and the Poetics of Passion*, Columbus.
Damschen, G. and Heil, A. (eds.) (2014), *Brill's Companion to Seneca: Philosopher and Dramatist*, Leiden.
Danese, R.M. (1992) *L'anticosmo di Eritto e il capivolgimento dell'inferno Virgiliano (Lucano, Phars. 6. 333 sgg)*, Roma.
Danese, R.M. (1995), "Eritto, la Belva umana", in: R. Raffaelli (ed.), *Vicende e figure femminili in Grecia e a Roma: atti del convengo Pesaro 28-30 aprile 1994*, Ancona, 425–434.
De Biasi, L., Ferrero, A.M., Malaspina, E., and Vottero, D. (ed.). (2009), *La clemenza - Apocolocyntosis - Epigrammi - Frammenti di Lucio Anneo Seneca*, Turin.
De Souza, P. (1999), *Piracy in the Graeco-Roman World*, Cambridge.
Dick, B.F. (1963), "The technique of prophecy in Lucan", in: *TAPhA* 94, 37–49
Dickie, M.W. (2001), *Magic and Magicians in the Greco-Roman World*, London.
Dietrich, B.C. (1965), *Death, Fate, and the Gods: The Development of a Religious Idea in Greek Popular Belief and in Homer*, London.
Dingel, J. (1974), *Seneca und die Dichtung*, Heidelberg.
Dinter, M. (2013), "Introduction: The Neronian (Literary) 'Renaissance'", in: E. Buckley and M. Dinter (eds.), 1–14.
Dodds, E.R. (1952), "A fragment of a Greek novel (P. Mich. inv. no. 5)", in: M.E. White (ed.), *Studies in Honour of Gilbert Norwood*, Toronto, 133–138.
Dölger, F. (1930), *Antike und Christentum: Kultur- und religionsgeschichtliche Studien*, Bd. 2, Münster.
Dominik, W.J. (1993), "Change or decline? Literature in the Early Principate", in: *AC* 36, 105–112.
Dudley, D.R. (1972), *Neronians and Flavians: Silver Latin I*, London.
Dupont, F. (1995), *Les Monstres de Sénèque: Pour une dramaturgie de la tragédie romaine*, Paris.
Edelstein, L. (1937), "Greek medicine in its relation to religion and magic", in: *Bulletin of the Institute of the History of Medicine* 5, 201–246.
Edmonds, R.G. III. (2019), *Drawing Down the Moon. Magic in the Graeco-Roman World*, Princeton.
Edwards, C. (2000), *Suetonius, Lives of the Caesars*, Oxford.
Egermann, F. (1940), "Seneca als Dichterphilosoph", in: *NJAB* 3, 18–36.
Eidinow, E. (2019), "Binding Spells on Tablets and Papyri", In: D. Frankfurter (ed.), *Guide to the Study of Ancient Magic*, Leiden, 351–387.
Eitrem, S. (1941). "La Magie Comme motif littéraire chez les grecs et les Romains", in: *SO* 21, 39–83.

Fahz, L. (1904), *De poetarum romanorum doctrina magica quaestiones selectae*, Giessen.
Faraone, C.A. (1999), *Ancient Greek Love Magic*, Cambridge MA.
Faraone, C.A. (2005), "Necromancy Goes Underground: The Disguise of Skull- and Corpse-Divination in the Paris Magical Papyri (PGM IV 1928-2144)", in: S.I. Johnston and P.T. Struck (eds.), *Mantike. Studies in Ancient Divination*, Leiden, 255–282.
Faraone, C.A. (2018), *The Transformation of Greek Amulets in Roman Imperial Times*, Philadelphia.
Faraone, C.A. (2022), "The Echenêis-fish and magic", in: J-C. Coulon and K. Dosoo (eds.), *Magikon zōon: Animal et magie dans l'Antiquité et au Moyen Âge*, Paris, 277–287.
Faraone, C.A. and Obbink, D. (eds.) (1991), *Magika Hiera: Ancient Greek Magic and Religion*, New York.
Fauth, W. (1975), "Die Bedeutung der Nekromantie-Szene in Lucans Pharsalia", in: *RhM* 118, 325–344.
Feeney, D.C. (1991), *The Gods in Epic: Poets and Critics of the Classical Tradition*, New York.
Ferri, R. (2003), *Octavia: A Play Attributed to Seneca*, Cambridge.
Fischer, S. (2008), *Seneca als Theologe. Studien zum Verhältnis von Philosophie und Tragödiendichtung*, Berlin.
Fitch, J.G. and McElduff, S. (2002), "Construction of the self in Senecan drama", in: *Mnemosyne* 55, 18–40.
Flint, V., Gordon, R., Luck, G., and Ogden D. (eds.) (1999), *Witchcraft and Magic in Europe, Volume 2: Ancient Greece and Rome*, Philadelphia.
Francese, C. (2007), *Ancient Rome in so Many Words*, New York.
Franek, J. and Urbanová, D. (2019), "'May their limbs melt, just *as this* lead shall melt...': sympathetic magic and *similia similibus* formulae in Greek and Latin curse tablets (Part 1)", in: *PhilClass* 14.1, 27–55.
Fratantuono, L. (2012), *Madness Triumphant: A Reading of Lucan's Pharsalia*, Lanham.
Frazer, J.G. (1925), *The Golden Bough: A Study in Magic and Religion* (abridged edition), London.
Freudenburg, K. (2017), "Petronius, realism, Nero", in: S. Bartsch, K. Freudenburg, and C.A.J. Littlewood (eds.), 107–120.
Frost, B.J. (2003), *The Essential Guide to Werewolf Literature*, London.
Gager, J.G. (1992), *Curse Tablets and Binding Spells from the Ancient World*, New York.
Garosi, R. (1976), "Indagine sulla formazione di concetto di magia nella cultura Romana," in: P. Xella (ed.), *Magia. Studi di Storia delle religioni in memoria di Raffaela Garosi*, Roma, 13–97.
Gill, C. (2013), "Stoic eros-is there such a thing?", in: E. Sanders, C. Thumiger, C. Carey, and N.J. Lowe (eds.), *Eros in Ancient Greece*, Oxford, 143–157.
Gloyn, L. (2017), *The Ethics of the Family in Seneca*, New York.
Gordon, R. (1987a), "Lucan's Erictho", in: M. Whitby, P. Hardie, and M. Whitby (eds.), *Homo Viator: Classical Essays in honour of John Bramble*, Bristol, 231–241.
Gordon, R. (1987b), "Aelian's Peony: The location of magic in Graeco-Roman tradition", in: *Comparative Criticism* 9, 59–95.
Gordon, R. (2008), "Superstitio, superstition and religious repression in the Late Roman Republic and Principate (100 BCE-300 CE)", in: S.A. Smith and A. Knight (eds.), *The Religion of Fools? Superstition Past and Present*, Oxford, 72–94.
Gordon, R. (2009), "Magic as a topos in augustan poetry: discourse, reality and distance", in: *Archiv für Religionsgeschichte* 11.1, 209–228.
Gordon, R. (2015), "Good to think: wolves and wolf-men in the Graeco-Roman world", in: W. de Blécourt (ed.), *Werewolf Histories*, London, 25–60.
Graf, F. (1991), "Prayer in magic and religious ritual", in: C.A. Faraone and D. Obbink (eds.), 188–213.
Graf, F. (1997a), *Magic in the Ancient World*, tr. F. Philip, Cambridge MA.
Graf, F. (1997b), "Medea the enchantress from afar. Remarks on a well-known myth", in: J.J. Clauss and S.I. Johnston (eds.), 21–43.

Graf, F. (2007), "Untimely death, witchcraft, and divine vengeance. A reasoned epigraphical catalog", in: *ZPE* 162, 139–150.
Green, C.M.C. (2007), *Roman Religion and the Cult of Diana at Aricia*, Cambridge.
Griffin, M. (1984), *Nero: The End of a Dynasty*, London.
Griffiths, E. (2006), *Medea*, London.
Grondona, M. (1980), *La religione et la superstizione nella Cena Trimalchionis*, Brussels.
Guastella, G. (2001), "Virgo, Coniunx, Mater", in: *ClAnt* 20.2, 197–219.
Gummere, R.M. (1917–1925), *Seneca. Ad Lucilium Epistulae Morales*, 3 vols., London.
Haase, F. (1862), *L. Annaei Senecae. Opera quae supersunt*, vols. I and II, Leipzig.
Hardie, P.R. (1993), *The Epic Successors of Virgil: A Study in the Dynamics of a Tradition*, Cambridge.
Haskins, C.H. (1887), *M. Annaei Lucani Pharsalia*, London.
Heinze, R. (1899), "Petron und der griechische Roman", in: *Hermes* 34, 494–519.
Hermes, E. (1923), *L. Annaei Senecae Dialogorum libri XII*, Leipzig.
Hickson, F.V. (1993), *Roman Prayer Language. Livy and the Aeneid of Vergil*, Stuttgart.
Highet, G. (1941), "Petronius the moralist", in: *TAPhA* 72, 176–194.
Hill, D.H. (1973), "The Thessalian trick", in: *RhM* 116, 221–238.
Hine, H.M. (1989), "Medea versus the Chorus: Seneca's *Medea* 1–115", in: *Mnemosyne* 42, 413–419.
Hine, H.M. (2000), *Seneca: Medea*, Warminster.
Hollis, A. (2009), *Callimachus: Hecale*, Oxford.
Hopfner, T. (1921–1924), *Griechisch-ägyptischer Offenbarungszauber*, 2 vols., Leipzig.
Horsfall, N. (1989), "The uses of literacy and the *Cena Trimalchionis: II*", in: *G&R* 36, 194–209.
Housman, A.E. (1958), *Lucan*, Oxford.
Jensson, G. (2004), *The Recollections of Encolpius: the Satyrica of Petronius as Milesian Fiction*, Groningen.
Johns, C. (1982), *Sex or Symbol?: Erotic Images of Greece and Rome*, New York.
Johnson, W.R. (1987), *Momentary Monsters: Lucan and his Heroes*, Ithaca.
Johnston, S.I. (1990), *Hekate Soteira: A Study of Hekate's Roles in the Chaldean Oracles and Related Literature*, Atlanta.
Johnston, S.I. (1995), "Defining the dreadful: Remarks on the Greek child-killing demon", in: M. Meyer, and P. Mirecki (eds.), *Ancient Magic and Ritual Power*, Leiden, 361–387.
Johnston, S.I. (2004), *Religions of the Ancient World*, Cambridge MA.
Jones, F. (1991), "Realism in Petronius", in: *Groningen Colloquia on the Novel* 4, 105–120.
Jordan, D. R. (1985), "*Defixiones* from a well near the Southwest corner of the Athenian agora", in: *Hesperia* 54, 205–255.
Kagarow, E. (1929), *Griechische Fluchtafeln*, Paris.
Klebs, E. (1889), "Zur Composition von Petronius *Satirae*", in: *Philologus* 47, 623–635.
Kohn, T. (2013), *The Dramaturgy of Senecan Drama*, Ann Arbor.
Korenjak, M. (1996), *Die Erichthoszene in Lukans Pharsalia: Einleitung, Text, Übersetzung, Kommentar*, Frankfurt am Main.
Lapidge, M. (1979), "Lucan's imagery of cosmic dissolution", in: *Hermes* 107, 344–370.
Laroche, R. (1995), "Popular, symbolic/ mystical numbers in antiquity", in: *Latomus* 54, 568–576.
Lawall, G. (1995), *Petronius. Selections from the Satyricon*, Wauconda.
Lease, E.B. (1919), "The number three, mysterious, mystic, magic", in: *CPh* 14, 56–73.
Le Bonniec, H. (1970), "Lucain et la religion", in: M. Durry (ed.), Lucain. *Sept exposés suivis de discussions*, Genève, 161–195.
Lecocq, F. (2016), "Inventing the Phoenix: a myth in the making through words and images", in: P. Johnston, A. Mastrocinque, and S. Papaioannou (eds.), *Animals in Greek and Roman Religion and Myth*, Newcastle upon Tyne, 449–478.

Lefèvre, E. (2002), "Die Konzeption der 'verkehrten Welt' in Senecas Tragödien", in: L. Castagna and G. Vogt-Spira (eds.), 105–122.
Lennon, J.J. (2014), *Pollution and Religion in Ancient Rome*, Cambridge.
Littlewood, C.A.J. (2017), "Post-Augustan revisionism", in: S. Bartsch, K. Freudenburg and C.A.J. Littlewood (eds.), 79–92.
Lo Cascio, E. and Tacoma, L.E. (eds.) (2016), *The Impact of Mobility and Migration in the Roman Empire*, Leiden.
Loupiac, A. (1991), "La poétique des éléments dans la Pharsale", in: *BAGB* 3, 247–266.
Luck, G. (1999), "Witches and sorcerers in classical literature", in: V. Flint, R. Gordon, G. Luck, and D. Ogden (eds.), 91–158.
Lugli, U. (1987–1988), "La formazione del concetto di stregoneria in Lucano", *Sandalion* 10–11, 91–99.
MacL. Currie, H. (1985), *Silver Latin Epic*, Bristol.
Makowski, J.F. (1977), "*Oracula mortis* in the *Pharsalia*", in: *CPh* 72, 193–202.
Maltby, R. (1991), *A Lexicon of Ancient Latin Etymologies*, Leeds.
Manuwald, G. (2013), "Medea: transformations of a Greek figure in Latin literature", in: *G&R* 60, 114–135.
Markus, D. (2000), "Seneca, *Medea* 680: an addendum to *ZPE* 117 (1997) 73–80", in: *ZPE* 132, 149–150.
Marti, B. (1945a) "The meaning of the *Pharsalia*", in: *AJPh* 66, 352–376.
Marti, B. (1945b), "Seneca's tragedies: a new interpretation", in: *TAPhA* 76, 216–245.
Martin, D.B. (2004), *Inventing Superstition. From the Hippocratics to the Christians*, Cambridge MA.
Martin, R. (1988), "La Cena Trimalchionis: les trois niveaux d'un festin", in: *BAGB* 1988 (3), 232–247.
Martín Hernández, R. (2024), "Practice Your Spells When It Suits You Best. The "Cycles of the Moon" Transmitted in GEMF 74/PGM VII and GEMF 55/PGM III", In: R.G. Edmonds III, C. López-Ruiz, and S. Torallas-Tovar (eds.), *Magic and Religion in the Ancient Mediterranean World: Studies in Honor of Christopher A. Faraone*, New York, 90–108.
Martindale, C.A. (1977), "Three notes on Lucan VI", in: *Mnemosyne* 30, 375–387.
Martindale, C.A. (1980), "Lucan's *Nekuia*", in: C. Deroux (ed.). *Studies in Latin Literature and Roman History II*, Bruxelles, 367–377.
Martinez, D.G. (1991), *P. Michigan XVI: A Greek Love Charm from Egypt*, Atlanta.
Marx, F. (1905), *C. Lucilii Carminum Reliquiae*, Leipzig.
Massoneau, E. (1934), *La magie dans l'antiquité romaine: la magie dans la littérature et les moeurs romaines; le répression de la magie*, Paris.
Masters, J. (1992), *Poetry and Civil War in Lucan's Bellum Civile*, Cambridge.
Mayor, A. (2009), *Greek Fire, Poison Arrows, and Scorpion Bombs: Biological and Chemical Warfare in the Ancient World*, Woodstock.
McKie, S. (2022), *Living and Cursing in the Roman West*, London.
McMahon, J. (1998), *Paralysin Cave: Impotence, Perception, and Text in the Satyrica of Petronius*, Leiden.
Meggitt, J.J. (2013), "Did magic matter? The saliency of magic in the early Roman Empire", in: *Journal of Ancient History* 1.2, 170–229.
Miller, F.J. (1951–1956), *Ovid. Metamorphoses*, Cambridge MA.
Morenz, S. (1975), "Anubis mit dem Schlussel", in: S. Morenz, E. Blumenthal, S. Herrmann, and A. Onasch (eds.), *Religion und Geschichte des alten Ägypten: Gesammelte Aufsätze*, Köln, 510–520.
Morford, M.P.O. (1967), *The Poet Lucan: Studies in Rhetorical Epic*, Oxford.
Morford, M.P.O. (1973), "The Neronian literary revolution", in: *CJ* 68.3, 210–215.
Morford, M.P.O. (1985), "Nero's patronage and participation in literature and the arts", in: *ANRW* II.32.3, 2003–2031.
Mouritsen, H. (2015), *The Freedmen in the Roman World*, Cambridge.

Müller, K. (ed.) (2009), Petronius, *Satyricon Reliquiae*, Berlin.
Narducci, E. (1979), *La provvidenza crudele: Lucano e la distruzione dei miti augustei*, Pisa.
Newlands, C. (1997), "The Metamorphosis of Ovid's Medea", in: J.J. Clauss and S.I. Johnston (eds.), 178–208.
Nisard, D. (1834), *Études de Mœurs et de Critique sur les Poètes Latins de la Décadence*, 3 vols., Paris.
Nock, A.D. (1972), *Essays on Religion and the Ancient World*, Vol. I, Cambridge MA.
Noy, D. (2000), *Foreigners at Rome: Citizens and Strangers*, London.
Nussbaum, M. (1993), "Poetry and the passions: two stoic views", in: J. Brunschwig and M. Nussbaum (eds.), *Passions & Perceptions: Studies in Hellenistic Philosophy of Mind: Proceedings of the Fifth Symposium Hellenisticum*, Cambridge, 97–149.
Ogden, D. (1999), *"Binding Spells: Curse Tablets and Voodoo Dolls in the Greek and Roman Worlds"*, in: V. Flint, R. Gordon, G. Luck, and D. Ogden (eds.), 3–90.
Ogden, D. (2001), *Greek and Roman Necromancy*, Princeton.
Ogden, D. (2002a), *Magic, Witchcraft, and Ghosts in the Greek and Roman Worlds: A Sourcebook*, New York
Ogden, D. (2002b), "Lucan's Sextus Pompeius episode: its necromantic, political and literary background", in: A. Powell, K. Welch, and A.M. Gowing (eds.), 249–272.
Ogden, D. (2013), *Drakōn: Dragon Myth and Serpent Cult in the Greek and Roman Worlds*, Oxford.
Ogden, D. (2021), *The Werewolf in the Ancient World*, Oxford.
Oliphant, S.G. (1913), "The story of the strix. Ancient", in: *TAPhA* 44, 133–149.
Oliphant, S.G. (1914), "The story of the strix: Isidorus and the Glossographers", in: *TAPhA* 45, 49–63.
Pachoumi, E. (2017), *The Concepts of the Divine in the Greek Magical Papyri*, Tübingen.
Panayotakis, C. (1995), *Theatrum Arbitri: Theatrical Elements in the Satyrica of Petronius*, Leiden.
Panayotakis, C. (2015), "Encolpius and the Charlatans", in: S. Panayotakis, G. Schmeling, and M. Paschalis (eds.), *Holy Men and Charlatans in the Ancient Novel*, Eelde, 31–46.
Panoussi, V. (2019), *Brides, Mourners, Bacchae: Women's Rituals in Roman Literature*, Baltimore, MD.
Paoletti, L. (1963), "Lucano magico e Virgilio", in: *A&R* 8, 11–26.
Perry, B.E. (1925), "Petronius and the Comic Romance", in: *CPh* 20, 31–49.
Pharr, C. (1932), "The interdiction of magic in Roman law", in: *TAPhA* 63, 269–295.
Pichon, R. (1912), *Les Sources de Lucain*, Paris.
Pinna, T. (1978), "Un'ipotesi sul rituale di Quartilla (Satyricon, XVI–XXVI)", in: *AFMC* 3, 215–259.
Plaza, M. (2000), *Laughter and Derision in Petronius' Satyrica: A Literary Study*, Stockholm.
Powell, A., Welch, K. and Gowing, A.M. (eds.) (2002), *Sextus Pompeius*, London.
Pratt, N.T. (1948), "The Stoic Base of Senecan Drama", In: *TAPhA* 79, 1–11.
Rackham, H., Jones, W.H.S., and Eichholz, D.E. (1938–1962), *Pliny. Natural History*, 10 vols., revised ed., Cambridge MA.
Ramsay, G.G. (1957), *Juvenal and Persius*, London.
Rankin, H.D. (1971), *Petronius the Artist: Essays on the Satyricon and its Author*, The Hague.
Reif, M. (2016), De arte magorum. *Erklärung und Deutung ausgewählter Hexenszenen bei Theokrit, Vergil, Horaz, Ovid, Seneca und Lucan unter Berücksichtigung des Ritualaufbaus und der Relation zu den Zauberpapyri*, Tübingen.
Reiner, E. (1995), *Astral Magic in Babylonia*, Philadelphia.
Renehan, R. (1992), "The staunching of Odysseus' blood: the healing power of magic", in: *AJPh* 113, 1–4.
Rimell, V. (2002), *Petronius and the Anatomy of Fiction*, Cambridge.
Rini, A. (1929), "Popular superstitions in Petronius and Italian superstitions of to-day", in: *CW* 22, 83–86.
Roche, P. (2019), *Lucan. De Bello Civili*. Book VII, Cambridge.
Rolfe, J.C. (1950), *Suetonius, The Lives of the Caesars*, Vol. II, Cambridge MA.
Rose, H.J. (1913), "The witch scene in Lucan (VI 419 sqq.)", in: *TAPhA* 44, I–liii.

Rose, H.J. (1922), "Asinus in tegulis", in: *Folklore* 33.1, 34–56.
Rose, H.J. (1936), *A Handbook of Latin Literature: From the Earliest Times to the Death of St. Augustine*, London.
Rose, K.F.C. (1971), *The Date and Author of the 'Satyricon'*, Leiden.
Rosenmeyer, T.G. (1989), *Senecan Drama and Stoic Cosmology*, Berkeley.
Rosner-Siegel, J.A. (1982), "Amor. Metamorphosis and magic: Ovid's Medea (*Met.* 7.1.424)", in: *CJ* 77.3, 231–243.
Sambursky, S. (1987), *Physics of the Stoics*, Princeton.
Sandbach, F.H. (1975), *The Stoics*, London.
Sandy, G.N. (1969), "Satire in the *Satyricon*", in: *AJPh* 90.3, 293–303.
Santangelo, F. (2015), "Testing boundaries: divination and prophecy in Lucan", in: *G&R* 62.2, 177–188.
Schaaf, I. (2014), *Magie und Ritual bei Apollonios Rhodios: Studien zu ihrer Form und Funktion in den Argonautika*, Berlin.
Scheid, J. (2003), *An Introduction to Roman Religion*, Edinburgh.
Schmeling, G. (1969), "Petronius: satirist, moralist, epicurean, artist", in: *CB* 45, 49–50; 64.
Schmeling, G. (1996), *The Novel in the Ancient World*, Leiden.
Schmeling, G. and Setaioli, A. (2011), *A Commentary on the Satyrica of Petronius*, Oxford.
Schuster, M. (1930), "Der Werwolf und die Hexen: Zwei Schauermärchen bei Petronius", in: *WS* 48, 149–178.
Scobie, A. (1975), *Apuleius Metamorphoses (Asinus Aureus). A Commentary*, Meisenheim am Glan.
Scobie, A. (1978), "Strigiform witches in Roman and other cultures", in: *Fabula* 19.1, 74–101.
Segal, C. (2002), "Black and white magic in Ovid's *Metamorphoses*: passion, love, and art", in: *Arion* 9.3, 1–34.
Setaioli, A. (2000), "La scena di magia in Petr. Sat. 131.4-6", in: *Prometheus* 26, 159–172.
Setaioli, A. (2007), "Seneca and the divine: stoic tradition and personal developments", in: *IJCT* 13, 333–68.
Setaioli, A. (2011), *Arbitri Nugae. Petronius' Short Poems in the Satyrica*, Frankfurt am Main.
Setaioli, A. (2014), "Physics III: Theology", in: G. Damschen and A. Heil (eds.), 379–401.
Shipley, F. W. (1961), *Velleius Paterculus. Compendium of Roman History*, London.
Sklenár, R. (2003), *The Taste for Nothingness: A Study of Virtus and Related Themes in Lucan's Bellum Ciuile*, Ann Arbor.
Slater, N.W. (1990), *Reading Petronius*, Baltimore.
Smith, M.S. (1975), *Petronii Arbitri Cena Trimalchionis*, Oxford.
Staley, G.A. (2010), *Seneca and the Idea of Tragedy*, Oxford.
Stanley Spaeth, B. (2010), "'The terror that comes in the night': the night hag and supernatural assault in Latin literature", in: E. Scioli and C. Walde (eds.), *Sub Imagine Somni: Nighttime Phenomena in Greco-Roman Culture*, Pisa, 231–258.
Stanley Spaeth, B. (2014), "From goddess to hag: the Greek and the Roman witch in the classical literature", in: K.B. Stratton and D.S. Kalleres (eds.), 41–70.
Star, C. (2006), "Commanding *Constantia* in Senecan Tragedy", *TAPhA* 136, 207–244.
Star, C. (2012), *The Empire of the Self: Self-Command and Political Speech in Seneca and Petronius*, Baltimore.
Šterbenc Erker, D. (2013), "Religion", in: E. Buckley and M. Dinter (eds.), 118–133.
Stratton, K.B. and Kalleres, D.S. (eds.) (2014), *Daughters of Hecate: Women and Magic in the Ancient World*, Oxford.
Stratton, K.B. (2014), "Magic, abjection, and gender in Roman literature", in: K.B. Stratton and D.S. Kalleres (eds.), 152–181.
Suárez de la Torre, E. (2021), *Eros mágico. Recetas eróticas mágicas del mundo antiguo*, Zaragoza.

Sullivan, J.P. (1963), "Satire and realism in Petronius", in: J.P. Sullivan (ed.), *Critical Essays on Roman Literature: Satire*, London, 73–92.
Sullivan, J.P. (1967), "Petronius: artist or moralist?", in: *Arion* 6.1, 71–88.
Sullivan, J.P. (1968a), *The Satyricon of Petronius: A Literary Study*, London.
Sullivan, J.P. (1968b), "Petronius, Seneca, and Lucan: a neronian literary feud?", in: *TAPhA* 99, 453–467.
Sullivan, J.P. (1985), *Literature and Politics in the Age of Nero*, Ithaca.
Tacoma, L.E. (2016), *Moving Romans: Migration to Rome in the Principate*, Oxford.
Tarrant, R.J. (2006), "Seeing Seneca whole?", in: K. Volk, and G.D. Williams (eds.), *Seeing Seneca Whole: Perspectives on Philosophy, Poetry and Politics*, Leiden, 1–17.
Tavenner, E. (1916), "Three as a magic number in Latin literature", in: *TAPhA* 47, 117–143.
Tesoriero, C. (2000), *A Commentary on Lucan Bellum Civile 6.333–830*, PhD. Diss.
Tesoriero, C. (2002), "*Magno proles indigna parente*: The role of Sextus Pompeius in Lucan's *Bellum Civile*", in: A. Powell, K. Welch, and A.M. Gowing (eds.), 229–249.
Tesoriero, C. (2004), "The middle in Lucan", in: S. Kyriakidis, and F. De Martino (eds.), *Middles in Latin Poetry*, Bari, 183–215.
Thilo, G. (ed.) (1881), *Servii Grammatici qui feruntur in Vergilii carmina commentarii*, Vol. I, Leipzig.
Trinacty, C. V. (2014), *Senecan Tragedy and the Reception of Augustan Poetry*. Oxford.
Tupet, A.-M. (1988), "La Scène de magie dans la pharsale: Essai de problématique", in: D. Porte, J.-P. Neraudau (eds.), *Hommages à Henri le Bonniec: Res Sacrae*, Bruxelles, 419–427.
Tupet, A.-M. (1976), *La magie dans la poésie latine*, Paris.
Tylor, E.B. (1871), *Primitive Culture: Researches into the Development of Mythology, Philosophy, Religion, Art, and Custom*, 2 vols., London.
Urbanová, D. (2018), *Latin Curse Tablets of the Roman Empire*, Innsbruck.
Usener, H. (1869), *M. Annaei Lucani Commenta Bernensia*, Leipzig.
van der Horst, P.W. (1994), "Silent prayer in antiquity", in: *Numen* 41, 1–25.
Veenstra, J.R. (2002), "The ever-changing nature of the beast. Cultural change, lycanthropy and the question of substantial transformation (from Petronius to Del Rio)", in: J.N. Bremmer and J.R. Veenstra (eds.), *The Metamorphosis of Magic from Late Antiquity to the Early Modern Period*, Leuven, 133–166.
Versnel, H.S. (1991), "Beyond cursing: the appeal for justice in judicial prayers", in: C.A. Faraone and D. Obbink (eds.), 60–106.
Versnel, H.S. (2002), "The poetics of the magical charm. An essay in the power of words", in: P. Mirecki and M. Meyer (eds.), *Magic and Ritual in the Ancient World*, Leiden, 105–159.
Versnel, H.S. (2010), "Prayers for justice, East and West: recent finds and publications since 1990", in: R.L. Gordon and M.F. Simón (eds.), *Magical practice in the Latin West: Papers from the international conference held at the University of Zaragoza, 30 Sept.-1 Oct. 2005*, Boston, 275–354.
Volpilhac, J. (1978), "Lucain et l'Égypte dans la scène de nécromancie de la Pharsale vi.413–830 à la lumière des papyri grecs magiques", in: *REL* 56, 272–288.
Vottero, D. (1998), *Lucio Anneo Seneca: I frammenti*, Bologna.
Wallis Budge, E.A. (1902), *A History of Egypt from the End of the Neolithic Period to the Death of Cleopatra VII B.C. 30*, Vol. III, London.
Walsh, L. (2012), "The Metamorphoses of Seneca's *Medea*", in: *Ramus* 41, 71–93.
Walsh, P.G. (1970), *The Roman Novel: The 'Satyricon' of Petronius and the 'Metamorphoses' of Apuleius*, Cambridge.
Walsh, P.G. (1974), "Was Petronius a moralist?", in: *G&R* 21.2, 181–190.
Watson, L. (1991), *Arae: The Curse Poetry of Antiquity*, Leeds.
Watson, L. (2004), "Making water not love: Apuleius, *Metamorphoses* 1.13–14", in: *CQ* 54.2, 651–655.

Watson, L. (2010), "The Echeneis and erotic magic", in: *CQ* 60, 639–646.
Watson, L. (2019), *Magic in Ancient Greece and Rome*, London.
Weinreich, O. (1909), *Antike Heilungswunder*, Giesen.
West, M.L. (1974), *Studies in Greek Elegy and Iambus*, Berlin.
Wiener, C. (2006), *Stoische Doktrin in römischer Belletristik: Das Problem von Entscheidungsfreiheit und Determinismus in Senecas Tragödien und Lucans Pharsalia*, München.
Wiener, C. (2010), "Stoische Erneuerung der epischen Tradition - Der Bürgerkrieg als Schicksal und die Entscheidungsfreiheit zum Verbrechen", in: N. Hömke and C. Reitz (eds.), *Lucan's Bellum Civile: Between Epic Tradition and Aesthetic Innovation*, Berlin, 155–173.
Wilburn, A.T. (2012), *Materia Magica: The Archaeology of Magic in Roman Egypt, Cyprus, and Spain*, Ann Arbor.
Wildberger, J. (2006), *Seneca und die Stoa: Der Platz des Menschen in der Welt*, 2 vols., Berlin.
Williams, G. (1978), *Change and Decline: Roman Literature in the Early Empire*, Berkeley.
Wortmann, D. (1968), "Neue magische Texte", in: *BJ* 168, 56–111.
Zanobi, A. (2014), *Seneca's Tragedies and the Aesthetics of Pantomime*, London.
Zeitlin, F. (1971), "Petronius as paradox: anarchy and artistic integrity", in: *TAPhA* 102, 631–684.
Zwierlein, O. (1986), *Seneca Tragoediae*, Oxford.

Index of Passages

Aëtius
6.11   89

Apollonius Rhodius
Argon.
4.1638–1688   18

Apuleius
Met.
1.13.8   86
2.30   92

Celsus
Med.
5.5   64 n.81
5.27.3c   24

Cicero
Clu.
194   3
Div.
2.18–19   48
Fin.
3.68   54
Rep.
2.9   49
Tusc.
4.38–39   51
Vat.
14   18 n.73, 92 n.64

CIL
II 172   10 n.42, 53

Diogenes Laertius
7.33   54
7.121   54
7.131   54
7.147   27

DT
1   7 n.29
3   7 n.29
5   10 n.40
9   7 n.29
10   7 n.29, 10 n.40
13   7 n.29, 9 n.37
18   7 n.29
22   6 n.23, 7 n.28–30
24   6 n.23, 7 n.28–30
26   6 n.23, 7 n.28–30
28–35   69 n.109
29   7 n.29
29–31   7 n.30
29–32   7 n.28
29–33   6 n.23
33   7 n.30
35   6 n.23, 7 n.28, 7 n.30
38   6 n.23
41   6 n.23
51   54
52   9 n.37
81   7 n.29
85a   95 n.77
74   7 n.29, 54
75   7 n.29
75A   54
92   9 n.37
96–98   7 n.28
97   7 n.28
100–101   7 n.28
111   7 n.29
129   9 n.37
135   54
139   7 n.29
140–141   9 n.37
161   7 n.29
163   7 n.29
187   9 n.37
190   7 n.28
191   7 n.29
198   7 n.28, 10 n.40
217–218   54
222   7 n.28
227   9
230   9
231   7 n.29
242   6 n.23

https://doi.org/10.1515/9783111429441-006

243	9 n.37	*Sat.*	
247	9 n.37	1.8	84 n.26
250	9 n.37	1.8.20–22	27 n.117
251	6 n.26	1.8.24–25	66
268–269	7 n.29		
270–271	9	**Hyginus**	
277	54	*Fab.*	
279	54	140	27
283–284	54		
288–289	7 n.29	**Julius Africanus**	
303	54	*Kestoi*	
		2.11	40 n.164
DTM			
1	53	**Juvenal**	
6	53	10.52–53	100

Euripides
Med.

		Lucan	
99	21	6.417–420	46
447	21	6.421–422	48–49
		6.423	75
Herodotus		6.423–424	46–47
4.105	83, 87	6.433–434	48
		6.434–506	50–58
Hippocrates		6.440–451	50–51
Morb. Sacr.		6.452–460	51–55
4.17–19	58	6.452–506	51–58
		6.457–458	51
Hippolytus		6.458	54
Haer.		6.462–484	55
4.37	58	6.487–491	56–57
		6.488–489	105
Hipponax		6.492–499	50–51
fr.78 W	101	6.499–506	57–58
fr.92 W	104	6.505	105
		6.510–569	58–59
Homer		6.589	48
Il.		6.592–601	75
14.214–215	99	6.596–598	47–48
		6.600–601	48
Horace		6.605–616	61
Epod.		6.607–615	48
5	XVI	6.615–616	75
17.29	24 n.101	6.621–623	75
		6.626	63
		6.630	62
		6.642	59
		6.666	48

6.667–684	62–66	*Met.*	
6.669	64	1.216–239	82
6.671–684	64–66	2.760–794	59–60
6.685–693	66–67	3.530	14
6.695–706	66–69	7.93–97	8
6.706–711	70	7.179–293	XVII
6.712–718	71	7.190–191	66
6.717	62–63	7.192–219	19, 26
6.719–729	104	7.192–287	19
6.722	64 n.80	7.199–202	21
6.726–727	59–60, 71–72	7.251	4
6.730–749	72–74	7.262–284	64
6.731	68 n.106	7.271–272	23
6.762–774	62, 74	7.285–287	64 n.83
6.770–773	75	7.294	4
6.773–774	74	7.294–296	20
6.782–815	75–76	7.296	41
6.822	62	7.394–395	19
6.827–828	60–61	7.404–424	13
10.70	54		
10.360–363	54	**Pausanias**	
		6.8.2	87
Lucilius		8.2.4–8.2.5	87
fr. 575–576 Marx	57		
		PDM	
Lucretius		xiv	
4.638–639	57	82–83	65 n.88
		428-450	85 n.29
New Testament		489–515	36
John		515	64 n.80
9.6	100	636–669	86 n.34
		956–960	86 n.34
Ovid		1070–1077	85 n.29
Am.		1155–1162	103
1.8.13–14	91 n.57	1194–1195	65 n.88
Ars Am.		lxi	
2.102	24 n.101, 57	58–62	103
Fast.		Suppl.	
6.141–142	91	60–101	38 n.157
6.141–145	XVI		
6.147–150	92 n.65	**Persius**	
Her.		1.30–36	XVI n.19
6.83–94	19	2.31–34	101
6.85–88	21		
6.91	4		
12.85–86	8		

Petronius
Sat.
17.9	78
30	78
61.4	88
62	81–89
62.6	88
62.14	88
63	90–95
63.1–2	88, 93–94
63.6	93
63.9	93
64.1	93–94
68–69	94
74	78
128.2	95, 98
129.10	95
131.2	96
131.4–7	99–102
131.7	96
133.4	96
134.1–2	103
134.1	96
134.8	96
134.12	97–98, 104–105
135.3–5	106
136.13	96
137.10	106–107
138.1–2	103–104
138.2	96
138.3	96
138.3–4	104

PGM
I
41–42	70 n.118
54–57	36
54–56	70 n. 118
56	22 n.92
69	4
188–191	26 n.110
222–231	29 n.120
223	65 n.91
279	22 n.95
285	65 n.91

II
43	85 n.32
54–55	73

III
24–26	85 n.28
304–306	36
338	85 n.32
455–456	85 n.32
626–632	74
703	23 n.97

IV
26	36
26–51	29 n.120
52–55	70 n.118
57	85 n.32
58–59	22 n.92
79–80	38 n.157
170	22 n.92
560–561	66 n.96
734–736	70 n.118
929	66 n.96
1006–1007	66 n.96
1035–1047	73
1099–1100	36
1247–1248	6 n.26
1460–1470	68 n.105
1462	68 n.104
1848–1858	74
1853	4
1928–2005	61, 85 n.29
1963–1964	68 n.104
2003–2004	23 n.97
2006–2125	61
2125–2139	62 n.76
2140–2144	62
2207–2208	38 n.157
2211–2212	23 n.97
2215–2221	85 n.28
2220–2221	85
2312–2330	73
2328	22 n.96
2468–2469	22 n.92
2577–2578	92 n.64
2578	65 n.86
2646	92 n.64
2690	65 n.86
2712	22 n.92

2857–2858	6 n.26	LXIX	
2871–2877	85 n.29	3	22 n.96
2875	65 n.86	LXX	
2943–2944	29, 65 n.91	6	22 n.96
2967–3006	28	LXXII	
3087–3124	26 n.109	6	22 n.92
V		XCIII	
283–285	73	1–6	38 n.157
VII		XCV	
184–185	102–104	7–13	29
203–207	65 n.88	XCVII	
226	4	1–6	102 n.107
260–271	100	7–9	29 n.120
767–774	66 n.96	CXXIII a-f	
874	64	69–71	65 n.88
981–982	36	**Philostratus**	
XIa		VA	
2	65 n.86	7.39	96 n.80
XII			
30–31	29	**Pindar**	
160	23 n.97	*Ol.*	
179–181	22 n.95	1.35–55	32
211	85 n.28	*Pyth.*	
401–444	35 n.143	2.21–48	32
XIII			
1–343	22	**Pliny the Elder**	
8	22 n.92	*HN*	
84–88	66 n.96	2.235–236	40 n.164
240–241	65 n.86	8.80–82	87
261–264	57	8.81	82
261–265	24	9.79	65 n.90
277–283	62	10.12	65 n.92
598–602	66 n.96	10.34	29 n.121
XXIIb		28.17–18	83 n.21
27	36	28.19	XII n.5
XXXVI		28.35–39	100
162–163	22 n.96	28.37–38	57
231–255	40 n.163	28.38	100
256–264	22 n.95	28.39	101 n.103
264–274	29 n.120	28.65–69	86
XXXVIII		28.99	65 n.88
1	36	28.122	65 n.87
LXI		28.150	65 n.89
5	22 n.92	28.185	65 n.89
LXII		28.235	65 n.89
32–36	73	28.241	65 n.89

29.20	65 n.91	4.32.1	48
29.29	65 n.94	5.13.4	15
29.67–73	23 n.97	5.17.5	47
29.82	29 n.121	6.25.2	53
29.99	65 n.86	6.35.1	47
29.119–122	23 n.97	6.38.1–5	4
30.1	17	7.16.6	47
30.2	96 n.80	*Brev. Vit.*	
30.6	50	5.3	47
30.6–7	XI n.4	13.6	56
30.14–17	XIII	*Clem.*	
30.22–23	23 n.97	2.5.1	15
30.24	65 n.91	*Constant.*	
32.1	65 n.90	15.3–5	47
33.41	XII n.5	*De Ira*	
36.39	65 n.92	1.16.1	15
36.129	64 n.81	2.27	27
36.146	64 n.81	2.31.7	54
		2.35	60
Pomponius Mela		3.15.3–4	76
2.14	83	*De superstitione*	
		F67–73	20 n. 86
Propertius		F68	38
4.5.5–18	84	F88	14, 48
		Ep.	
Ps. Dioscorides		7.4	56
Lap. 21.2	64 n.82	9.2–3	48
		9.6	53 n.41
Quintilian		9.16	15, 55
Decl. min.		10.5	4
385	2	15.1	47
Inst.		15.11	76
3.8.44	49	16.6	47
7.3.7	2	22.15	48
		30.5–17	76
Scholia in *Iliadem*		32.4	3
6.153	32	42.4	57
		66.42–43	76
Scholia in Theocritum		70.4–7	76
7.127a and b	101 n.103	71.15	76
		71.30	47
Seneca the younger		75.19	27
Ben.		77.6–13	76
1.6.3	14, 50	77.19	75
3.6.2	15	82.10–17	76
4.3.3–4.9.1	27	85.22–23	76
4.8	50	85.41	56

90.3	50	676	21–22
91.16	76	677–679	41
94.53	14	680	22
95.2–3	50	681–690	23–24
95.49	27	690	14
95.50	48	690–704	24–27
115.5	14, 50	705	105
121.4	48	706	14
123.16	15	707–730	27–28
Helv.		717–718	27
5.1	47	728–730	27–28
Marc.		731–736	28–29
19.5	76	737–739	29–30
Med.		738	34
1–17	5–8	740–751	31–32
1–55	12–15	740–848	30
2–4	8	752–753	34
7	6 n.23	752–770	32–34
7–8	10	760–770	105
8–9	7	771–772	36
11–12	7	771–784	34–36
12	14	785–796	36
13	17	797	22
15–16	17	797–811	37–38
17–18	9	804	34
17–26	8–10	807–811	38
25	7	817–840	39–41
32	13	874–878	22
32–36	14	880–887	41
35–36	13	910	21
37–39	10–11	970–971	41
44	15	1019–1020	41
44–50	11–12	1026–1027	13
46	15	1027	43
50	15	*Oct.*	
56–74	16–18	89	XII
116	18	240	XII
159	48	*Prov.*	
166	42	1.1.2	27
171	20	5.8	50
179–300	10	5.11	46
191	4, 21	*QNat.*	
203–251	10	3 pf. 14	3, 14, 47
670	30	*V.B.*	
670–676	21	5.3	47, 48
675	4	20.5	46
675–739	21		

Servius Danielis
ad *Aen.*
1.730   94

SGD
104   9 n.37

Strabo
1.2.8   2

Suetonius
Ner.
6   XIV
34.4   XIV
56   XIII

Tacitus
Ann.
12.52.3   96 n.80
16.18   80

Theocritus
Id.
6.39–40   101 n.103
7.126–127   101 n.103

Varro
Ling.
7.42   9

Vellius Paterculus
2.72.2   61 n.71

Vergil
Aen.
4.487–491   98
7.325–335   60
7.447–450   60
7.451   59
7.750–760   XVI
7.752–755   24
Ecl.
8   XVII
8.71   57
8.95–99   83

General Index

Acanthis 84, 90

Bellum Civile
– accuracy of magic ritual 45, 75
– didactic aspect 44, 51, 71, 76
– Erichtho's necromancy 61–74
– negative representation of magic 53–55, 57, 73–74
– and Ovid 59–60, 64
– parallels magic to civil war 45
– presenting magic as charlatanry 56–58

Circe 19, 59, 98, 105

Defixiones
– 'borderline *defixiones*' 4–5
– gods invoked in 6–7
– judicial curses 10 n.41
– 'prayers for justice' 7–9, 11
– punishments aimed at the target 9, 53–54
– reasons for casting 9–10
Dipsas 90, 91 n.57

Erichtho
– Allecto and Invidia, similarities with 59–61
– failure of 75–76
– models 58–61
– personification of *ira* and jealousy 60
Eumenides (Furies, Erinyes)
– agents of punishment for criminals 7, 13
– personified curses 7 n.30, 68

Magic
– amatory 52–53
– as anti-roman practice 49–51, 54, 61
– anti-social character of XVI, 42, 54
– as anti-stoic practice 14–15, 27, 50–51, 53–55, 76
– astrology, relation to 96
– beneficial aspect of 20, 23, 57

– as charlatanry 56–58, 105–107
– clashing with religion 15–18
– compulsive power of 22, 50, 69, 73
– as a destructive force 19, 41–42, 51, 55
– form of piety in 18, 36, 50 n.32, 70 n.118
– and *mala manus* 92
– medicine, relation to 23 n.97, 86 n.34, 89, 96 n.80
– as *nefas* 14
– proving ineffective 75–76, 104–105
– and roman law 49, 12 n.51, 83 n.21
– and shapeshifting 83–84, 90–92
– its subversive power 12–14, 17–18, 27, 33–34, 36, 40–41, 51, 53–55, 57, 73–74
– superstition, relation to XI, 20 n.86
Medea
– its 'apotropaic' function 2, 43
– 'essentials' of the myth 2, 19
– exclusively evil portrayal of the heroine 20–21
– the heroine's 'borderline curse' 4–12
– transformation of literary antecedents 18–21, 34, 41
Moeris 83

Nero
– as literary patron XV–XVI
– and magic/superstition XII–XIV
Neronian literature
– change in aesthetics XI, XVI–XVII
– and contemporary life XII, XV–XVI
– obsession with magic XI–XII
– realism of witchcraft scenes XVII

Ovid
– Aeson's rejuvenation XVII, 19–20, 64
– depictions of magic XVI–XVII, 4, 18–20, 26, 91

References are to page numbers. This index is selective.

https://doi.org/10.1515/9783111429441-007

PDM/PGM
- *diabolai* 70 n.118
- and Erichtho's necromancy 61–62, 64–69, 73–74
- *logoi epanankoi* 73–74
- *logos* and *praxis* 21, 30, 62, 66, 72, 99, 107
- and Medea's ritual 22–29, 33–40
- *paredros* 26, 40, 55, 73, 74
- and Proselenos' ritual 99–100, 102
- and the rites of Oenothea 103–104
- *voces magicae* 25 n.103, 66

Persius
- and popular superstitions 101

Petronius
- and edification 79
- Oenothea's ritual 103–104
- Oenothea and Proselenos as witch figures 96–97
- parody of literary motifs 79, 104–105
- parody of reality 79, 105 n.118
- Proselenos' ritual 98–102
- religious charlatans/charlatanry 105–107
- sexualization of rituals 78–79, 95–97, 102–104
- *strigae* 90–92
- and superstition 78–79, 93–94
- werewolf story 81–86

Pliny the Elder
- and human-wolf hybrids 82
- magic, views on XII–XIII
- origins of magic XI n.4, XIII, 96 n.80
- *quasi*-magical recipes 23 n.97, 65 n.86–94
- on superstition 86, 100

Prayer (Religious/Magical)
- *do ut des/da quia dedi* formula 11, 17, 32
- language 7, 12 n.53, 69
- silent 4, 18
- structure 5, 5 n.18, 11 n.47, 16, 67
- superstitious 3
- tone 7, 12, 50

Reader's response
- contrasts with credulity 88–89, 93–95, 107
- disgust 29, 38
- fear 14, 21, 30, 42, 105
- laughter/ridicule 87–88, 105
- suspicion 88–89, 94–95, 106

Realism
- creating the illusion of upcoming success 75
- feature of Neronian aesthetics XV n.18, XVIII
- function of XVIII, 3–4, 42–43, 44–46, 77, 79–80
- hinting at magic's failure 56, 105–107
- impact on the reader XVIII, 3, 10, 24, 28–29, 44, 49, 56–57, 75, 89, 94–95, 98, 108
- links reader, reality, and text XVIII

Seneca
- on magic 15, 20–21
- philosophical tragedy 1–2
- on superstition 20 n.86
- on theodicy 27, 45 n.8
- and Ovid 4, 18–21, 23–24, 26, 28–29, 41

Sextus Pompey
- emotions and motives 46–48
- anti-roman character 48–49
- anti-stoic figure 46–48

strix
- ill-omened bird 29 n.121, 91 n.56
- use in magic 29
- witches transform into XVI, 59, 90–91

Superstition
- definition of XI n.4, 15
- foreign cults and practices, relation to XIII, 86
- magic, relation to XI, XI n.4
- opposed to *religio* XI n.3, XIII, 15–16
- popular XIV, 78, 89, 93–95, 100–101, 86

Vergil
- depictions of magic XVI–XVII, 57, 83

Witches/magicians
- their anti-social behavior 18, 70, 92 n.61
- archetypes 3, 19, 98
- drawing the moon down 57–58, 95, 98, 105
- and the 'other' 2, 49, 83–84
- stereotypes 18, 59 n.62, 70, 91–92, 96, 105–106
- Thessalian 56–57
- physical resemblance to Eumenides 59

www.ingramcontent.com/pod-product-compliance
Lightning Source LLC
LaVergne TN
LVHW051818060925
820435LV00002B/23